Punk Crisis

Punk Crisis

THE GLOBAL PUNK ROCK REVOLUTION

RAYMOND A. PATTON

Oxford University Press is a department of the University of Oxford. It furthers the University's objective of excellence in research, scholarship, and education by publishing worldwide. Oxford is a registered trade mark of Oxford University Press in the UK and certain other countries.

Published in the United States of America by Oxford University Press
198 Madison Avenue, New York, NY 10016, United States of America.

© Oxford University Press 2018

All rights reserved. No part of this publication may be reproduced, stored in a retrieval system, or transmitted, in any form or by any means, without the prior permission in writing of Oxford University Press, or as expressly permitted by law, by license, or under terms agreed with the appropriate reproduction rights organization. Inquiries concerning reproduction outside the scope of the above should be sent to the Rights Department, Oxford University Press, at the address above.

You must not circulate this work in any other form
and you must impose this same condition on any acquirer.

Library of Congress Cataloging-in-Publication Data
Names: Patton, Raymond A. author.
Title: Punk crisis : the global punk rock revolution / Raymond A. Patton.
Description: New York, NY : Oxford University Press, [2018] |
Includes bibliographical references and index.
Identifiers: LCCN 2018002842 | ISBN 9780190872359 (cloth : alk. paper) |
ISBN 9780190872366 (pbk. : alk. paper) | ISBN 9780190872397 (oxford scholarship online)
Subjects: LCSH: Punk rock music—History and criticism. | Punk rock music—Political aspects.
Classification: LCC ML3534 .P375 2018 | DDC 781.6609/047—dc23
LC record available at https://lccn.loc.gov/2018002842

9 8 7 6 5 4 3 2 1

Paperback printed by WebCom, Inc., Canada
Hardback printed by Bridgeport National Bindery, Inc., United States of America

Contents

Acknowledgments vii

Introduction   1

1. Punk Ethnoscapes: New York–London–Kingston–Berlin–Warsaw–New York   13

2. Prophets of Postmodern Provocation   33

3. Subcultural Capital   53

4. The Politics of Aesthetics: Punk in the East and West   75

5. Thatcher, Reagan, Jaruzelski   99

6. Punk *Tiermondisme*, Punk Tribalism, and the Late Cold War Roots of Antiglobalization   127

7. Culture Wars   151

1989: Conclusion and Epilogue   173

Notes   187
Bibliography, Discography, and Videography   203
Index   213

Acknowledgments

This book project has undergone a number of crucial transformations over several years, guided by the generosity and insight of others. First, I would like to thank all those who helped make my intellectual journey possible before I ever imagined writing a book about punk. This includes my parents, engineers who nevertheless supported my obscure interests in music and the humanities. I am also indebted to my friends and teachers who introduced me to music from classical to jazz to indie rock to punk. Finally, I am grateful to my third-wave ska bandmates who embraced an oddball who didn't fit the 1990s punk stereotype.

At the University of Georgia, I would like to thank the Department of Philosophy and the Demosthenian Literary Society for developing my facility with argumentation—a skill that never ceases to be useful. I am also indebted to my undergraduate professors in the Department of History who kindled my unexpected interest in history, and particularly Douglas Northrop and Joshua Cole, both of whom I had the good fortune of working with again in graduate school at the University of Michigan. It was my fantastic teachers and mentors at the University of Michigan who cultivated my interest in punk as an object of inquiry. Without Piotr Westwalewicz, I would have never encountered the enigma of punk's golden age in martial law Poland. I would especially like to thank Geoff Eley, Ron Suny, Jay Cook, Geneviéve Zubrzycki, Valerie Kivelson, and my adviser, Brian Porter-Szűcs: I hope each of you can see the mark you have made on my work. I would also like to thank the Center for Russian, East European, and Eurasian Studies for its incredibly robust area studies programming, and the fantastic staff in the History Department office: I am indebted to your support and guidance through my graduate studies.

This project would have never made it out of the theoretical phase without guidance from countless individuals during my research in Poland. I'd like to thank Przemek Zieliński for guiding me through my first visits to Polish libraries and archives. I send my thanks also to Mirosław Makowski, Andrzej

Turczynowicz, Henryk Gajewski, and many others for responding to inquiries in awkward Polish from a US scholar. I'm also indebted to the archivists, librarians, and other helpful staff members at Biblioteka Narodowa, Archiwum Akt Nowych, and Archiwum Panstwowe w Kaliszu who treated my requests with friendliness and good humor (despite occasional missteps—like the time I requested materials written in Braille). Finally, I must thank the Polish winter for keeping me inside reading and writing—and Pub Frodo and Pub Lolek for when I just had to get out.

My five years at Drury University were a transformative phase in this project. I'd like to thank my colleagues in the Department of History, Philosophy, and Religion who supported my interest in reaching beyond my subfield to other disciplines and regions. I also want to thank my students, who took these journeys across disciplines and regions with me. It was the breadth of my teaching that showed me how the story I once assumed to be idiosyncratic to Eastern Europe was part of a much wider global narrative. I thank librarians (and interlibrary loan librarians everywhere!) for keeping me connected to the world of academic discourse regardless of my location. Thank you, Rich Schur and Greg Renoff, for keeping me grounded in the popular music discussion, and Shelley Wolbrink and Hueping Chin for support and guidance despite my insistence on constantly overextending myself participating in faculty governance. I am especially thankful for Dan Livesay, a role model for balancing scholarly rigor with intellectual humility and open-mindedness, for all the open-ended conversations we have shared, holding no academic cows sacred. Indeed, thank you to all my colleagues at Drury, who shared many a conversation about culture, politics, and globalization across disciplinary borders. You helped me think about my work, but also my life, both within and beyond the bounds of the traditional academic career trajectory. Your support helped shape my work and also prepared me for my latest great adventure in New York City, where this book project has come to fruition.

In New York, I would like to thank my faculty and staff colleagues at John Jay College of Criminal Justice, City University of New York, for welcoming a newcomer into the fold of those who are committed to teaching and learning while maintaining a scholarly agenda. The environment of scholarly excellence combined with a passion for justice has shaped my work. In particular, I want to thank Dean Dara Byrne for supporting my scholarly endeavors amid our myriad ambitious projects. I would also like to thank Suzanne Ryan at Oxford University Press for taking the time and effort to see the merit in this ambitious, idiosyncratic project, Susan Ecklund for fantastic copy editing, and the many others whose work has guided this book to its publication. I extend my thanks also to my anonymous reviewers (and one in particular)—I do not know who you are, but I hope you can see the indelible mark your valuable feedback made on the project.

Above all, I would like to thank those closest to me, who have joined me through all the stages of this intellectual journey. Thank you, Kerry, for your editorial guidance and for making time for me to work on the manuscript despite everything else going on in our lives. Thank you, Avery, for giving up an hour with dad each morning for the first several years of your life while I wrote (and thank you to the Corporation for Public Broadcasting for all those *Sesame Street* episodes). Finally, I would like to extend my gratitude to the countless others who have helped make this book project what it is. This includes punks and their fellow travelers around the world—the varied people who have sought out "something better" and continue to make the world a far more interesting place.

Introduction

In March 1977, John "Johnny Rotten" Lydon of the Sex Pistols stood on the west side of the Berlin wall and looked out over the gray, militarized landscape of East Berlin. It reminded him of home. He and the Sex Pistols had wanted to escape London because it felt like a prison camp, he recalled, so "the best thing we could do was to go set up in a prison camp somewhere else."[1] Looking to the East, the Pistols penned their third single, "Holidays in the Sun," expressing the masochistic pleasure of inhabiting the shadow of the Berlin Wall—"cheap holidays in other people's misery," as the cartoon on the single's front cover promised. Between the residual ruins from the bombing campaigns of the Second World War, the postwar tower block housing, and the onset of postindustrial urban blight, East Berlin was the doppelgänger of the Pistol's vision of London—the shadowy twin that prophesized its imminent demise. Lydon went up to the wall and extended his finger in a rude punk salute.

Lydon didn't know it, but young people in the East were looking back with just as much interest. Rumors of the antics of the Pistols and other punks—their outlandish dress, foul language, and penchant for disparaging the sacred symbols of God, queen, and country—crossed not only the English Channel but also the Iron Curtain. Media reports on punk circulating in the Eastern bloc served as proof of the degeneracy of capitalist culture and evidence of the disaffected youth of the West. For the disaffected youth of the East, the reports served an entirely different purpose: in Warsaw, Poland, burgeoning punks like Robert Brylewski repurposed the media's descriptions of punk's degenerate sounds and styles as an instruction manual.[2] Over the months that followed, scores, then hundreds, and eventually thousands of young people around the cities, towns, and villages of Eastern Europe would do the same.

Unlike their reputation, the Sex Pistols never made it to the other side of the Berlin Wall. Other punk bands did, though. Shortly after Brylewski read about punk in the Warsaw daily paper, a newly formed punk band called the Raincoats arrived from London to perform one of their first shows, at the invitation of Henryk Gajewski, Warsaw's self-styled version of Sex Pistols manager and punk impresario Malcolm McLaren. Before the Raincoats took their place among the most important innovators of the second wave of punk in London, they cut their teeth in Eastern Europe. Brylewski was not the only Pole in the audience who decided to start a band of his own after seeing the Raincoats, nor was Warsaw the only place in the Eastern bloc to develop a lively punk scene. Zagreb, Belgrade, and Ljubljana in Yugoslavia were also undergoing punk revolutions. Budapest, Talinn, and Prague would soon follow.

When the Raincoats returned from Poland, they found London erupting in a Rock Against Racism rally and concert, where some hundred thousand UK punks and Anglo-Caribbean immigrants marched into Victoria Park to the sound of X-Ray Spex, a punk band fronted by Afro-British Poly Styrene. Alongside punk performers like the Clash, Jimmy Pursey, and X-Ray Spex, the reggae band Steel Pulse showed up to contribute Jamaica's culture of reggae and Rastafarianism, providing a glimpse of the ongoing collaboration between punks and West Indian immigrants that developed over the late 1970s. The fusion of punk and reggae would prove just as potent in Eastern Europe when Rock Against Racism mainstays Misty in Roots headed to Poland and the Soviet Union, drawing crowds of East European punks and reggae fanatics who embraced the Jamaican music, style, and philosophy.

By the late 1970s, punk had become a global rebellion. At that time, anyone who went to school, read the newspaper, or watched television knew that the world was split into three parts: the capitalist "First World" in the West, the communist "Second World" in the East, and the anticolonialist "Third World" in the South. Over the twenty-five preceding years of the Cold War, each "world" had formed its own worldview that competed with the other two. From the perspective of the capitalist First World, the defining opposition was between the free people and free markets of capitalist democracy and the slavery of communism—a struggle of good versus evil. It was exactly the same for the communist Second World, but with the hero and villain reversed, the capitalist master and the masses of exploited slaves. For the Third World—the global South—it was the struggle of oppressed former colonies seeking independence, and sometimes assistance, from their oppressors in the First and Second Worlds. These three worldviews were locked in a struggle to define the world in their likeness.

And yet, when punks in the East swapped stories with their Western counterparts, they were surprised at the similarities between the worlds they described. Rhetoric of crisis and decline was ubiquitous. There were few jobs, and those that were available were repulsive to many young people: they could aspire to join the mass of colorless sooty laborers, or the mass of colorless suited businessmen and communist party hacks.[3] "No future" was coined in Britain by the Sex Pistols—"There is no future in England's dreaming"—but it spoke to Eastern Europe at least as well.[4] The increasingly effete empire of the United Kingdom and the increasingly hollow vision of communism in the East each utterly failed to match the reality punks saw around them.

Eric Hobsbawm described the mid-1970s as the beginning of the "crisis decades," but it didn't take a philosopher to perceive the existential crisis that spanned culture, politics, and society in all three worlds. When Robert Brylewski's pioneer Polish punk band Kryzys (Crisis) chose its name at the end of the decade, the term was ubiquitous; in fact, Brylewski assembled a collage-style playbill for the band entirely from press clippings of the word.[5] Punk latched onto the moment of global crisis and appropriated it. Like Lydon at the Berlin Wall, punks looked out at all three worlds and gave them the finger. Punk arose through connections between the three worlds of the Cold War era; its style and ethos defied their paradigms and transgressed their boundaries. Over time, punk played an important part in collapsing those boundaries and, ultimately, the framework of the Cold War world itself.

Making Sense of Punk: Post-subcultural Studies and the Cold War

By now, the story of how punk burst into the mainstream is familiar to the point of cliché. When the Sex Pistols' "Anarchy in the UK" hit the UK Top 40 the second week of December 1976, it sounded like nothing else on the radio. Nine of the top ten songs on the charts that week were about love; the Swedish pop band Abba served as the unlikely voice of dissent with the hit "Money." Besides pop, the music genres represented included progressive rock, disco, and a 1950s revival band. Over the previous two decades, pop and rock had traded spontaneity and vitality for complexity and polish. For some, rock had become bloated and unattainable—music created by professionals for sophisticated listeners. There were exceptions, of course: hard rock bands like the MC5, Iggy Pop and the Stooges, the New York Dolls (now often described anachronistically as "proto-punk"), and occasional airings of New York punk bands by John Peel on BBC-1, but they were confined mostly to cult followings.

Then, in late 1976, punk arrived in the mainstream, courtesy of the Sex Pistols' "Anarchy in the UK" on the radio. As though sensing his band was out of place at number forty-three on the week's hits list, Johnny Rotten laughs maniacally over a wall of overdriven guitar before snarling, "I am an Antichrist / I am an anarchist," forcing the two phrases to rhyme against their will.[6] The shock doubled for those who saw punk performed—cropped hair, straight pants, and a sneer instead of the flowing hair, bell-bottoms, and suave machismo that were standard for rock bands. Within a few weeks, "punk" became a household word after the Pistols' guitarist Steve Jones called *Today* show host Bill Grundy a "fucking rotter" on prime-time television.[7] The explosion of outrage that ensued could only be matched by the band's next hit, "God Save the Queen." Set against the Silver Jubilee of Queen Elizabeth II, the song refused to celebrate the "fascist regime" and instead reveled in its impending demise from a boat on the Thames in the midst of the festivities. It was so offensive that the band was attacked on the streets. The press went into a frenzy, factory workers went on strike, attorneys filed lawsuits, local councils scrambled to ban shows, and Members of Parliament raged with denunciations.

The story of punk in the East is less well known. News about punk first arrived in newspaper and television reports circulating salacious stories from the Western media. Like their Western counterparts, citizens of the East struggled to figure out what punk meant. Among communist elites, punk could be scorned as a symbol of the decadence and decay of capitalism, or cautiously admired (from afar) as a form of anticapitalist resistance. For anticommunists, punk could be seen either as a resource to harness for antigovernment rebellion or as a threat to the nation and its youth. Each of these interpretations existed across the Eastern bloc, with a variety of local factors determining which one dominated, as the chapters that follow will demonstrate.

Then punk dress and music arrived in the societies of Eastern Europe—thanks to brave pioneers inspired by news reports, smuggled records and fanzines, trips abroad, and foreign radio broadcasts. A few adventuresome DJs even played punk records on the radio. When bands began to form and appear at music festivals, the debate about punk became more urgent. As punk rose above the underground in Poland and public outcry reached panic levels, the state Ministry of Culture and the anticommunist Solidarity labor union each pondered what to do about it. Their conversations reverberated through the highest echelons of their respective organizations. Similar debates occurred in countries around the Eastern bloc.

East and West, as punk rose into mass consciousness, contemporaries tried to figure out whether it was a cultural, sociological, or political phenomenon, and where to locate it in their ideological frameworks. A multitude of voices joined in the conversation: intellectuals, unions, anarchists, socialists, nationalists, and white supremacists all tried to interpret punk in ways that supported their own claims about the world. This was true as well of highbrow intellectual attempts to make sense of it. Punk's rise paralleled the rise of subcultural theory, a body of work dedicated to understanding the sociological significance of popular culture, particularly the highly visible, style-oriented youth "subcultures" that proliferated in the postwar era.

Precisely as punk hit the mainstream in the United Kingdom, the Centre for Contemporary Cultural Studies (CCCS), founded in Birmingham, England, developed a theory of "youth subcultures," using a combination of a semiotics-heavy structuralist methodology and a neo-Marxist framework, reading style in terms of its symbolism and orientation to social class. This work culminated in 1976 with the publication of a volume edited by Stuart Hall and Tony Jefferson, *Resistance through Rituals: Youth Subcultures in Post-war Britain*.[8] While it was directed at the previous generation of subcultures—Teddy boys and mods—it provided a theoretical foundation that could be adapted to address punk. Subcultures, it argued, were symbolic attempts to recreate the working-class "parent" culture that was steadily dissolving in the postwar era. Seen through the neo-Marxist lens of the CCCS, this response was understandable, or even admirable, as these subcultures were directed against the dominant bourgeois culture—thus serving as "resistance." However, by operating in the realm of symbols, subcultural resistance was condemned to resolving contradictions in the realm of the "imaginary" rather than fighting out real (material) struggles. Two years later, CCCS scholar Dick Hebdige's *Subculture: The Meaning of Style* addressed punk explicitly. Adapting the subcultural studies model to include race as a relevant factor, Hebdige argued that punk challenged the dominant order through the symbolic act of negation, serving as the white counterpart to black Anglo-Caribbean culture. These subcultural studies interpretations would continue to influence scholarship on punk for decades.

Subcultural theory designed for analysis of the capitalist West quickly found its way into the Eastern bloc, much like punk itself. In Poland, scholars and journalists translated and applied the latest theories to the Polish context (as we will see, in 1981, some of this work found its way into the Central Committee's Division of Culture; by the late 1980s, the terminology of cultural studies was part of the routine vocabulary of the security service). For some, "youth subcultures" (*mlodzieżowe podkultury*) were a sign of the degradation of communism in Poland; for others, they indicated the moral decay of the nation and its youth. For others still, they represented the local incarnation of a growing transnational community that rejected corrupt modern Western civilization in any of its ideological guises.

The question of the meaning of an ostensibly Western cultural form like punk in the communist East remained unresolved through much of the 1980s. However, with the fall of communism in 1989, the enigma of punk's meaning in the East seemingly untangled. As the 1980s were recast as an era of struggle between the communist state and a hostile society, a flurry of accounts lumped punk in with the latter, where it has largely remained ever since. Once again, a number of the same concepts and approaches that defined cultural studies in the West—hegemony, subculture, and above all, resistance—were readily applied to the East.[9]

Despite sharing a framework based on subcultures and resistance, however, analyses of punk in the East and West have differed in their assumptions and conclusions, which have been shaped by the categories of the Cold War. While scholars typically eschew the Manichaean language of Cold War politics, the structure of academia has allowed Cold War intellectual paradigms to endure by ghettoizing Eastern Europe in a separate field of study, making cross-regional comparison difficult and atypical. For those studying punk in the West, analysis has typically rested on the question of whether punk was left-wing or right-wing, in terms of political economy or racial and gender politics.[10] Were punks working-class or bourgeois? Did they oppose the forces of capital or collaborate with them? Were they antiracist or racist? Gender benders or homophobic? Feminist or misogynistic? The conversation about punk in the East is most often framed as the people against the state—that is, whether punk was a successful or co-opted anticommunist rebellion.[11] Was punk anticommunist, or cleverly incorporated into communist strategies of governing?

These categories are ideologically rigid, binary, and highly normative, casting popular culture in service of heroes and villains. Further, they offer little to help us understand punks. Those looking through punk scenes (East or West) for checklists of progressive political purity and those who seek to critique punks as neo-Nazis are equally likely to be disappointed. Punks spoke with complex, differing voices. To borrow a term from Tricia Rose's study of hip-hop, punk was polyvocal, and its scenes were venues for conversation, contestation, and expression that seldom lined up squarely with mainstream ideological categories.[12]

In part for this reason, the subcultural studies paradigm has increasingly come under fire over the last two decades from scholars searching for new ways to approach the relationship between culture and society. Rather than canvassing subcultures in search of symbolic resistance, "post-subcultural studies" approaches have turned to conducting ethnographies of "scenes" and "tribes" in the West, and describing "currents" and "phenomena" in the East.[13] Moving from theory and politics to gathering and cataloging empirical data, these accounts have eschewed explicitly linking punk to the sociopolitical frameworks in which it emerged. Meanwhile, beyond the academy, in a reaction against formulaic readings from outside experts, self-identified punks have asserted their own heterogeneous interpretation of their experiences. If the 1980s and 1990s were dominated by the erudite, theoretical, totalizing approach of the CCCS, the decade that followed was the heyday of collections of data points and voices—ethnographies and stories with nary an attempt to pull them together (indeed, sneering at any attempt to do so).[14]

The post-subcultural studies critique of Cold War subcultural studies is merited in many respects, for the reasons just described. However, the fall of the CCCS-based resistance model has left a conspicuous gap in studies of culture, and of punk in particular. The utility of post-subcultural studies ethnographic approaches is concentrated at the micro level; when questions of broader social significance arise, the same old vocabulary of resistance and incorporation returns. As Nan Enstad observed in 2008, despite the nuance infused into recent work in cultural studies, the conversation doggedly turns back to "the opposition between corroboration with power and resistance."[15] Scholars of Eastern Europe continue to default to "rock against the state," as scholars of Western Europe and the United States churn out works about resistance and co-optation with respect to political economy, gender, and race. In short, the post-subcultural studies approaches of the late twentieth century and early twenty-first century left us with a resistance-based subcultural studies model that will no longer stand, but no compelling alternative model to explain the sociopolitical relevance of a cultural phenomenon like punk. This omission is doubly problematic in light of the schizophrenic tendency to isolate scholarship on punk (and popular culture in general) in the West from scholarship on the East. While significant differences existed between the First and Second Worlds, isolation of studies of the capitalist West and communist East (not to mention the Third World) has unduly polarized the discussion, artificially reinforcing Cold War categories and sustaining them beyond the duration of the Cold War itself.

What we need now is an account of punk that examines its development in both the East and the West, addressing punk as the global phenomenon that it was and offering an analysis that grasps its significance in historical and social context while avoiding the pitfalls of the subcultural studies resistance model. On the cutting edge of scholarship, the sharp delineation assumed to exist between popular culture in the East and West is already under interrogation. In a recent collection, scholar of French punk Jonathyne Briggs asks whether the issues underlying youth culture in the West and East are really so different.[16] Scholars of popular culture in Eastern Europe have begun exploring the extensive connections between the Eastern bloc and the global spread of popular culture, going beyond the assumption that culture is best understood as a form of resistance to the communist state.[17] They show that popular culture in the East emerged not simply as a copy of Western culture but, rather, in conversation with it, through shared experiences and conversations in an increasingly interconnected, globalizing world. As they argue, and this account confirms, there are many surprising similarities and connections that emerge for those willing to examine punk in the East and West side by side.

Indeed, the first scholarship on punk as a global phenomenon has now begun to appear, most notably Kevin Dunn's *Global Punk: Resistance and Rebellion in Everyday Life* (2016).[18] Dunn hews closely to the lived experience of punks, focusing on the daily practice of punk as a form of "do-it-yourself" (DIY) expression rather than high politics. Dunn nonetheless argues that "punk matters," providing a means for self-expression and local empowerment against the totalizing forces of corporate-led globalization. But what were the conditions in which punk practices proliferated across its varied but interconnected scenes? How was punk interpreted by the different societies in which it emerged—particularly when punk moved from the sphere of DIY to its explosive intersection with mass media in the First and Second Worlds? Dunn claims that "punk has changed the world and continues to do so, at the individual, local, and global levels." The account that follows confirms this claim—albeit not necessarily in the way that terms like "resistance" and "rebellion" might suggest.

The World Punk Crisis and the Late Cold War Era

There were tremendous shifts taking place around the world in the 1970s and 1980s, and these changes were intertwined with punk. To make sense of this conjuncture, scholars of punk have begun to selectively recuperate some of the more useful insights and approaches generated by the CCCS tradition—above all, its insistence on seeing popular culture as intertwined with broader social, political, and economic structures.[19] In fact, the best of CCCS scholarship was already grappling with the limitations of the subcultural studies approach in the early 1980s, as astute observers like Stuart Hall perceived the transformation of their societies—in part, through and around punk. Hall noticed that seemingly repressive symbols like swastikas had lost their meaning through punk appropriation, even as the seemingly liberating concept of "the people" was co-opted by Conservative prime minister Margaret Thatcher. Meanwhile, he observed, the punk subgenre of 2 Tone was constructing a new cross-racial alliance by anglicizing ska and Caribbean culture even as it "Caribbeanized" punk and English culture.[20] These new formations defied the conventional logic of the ideological spectrum and Cold War world order alike, demanding a new, flexible way of understanding the significance of how people identified and oriented themselves with respect to culture.

Besides his foresight in calling for scrapping "resistance" and "encapsulation" as categories of analysis—a call that would be echoed decades later by post-subcultural studies critics—Hall's insistence on looking beyond the ideological content of culture to the way people identified and oriented themselves around it is quite useful. Punk inspired some people, but it also provoked the rest of society to choose sides: it produced a powerful group of enemies and, eventually, some powerful allies in cultural and political institutions. Yet, the sides they took and the way they defined and oriented themselves to punk bypassed the ideological categories of the Cold War world, instead fueling an emergent sociopolitical realignment away from a Cold War world based on class and ideology and toward a new world order framed in terms of culture and identity.

Punk was thus part of a broader global moment—a moment Michael Denning has identified as the end of the era of "three worlds." The Cold War era of three worlds was characterized by an interconnected global economy and cultural arena, but with sharp differences in the ways in which those global connections were experienced in the (capitalist) West, (communist) East, and (nonaligned) South.[21] This world order was briefly challenged by the global rebellions of 1968, and by the 1970s, it was gradually overlain by a growing global discourse of neoliberal capitalism, with disagreements expressed in terms of identity rather than ideology. This book focuses on this final period in the era of three worlds—here referred to as the "late Cold War world." While "late" might seem an anachronism that makes sense only in hindsight, many punks did see their world as irredeemably corrupt, teetering on the verge of destruction. This Cold War world was also "late" in this second sense—dead and fading into the past, to be succeeded by the world of globalization and the brief triumph of neoliberalism.

This book argues that punk developed out of and contributed to this global transition from approximately 1976 to 1989, moving from the late Cold War era to the globalized world that followed. Punk and the late Cold War world were intertwined in at least four related respects. First, punk emerged from and contributed to the third wave of globalization of the 1970s, as the Second and Third Worlds gradually merged into the global capitalist economy. The first chapter follows the intertwined stories of punks with roots in each of the three worlds, showing how they formed communities in the diverse, interconnected "ethnoscapes" of the late Cold War world.[22] While each scene developed in its specific local "habitus," punks and the impresarios they worked with recognized themselves as facing conditions similar to those of their counterparts around the world. Besides shedding new light on punk's transnational development, these stories show that the cultural exchanges that appear from a distance like disembodied "flows" in fact began as individuals interacting in personal networks that they themselves cultivated.[23] While scholarship on globalization emphasizes international corporations, punks and the impresarios who often guided them (the topic of the second chapter) were connected through global DIY networks of their own making.

Thanks to punk's artistic connections, it also became intertwined with a second, related development—the cultural watershed often described as the era of postmodernity and postmodern culture.[24] Like globalization, "postmodern" is a word that has come to mean everything and thus nothing. However, also like that term, it suggests a momentous transformation that is important for contextualizing punk amid contemporary developments in popular culture and avant-garde artistic circles—particularly the blurring of high and low culture, the integration of the aesthetic and the everyday, and the collapse of metanarratives structuring the modern world. These changes also contributed to a transformation of subcultures—the third coordinate of punk's rise in the late Cold War world. As the third chapter demonstrates, subcultures and subcultural theory alike transformed over the late 1970s, 1980s, and 1990s, spurred on by the globalization of the music industry, the spread of market capitalism, and the advent of postmodern culture. These global developments colored punk scenes around the world with parallel—albeit locally distinctive—struggles for subcultural capital.[25]

These conditions contributed to the development of a fourth key characteristic of punk and the late Cold War world—a transformation in the relationships between politics and culture that might be described as the aestheticization of politics and the politicization of aesthetics. As punk scenes around the world developed in a spectacular relationship with (and against) the globalizing music industry, social and political elites took notice. As the fourth chapter shows, punk initially confounded politicians precisely because it did not align with Cold War categories—defying conventional understandings of right and left, capitalism and communism. However, as the fifth chapter demonstrates, a global reaction erupted around punk, redefining politics in terms of culture and forging a conservative identity that drew strength by opposing the threat punk and other "deviant" culture represented to society. Chapter 6 describes how, over the first half of the 1980s, punk scenes also divided along cultural lines, coalescing into groups of punks who embraced progressive culture and multiculturalism in a new punk *tiermondisme*, and those who turned to an insular and xenophobic punk tribalism.

By the mid-1980s, chapter 7 demonstrates, punk scenes in the East and West alike were tied up in all-out culture wars that they had helped provoke, scrambling conventional political identities but also spawning new coalitions of progressives and conservatives—the political categories that would come to define the post–Cold War world.[26] Following Jonathan Clover's suggestion that the significance of 1989 can be discerned in popular culture, this account shows that this global moment was not so much a political about-face as a protracted sociocultural transition taking place through and around popular culture like punk.[27] If punk was a defining feature of the late Cold War world, it also was intertwined with the global transition from the late Cold War world to a new era, defined by global neoliberalism and politics expressed primarily in terms of cultural identity rather than socioeconomics. Punks played a part in this transition not only by pushing societies to realign around cultural identities but also through their own embrace of identity and individualism as defining characteristics. While in some respects punk resembled a social movement, its preoccupation with identity was also amenable to the privatization of citizenship in the Reagan years described by Lauren Berlant.[28]

This book offers a global narrative of the rise of punk and its sociopolitical significance. Focusing on interaction between the United Kingdom, the United States, Poland, and Jamaica, but drawing comparisons with other countries around the world, it tells the story of how punk scenes in the East and West arose amid analogous conditions, in dialogue with each other and with the Third World. Its purpose is not a quixotic mission to define punk, but to place punk scenes and the changing world in which they emerged side by side, using each to illuminate the other. Seeing punk in this way reminds us that the development of punk in the communist Second World is crucial to the wider story of punk. It shows how punk is part of a larger narrative about the late Cold War world and globalization and affords the opportunity to rethink the relationship between culture, politics, and society. The stories that follow are certainly not the only ones that might be told about punk; many more exist, with different protagonists in different scenes. Some of them are familiar, others are virtually unknown—but their intertwined paths have been obscured by the shadow of the Cold War. Reconnecting these stories across the boundaries of the late Cold War world shows how punk and the global transition that coincided with it emerged and shaped our world.

1

Punk Ethnoscapes

New York–London–Kingston–Berlin–Warsaw–New York

Johnny Rotten wasn't the first to give the Berlin Wall the finger. The young actress and singer Nina Hagen had been making the same gesture for years, albeit from the other side. The edifice had divided Berlin into Eastern and Western portions since its construction in 1961, when Nina was six. Living on the wall's Eastern side, she managed to tap in to West German broadcasts of soul and rhythm and blues (R & B) and to procure a photo of the Rolling Stones' Brian Jones to carry around in her pocket—a symbol of her alternative identity like the bindi she wore on her forehead.[1] Hagen spent much of her early adult life in East Germany experimenting with hippy counterculture and hatching schemes to emigrate to somewhere with a livelier rock and roll scene. On her journey over the next decade and a half, she found precisely that, stopping in Warsaw, London, Amsterdam, and Los Angeles.

Along the way, her path crossed those of other world travelers from the First, Second, and Third Worlds who would go on to become leading figures in punk: Dee Dee Ramone, Joe Strummer of the Clash, Ari Up of the Slits, Roxy DJ Donovan Letts, UK-émigré-turned-Polish-new-wave-star John Porter, and pioneering Polish punk Walek Dzedzej. They may have come from different worlds, but when their fates collided in punk, they recognized that they had a lot in common. Like thousands of others to the East and West, they chose to embrace identities as punks, looking to each other and transgressing the boundaries and categories that defined the late Cold War world.

Hagen's story is unique, but typical of punk in its mobility and interconnectedness. Punks emerged from the mobile, diverse populations characteristic of the late Cold War era—what scholars of globalization call the "ethnoscapes" of cities like New York, London, Berlin, Warsaw, and Kingston.[2] Global studies scholarship has emphasized the importance of "flows" of people, capital, and information, resulting in exchange, hybridity, and diversity. However, contrary to the abstract, disembodied process suggested by the term "flows," punk's interconnected scenes formed through the connections, movements, and decisions of specific individuals, grounded in particular local contexts.

There has been some debate over whether punk is best understood in global or local terms. As the trend in cultural studies has shifted from the universalist, class-based Centre for Contemporary Cultural Studies (CCCS) approach toward a post-subcultural studies emphasis on each scene's unique "habitus," some scholars have resisted interpreting punk as a global phenomenon.[3] In contrast to the universalizing ambition of the concept of "subcultures," alternative terms like "tribes" and "scenes" evoke acutely local identities. We need not choose between punk's local and global aspects, however. As Anoop Nayak convincingly argues, "global" and "local" ought not be read as mutually exclusive alternatives but rather as complementary aspects that coexist within the same culture.[4] The local is often informed by global trends, and the global is almost always experienced in local context—a process that Rupa Huq identifies as "glocalization" in her study of late twentieth-century popular culture.[5]

This chapter demonstrates precisely this combination of local particularities and global connections by examining the intertwined lives of influential punks in the globalizing cities of the late Cold War world. Some of the stories are new, while others are familiar—but only as individual, disconnected biographies and scenes. When placed side by side, these stories reveal the contours of punk's networks in the interconnected ethnoscapes of the late Cold War world. These punks' lives were ordinary but also distinctive; their experiences enabled them to recognize the strangeness and contingency of their immediate surroundings by looking abroad to the East, West, and South. Their stories show that punk and the immigrant experience were inextricably intertwined, a connection that has only recently begun to be recognized.[6] Punks were also socially diverse, coming from and mingling with working-class communities, circles of avant-garde artists, art school dropouts, and bohemian squatters. While punk scenes were by no means multiracial, mixed-class utopias, punk emerged through creative fusions and tensions of the ethnoscapes of the late Cold War world, enabling punks to see their surroundings from the vantage point of outsiders.

Dee Dee Ramone

As a child in East Berlin, Nina Hagen would never have guessed that a boy who would become a key punk innovator lived just a few kilometers away, on the other side of the wall. Douglas Colvin spent many of his first fourteen years in West Berlin with his American military family. Like Hagen, he sought out British rock from across the channel—albeit the Beatles rather than the Rolling Stones. He spent the rest of his time scouring battlefields for remnants of the war to keep as souvenirs—dark symbols that remained with him on his move to New York in 1966, and later when he helped create its punk scene.[7]

New York had long served as an entry point for the world's migrants, dating back to its seventeenth-century roots as New Amsterdam, a multiethnic trading post for the Dutch West India Company. Immigration increased dramatically over the nineteenth century and into the twentieth, packing people from around the world into close proximity. While social tensions and problems existed (often experienced and expressed along socioracial lines), so too did a flurry of hybrid cultures. By the mid-twentieth century, New York's diverse cultural landscape made it a hot spot for avant-garde art movements, particularly in Greenwich Village, known for its clubs that provided a home for the beat and folk revival movements.

In the early 1970s, the pop cultural phenomenon of the moment was the "glitter rock" band the New York Dolls, which performed frequently at the Mercer Arts Center. The Dolls were as eclectic as New York itself: they were all men, among them New York natives, an Egyptian Jew, and a Colombian. They combined camp, glamour, sexual deviance, and use of incompatible symbols (cross-dressing and swastikas)—all of which fit with Douglas Colvin's idiosyncratic tastes and would influence punk in the coming years.[8] Most important, they played simple, brutal hard rock that only a few other bands played at the time—among them, Iggy Pop and the Stooges, another of Colvin's favorites. That alone was enough to draw Colvin from his Queens neighborhood of Forest Hills regularly to the Mercer Center to see the Dolls play.

By the mid-1970s, though, the glitter and flamboyance of the New York Dolls was conspicuously out of step with the city's dire economic situation: New York faced bankruptcy in 1975, and President Gerald Ford declined to offer federal assistance (effectively leaving the city to "Drop Dead," as the *New York Daily News* famously reported it). As the Dolls faded into managerial feuding and drug abuse, Colvin and a group of neighbors in Forest Hills put together a band of their own. They abandoned the flamboyance of glam and glitter rock for simple, tough jeans and leather jackets—and an equally simple, tough sound. They named themselves the Ramones—Dee Dee, Johnny, Joey, and Tommy. Performing at the East Village club CBGB, which opened in 1974, the Ramones became the prophets of the next cutting edge of fashion and music—a strange new phenomenon that would come to be called punk.

The Ramones' combination of quintessential American style (jeans and leather jackets) and international symbolism (fascist paraphernalia and titles like "Blitzkrieg Bop" and "Rocket to Russia") can only be understood through the bifocal lens of their uniquely local and utterly global migrant experiences. The band members' stereotypically American stage names belied the international heritage of not just Dee Dee but also Tommy, born in Hungary in 1949 at the conclusion of the cruelest decade in modern East European history. "Tommy" Ramone (Tamás Erdélyi) entered the world six years after the climax of the Holocaust (when he and his Jewish family had gone into hiding), four years after the communist takeover, and precisely at the peak of the Stalinist terror.⁹ Eight years later, following the Hungarian Revolution—brutally suppressed by Soviet forces—Erdélyi immigrated with his family to the United States with a catalog of images and experiences to complement Colvin's fascination with totalitarian imagery.¹⁰

The Ramones were joined in the early CBGB's punk scene by Patti Smith, who captured the attention of Dee Dee and the other Ramones with her intense, emotional performance art. Smith's band acquired its own Central European presence via bassist Ivan Král. Born in Prague, the young multi-instrumentalist made it into the Top 10 Hit Parade in Czechoslovakia in 1964 with the song "Pierot," performed by his band Saze.¹¹ Two years later, he traveled with his family to the United States. When the hope of liberalization was crushed in the Soviet response to the Prague Spring, the Král family decided to stay for good. The Czech refugee (he would maintain refugee status through his first few punk years, until 1981) joined the early punk outfit Blondie—another CBGB mainstay—and then Patti Smith's band shortly after, in 1975. A decade later, he would form the aptly named punk band Eastern Bloc. Rounding out the incipient New York punk scene, the band Television became a regular fixture at CBGB, with bass guitarist Richard Hell (also an immigrant of sorts, from the distant land of Kentucky), wearing his iconic homemade "Please Kill Me" T-shirt with a bullseye on the front. The band's song "Blank Generation" became an anthem for early punks much as the Who's "My Generation" had for counterculture in the 1960s.

The conglomeration of new looks and sounds coming out of New York's nascent punk scene was so distinct from that of progressive rock and lingering vestiges of 1960s hippie culture that it might as well have come from another world—and in some respects, it did, shaped by the diverse, global backgrounds of its participants. Even with minimal promotion, it made waves across the country to spawn punk scenes in Los Angeles and San Francisco—and across the Atlantic to London, most notably by a young art school dropout named Malcolm McLaren and the Sex Pistols, whose story will return in chapter 2. Well before that, however, the first seeds of punk were sown across the Atlantic in the fertile ethnoscape of London, where a young man named John "Woody" Mellor watched the New York Dolls perform on the program *Old Grey Whistle Test* from his pub stool in 1973.¹² Within three years, he would transform into Joe Strummer, front man of the Clash.

Joe Strummer

John Mellor's biography epitomizes the diversity and mobility of London's punk ethnoscape. Mellor's early years read like an almanac of decolonization and the Cold War. His parents had met in India (where his father grew up under Britain's colonial rule before serving in the prestigious British Foreign Service). He was born in Turkey in 1952, just after President Harry Truman's speech made it one of the first hot spots of the Cold War, a focal point in the battle between capitalism and communism. He was toddling in Egypt as anticolonialist president Gamal Abdel Nasser rose in fame and notoriety, eventually nationalizing the Suez Canal, inspiring awe among Third World revolutionaries and dismay among European investors. He spent a year in Mexico shortly after the release of the film *Viva Zapata!* and became a fan of Mexican revolutionary Emiliano Zapata. He bought his first rock and roll LP (by bluesy African American guitarist Chuck Berry) in Teheran, where the US Central Intelligence Agency had recently orchestrated the overthrow of nativist Mohammad Mossadeq and helped install the Western-friendly Shah.[13] When the sixteen-year-old Mellor saw "the world exploding" (as he later described it) in a series of popular rebellions in 1968, he had a wide (if not necessarily deep) perspective of how the world worked, who had power, and how it was intertwined with culture.[14] That early experience would guide him as he and his bandmates sculpted the ethos of the Clash.

Mellor's international experiences and connections were more explicit than those of many of his fellow British citizens, but they weren't anomalous. Like generations before him, Mellor was raised on the fruits of empire—without which, Prime Minister Joseph Chamberlain had warned at the beginning of the century, they would all surely starve. Culture and people moved back and forth along the same lines as goods. Decades before the New York Dolls, African American R & B had arrived in the United Kingdom from across the Atlantic at the ports with sailors, inspiring British rock and roll bands to repackage it for consumption by affluent white audiences. Connections with the East were at least as significant, particularly given the British colonial stronghold of Southeast Asia. By the twentieth century, European, African, American, Caribbean, and Asian cultures were deeply intertwined and hybridized. There was no pure black, white, or Asian culture, only the cultures that various populations recombined and appropriated at a given moment. Of course, race could be used to indicate authenticity and "coolness," as it was for Teddy boys, the 1950s working-class youth subculture that combined taste for African American R & B with Edwardian dress. It could also be used for political capital among those who fretted over the influx of "colonials" from around the world to the metropole in search of new opportunities. Some argued that English culture was threatened by these new residents, as MP Enoch Powell notoriously envisioned in a 1968 speech predicting an inevitable conflict between Britain's ethnicities, flowing in "rivers of blood"—a fear that was compounded by a mugging scare in 1972 that took on ubiquitous racial overtones in the media.

An inveterate traveler, Mellor eschewed such concerns (indeed, his future bands would be indebted to these interethnic contacts). After a stint in art school, he went busking around Western Europe and the United Kingdom, staying with friends in Newport and visiting reggae clubs in the multicultural port city of Cardiff before finally returning to London, taking up residence at a squat at 101 Wallerton and cultivating his musical persona in a rock band called the 101ers.[15] Like Mellor, the 101ers made the most of London's diverse ethnoscape: their first show was opening for the Reggae Men, an early incarnation of the Anglo-Caribbean reggae act Matumbi, whose guitarist, Dennis Bovell, would produce punk records a couple of years later. The gig was a benefit concert spotted by the 101ers' two Chilean members, protesting the recent US-backed coup overthrowing democratically elected socialist Salvador Allende and installing authoritarian dictator Augusto Pinochet. The violence made a particular impression on Mellor because the junta killed folk singer Victor Jara, as the Clash would remind the world a few years later in the song "Washington Bullets."

Not long after, Mellor saw the Sex Pistols perform. The 101ers had been building their publicity in the London pub rock scene, but playing next to the Pistols, they suddenly seemed quaint in comparison. And so Woody Mellor the zoot-suited pub rocker became Joe Strummer the punk. His new punk band, the Clash, offered a new venue for Mellor's globally minded critique. His bandmate guitarist Mick Jones was also obsessed with the New York Dolls and Patti Smith. Jones and bassist Paul Simonon provided the working-class credibility that was the local counterpoint to Strummer's global vision. Simonon's family was global too—but instead of the Foreign Service, tours of Europe, and New York cult bands, Simonon got his experience of the British Empire from Kingston by way of Brixton, London's hub for West Indian immigrants. When Strummer's father was performing diplomatic duties in Egypt, Simonon's was a grunt a bit farther south in Africa, fighting to preserve the empire against the Mau Mau rebellion. Coming from a poor, heavily immigrant neighborhood like Brixton and fighting to support empire was evidently deeply contradictory: Paul's father became a communist and sent his son around the neighborhood delivering flyers and pamphlets.[16] Paul took up the look of a skinhead—the working-class subculture built around snappy dress, street smarts, and a mania for ska, all borrowed from Britain's former Caribbean colony of Jamaica.

Donovan Letts

Punk in the United Kingdom (and particularly the repertoire of the Clash) was thoroughly intertwined with West Indian style and music. While the Sex Pistols' infamous look derived from Malcolm McLaren and Vivienne Westwood's shop Sex, the Clash's Paul Simonon and Joe Strummer spent their free time at Acme Apparel, which was cheaper, less prescriptive, and less Eurocentric—largely thanks to its hip Anglo-Jamaican manager, Donovan Letts. Letts's eclectic music, fashion, and lifestyle made the shop a major attraction among the burgeoning community of punks in London. Part of the store's appeal was the same cachet that black culture had long held for white people looking for alternative ideas and identities, but Letts was far more than just a prop (like the scooter parked in the center of the shop floor) and brought a keen sense for fashion and music.[17] Upstairs from Acme, Letts inspired future Clash manager Bernie Rhodes to add rude boys, dreads, and zoot suits to the "in" list on his famous "You're Gonna Wake Up One Morning and Know What Side of the Bed You've Been Lying On" shirt that he made for McLaren's shop. Letts became renowned among London punks for his compilation tapes, which included music from the New York scene—MC5, the Stooges, the Ramones, and the New York Dolls—and also the latest reggae and dub coming out of Jamaica. After the Sex Pistols' show at the London venue the Nashville in April 1976 (the same one that inspired John Mellor to turn to punk), the band returned to Letts's house to talk about reggae and Jamaican culture. Between his time at Acme and his new job as the DJ at the Roxy (London's punk headquarters), Letts became one of the most influential shapers of the style of London punk, which he inflected with a potent dose of Jamaican culture.

While Strummer's and Simonon's fathers traveled from the capital to the colonies in service of empire, Don Letts's parents made a one-way voyage in the opposite direction. Like many fellow immigrants from the West Indies, they traveled from Jamaica to the United Kingdom via Brixton, the same London neighborhood where the Clash's Simonon and Mick Jones lived, contributing to the city's urban ethnoscape.[18] Jamaica (like the other colonies in the Caribbean) had a complex history of hybridized popular musical culture from African, European, and new North American roots—Pocomania (with roots in Africa), quadrille (inspired by European dance), calypso (from Trinidad), the blues (the US African diaspora), and mento (native Jamaican folk music). As R & B made its way to Eastern and Western European port cities like Liverpool, Hamburg, and Gdańsk in the 1950s, it also turned up in Kingston, Jamaica, via the ports, migrant workers, and airwaves from Miami. With the addition of R & B to the already complex Caribbean sound palette, Jamaican popular music gave rise to the hybrid genre ska, popularized by artists like Toots and the Maytals and Prince Buster for its uptempo, danceable rhythm and vibrant sound.[19]

Although Jamaica was a colony of Great Britain until 1962, it was anything but peripheral to popular culture in the United Kingdom. The sounds of Jamaican ska traveled from the colony back to the United Kingdom, where hundreds of singles by Jamaican bands and producers such as Prince Buster were imported in the 1960s by the Blue Beat record label. The fashion styles associated with ska and rocksteady in Britain's black community inspired a whole range of subcultures among white British youth from zoot-suited hipsters to skinheads in the 1960s. The look also came with an attitude based on the Jamaican trope of the "rude boy" or "rudy," the young, tough, self-sufficient man who fought back against the threats to his person or status in the streets of Kingston. It appealed just as much, however, to many young people in cities across the ocean such as London—including alienated black youths like Donovan Letts and alienated white youths like Paul Simonon.

Growing up in the United Kingdom, Donovan Letts developed a sense of injustice at England's ubiquitous but diffuse racism. Enoch Powell's alarmist immigration speech in 1968 made a lasting impression. Letts found the antidote coming from the black community in the United States, in James Brown's "Say It Loud—I'm Black and I'm Proud" and books by Black Panthers Eldridge Cleaver, Bobby Seale, and George Jackson (he also attended a meeting of the local UK Black Panther chapter).[20] Like many black Britons, Letts developed a politicized black identity by turning to other black diaspora communities—first looking to black nationalism in the United States, and eventually searching for inspiration from his Caribbean homeland, Jamaica.

In Jamaica, the popularity of Third World radicalism, Afrocentric Rastafarianism, and roots reggae peaked in the early 1970s. They spoke not only to native Jamaicans, however, but also to the immigrant community in the United Kingdom. Compared with the soul music coming out of the United States, Letts found that reggae "seemed a whole lot more attractive and a whole lot more relevant" to his situation in Britain, where black residents like him were "alienated, downtrodden and oppressed."[21] Letts traded his cultural ties to the United States for ties to the Third World, drawing from the Jamaican rude boy look for his own sense of style. Letts took an interest in Rastafarianism, grew dreads, and briefly attended an Ethiopian Doctrine Church—the former of which became a lasting part of his self-image, unlike the latter. He even got some help from friends in high places. When Jamaican (and, increasingly, international) reggae icon Bob Marley came to the United Kingdom, Letts not only attended a concert but also followed Marley back to his room and waited to reason with Marley over a joint. After that, Marley always stopped to see Letts when he came through London.

When Letts began working at Acme, he introduced punks to the radical, apocalyptic reggae and dub coming from Jamaica. He also provided a still more visceral experience that would define the identity and outlook of Strummer and the Clash for the rest of their career when he brought them to the Notting Hill carnival. The carnival was typically a safe space where the West Indian community of London could gather and avoid harassment under the notorious "SUS" law (referring to a provision granting police license to stop and question any "suspected person" under the Vagrancy Act 1824). On a hot summer day in 1976, however, the carnival turned into a near riot when police detained a black youth as a suspected pickpocket. Letts and the Clash were there amid the hail of bricks and bottles, a moment famously captured on the first Clash album in a photograph of Letts striding across the street between the opposing groups—the people versus the police. Standing with Letts, there was no doubt which side Strummer and the Clash saw themselves on.[22] The experience at the carnival made the Clash into the band that they were and forged an early link between counterculture of the First and Third Worlds. It wasn't quite biracial—that would wait another couple of years for Rock Against Racism, and especially 2 Tone. Instead, Strummer penned the band's first single (and the name for the subsequent tour), the song "White Riot"—calling for a white riot emulating the black crowds that weren't afraid to "throw a brick."

For his part, Letts rapidly became a fixture of the London punk scene thanks not only to his impeccable taste in music and fashion but also to his job as a DJ at the hottest new punk club, the Roxy. Letts had gotten the job by attracting the attention of Anglo-Polish Andy Czezowski—another key immigrant in London's punk ethnoscape, who worked as an accountant for Malcolm McLaren, manager of punk band Generation X, and proprietor of the Roxy. There, Letts used reggae and dub music from his family's native Jamaica to balance out the frenetic, treble-heavy sound of live punk sets, inspiring punk groups like the Clash to infuse reggae's slow, bass-heavy, rhythmic sound into their music.

More than anyone else in the London punk scene, Donovan Letts established the mutual affinity between punk and reggae, bringing out punk's transnational roots and cultivating a sense of shared struggle between First World and Third World alternative cultures. He also personally found a lot to identify with in punk. While the situation of black punks like Letts wasn't quite the same ("For the punks it was a choice. We were black and had no choice," he noted), punk and reggae shared a "revolutionary stance and ruthless hate of the establishment."[23] He valued the function of punk as "musical reportage," the same quality of social realism he admired in reggae. Although he arrived at it from the opposite direction, his Anglicized rude boy look converged with the skinhead look Paul Simonon had tried out, and the zoot suit Woody wore while performing with the 101ers. Black punks weren't typical, but he wasn't alone: Poly Styrene from X-Ray Spex was part Somali, and when Rock Against Racism and then 2 Tone hit in the late 1970s, cross-racial connections became still more prominent.

Letts even tried his hand at managing a punk band, the Slits, which used Joe Strummer's squat at 101 Wallerton as a rehearsal space. Besides sharing an interest in punk, Letts and the Slits shared the immigrant experience. Vocalist Ariane Forster, who had immigrated from West Germany with her mother, found punk and the Slits after hearing Patti Smith in the summer of 1976. Drummer Paloma Romero had come to London from Spain in 1972 and found the road to punk alongside Woody Mellor at the 101 Wallerton squat (they met when she came to see the 101ers at the invitation of drummer Richard Dudanski—born Richard Nother, but taking a conspicuously Polish surname in a punk gesture of solidarity with the underdog). The local punk community welcomed Ariane and Paloma: Ariane became "Ari Up," and Paloma was rechristened "Palmolive" (a mispronunciation coined by Clash bassist Paul Simonon). Between the global experience of the Clash and the heritage of Letts and the Slits, the cast was truly global. All that was missing was the influence of the Second World—until a young woman showed up at 101 Wallerton during a Slits rehearsal. "One day she was standing there," Ari Up recalled, "like from another planet."[24]

Nina Hagen

The woman was Nina Hagen, and the planet was East Berlin, gateway to (and from) the communist Second World. A couple of months earlier, Hagen had crossed the Iron Curtain for Hamburg, where CBS in West Germany was interested in her talent and her stepfather, the dissident songwriter Wolf Biermann. Soon, though, it became clear that West German music executives had no idea what to do with a strong-willed, creative woman trained as an East German pop star and actress. Hagen resented the recording studio's emphasis on her image over her artistry, deeming her insufficiently chic for the capitalist world. The record company sent her off to London for a style makeover—a decision the company might have reconsidered had it known about the new phenomenon that was about to sweep the city.

Hagen had been searching for something like punk for years. As a child, she was attracted to the soulful music of her US namesake, Nina Simone, that slipped over the wall via West Berlin radio waves. Simone had some of the traits that would come to define Hagen: a distinctive, powerful voice; engaging live performance skills; and a willingness to sing out about issues that others shied away from, including racism and civil rights. The closest substitute Nina could find at home was the rock and roll music that swept across the Eastern bloc in the late 1950s. In 1946, Winston Churchill had declared that Eastern Europe had been cordoned off from the free world by an "Iron Curtain." Yet, rock and roll arrived with sailors, tourists, and care packages in port cities like Gdańsk and Talinn; then in metropolitan centers like Berlin, Warsaw, Budapest, Prague, and Lviv; and eventually the towns and villages in between. Rock and roll also made it to the USSR, where young people deemed "stylists" (*stilyagi*) modeled their fashion on snippets of black hipster culture, collecting music scratched into used X-ray plates in the absence of official record manufacturers willing to press rock.

Rock provoked alarm around Eastern Europe. Of course, it had also inspired panic in England and the United States, where rock stars like Elvis and the Beatles were scrutinized by cultural and political elites. The uncertainty over the new form of youth culture was particularly acute in Eastern Europe, though, where authorities dithered between openness and repression as they struggled to preserve communism in the wake of Stalin. Many were wary of jazz, let alone rock (indeed, Soviet officials notoriously had trouble distinguishing between the two). From the local level up to the top echelons of power, attitudes toward rock shifted between cautious support, reluctant toleration, and outright suppression. Some elites bolstered their authority by casting themselves as heroes defending youth and culture from the Western bourgeois influence they feared in rock. Others saw it as a benign diversion and cautiously sided with young rock fans against conservative elites—like the first secretary of the Hungarian youth organization, who decried in the 1950s that viewing the ecstatic behavior of rock fans as political protest was "more harmful than the 'ecstasy' itself." When the anti-Soviet revolution came in 1956, one response was to import jukeboxes with Western music to defuse the rebellious impulses of youth.[25]

Rock's supporters did what they could to help ease the tension. Journalists used the euphemism "beat" or "big beat," sometimes translated into the local language, to remove the taint of foreign influence carried by the term "rock." In Poland, the band Niebiesko-Czarny (Blue-Red) assuaged fears of foreign cultural influence by using Polish lyrics and the patriotic slogan "Polish youth sing Polish songs."[26] The overture worked: rock bands made it into the Exposition of Young Talents in 1962 and eventually the prestigious national song festival in Opole. In 1966, the rock and roll band Czerwono-Czarny (Red-Black) even received an award from the state's Committee on Matters of Radio and Television.

By then, Beatlemania had reached full force in the Eastern bloc, finding footholds in even the most culturally cautious states. In 1964, when Hagen was nine, the Deutschlandtreffen festival allowed rock for the first time after the newspaper of the Communist Party came to the defense of young musicians facing restrictions from petty local authorities. The Beatles-inspired band Olympic formed in Czechoslovakia in 1963; by 1967, there was a beat music festival. In 1965, East German record label Amiga pressed a Beatles album. The same year, the film *A Hard Day's Night* opened in Warsaw, and by 1967, Soviet authorities were alarmed to note that young people were dancing the twist in Moscow's Red Square.[27] In 1968, the Beatles-inspired art-rock band the Plastic People of the Universe won a prize amid reform efforts in Prague as the party sought to return to the original humanitarian vision of socialism, a "socialism with a human face" that attracted sympathy from observers around the world, including Nina Hagen and her stepfather Wolf Biermann in Berlin.

However, gateways for rock could close as quickly and unpredictably as they opened—as Hagen and Biermann learned from personal experience. In late 1965, an East German party plenum resulted in a new, tighter line in cultural policy that specifically forbade Biermann from making public performances.[28] Biermann had made a name for himself over the 1960s as a folk performer. He was dedicated enough to communism to relocate to East Germany from West German Hamburg in 1953. Like many true believers, though, Biermann had his own idea of communism that didn't always fit the party line. For him, communism was an empowering, humane, egalitarian philosophy. In his music, its ideals inspired critiques of capitalism—but also of the authoritarian regimes of bureaucrats, technocrats, and careerists that came to dominate Eastern Europe and the USSR. However, Biermann also kept in touch with intellectuals and artists in the West like Heinrich Boll, F. J. Degenhardt, and Rudi Dutschke, who were dissatisfied with West Germany marching lockstep with the United States toward consumer capitalism.

Biermann's household was like a gateway between East and West, and Nina grew up hearing critiques from dissident intellectuals on both sides. In 1968, as students in Paris and elsewhere launched strikes, Nina took up similar causes in the East. Feeling close kinship with the Prague Spring, a movement for a more humane version of communism, thirteen-year-old Nina listened to broadcasts with her stepfather and distributed flyers in support of the uprising. Like teenagers in the West, Nina and her hippy-inspired friends went on camping expeditions, played rock and roll for each other, and experimented with sex and drug use. By the 1970s, her sense of adventure and curiosity about the world inspired her to leave East Germany altogether—not to the West (a difficult feat in the early 1970s) but farther east to Warsaw, Poland.[29]

Warsaw's rock and roll scene thrived long after the window closed on rock in East Berlin in 1965. In 1966, the state artistic agency invited the UK rock band the Animals to tour the Baltic coast (alongside Czech and Polish Beatles-inspired bands). The following year, Nina's idols the Rolling Stones entertained Warsaw with a concert that guitarist Keith Richards deemed one of their most outrageous ever. Adding to the outrage, it took place at the hall where the Communist Party held its Congresses, located in the Palace of Culture and Science ("in the Name of Josef Stalin," the stone carving read, until it was strategically obscured by a neon sign in the post-Stalin era).[30] Poland also had native rockers who, like the Stones and Beatles, joined the countercultural explosion circling the world in the late 1960s. In the same years that Biermann was confined to performing in his living room, Poland's Czesław Niemen used his powerful voice (inspired by black American soul singer Ray Charles) to address many of the urgent issues facing the East and West alike, from social injustice to nuclear war. He was an international star by the middle of the decade, performing with American star Dionne Warwick, securing contracts with West European music companies, and touring the United States and Western Europe in the late 1960s.[31]

And so it was in Warsaw that Hagen got her first hands-on introduction to rock and roll. Although she didn't know Polish, she could communicate with the locals using Russian—the Cold War lingua franca of the Eastern bloc. But the more important language for her as a performer was English. She met a drummer and joined a band with a classic Orwellian name, Grupa System (System Group), performing Western songs by Janis Joplin, Bob Dylan, Jimi Hendrix, and James Brown. She even had a chance to jam with the guitarist for Niemen's band, who showed her some of his repertoire of the black American blues that she had grown up loving.[32]

Performing with a rock band was an experience that stayed with Nina even when she returned to East Berlin a few months later. She performed a Bob Dylan song to get a license as a musical performer (she passed), and, since cultural policy had loosened up by the mid-1970s, she not only found success as a film actress but also finally found a rock band to perform with. Her first hit with Automobil was the cabaret-style "You Forgot the Color Film," which showcased Hagen's formidable talents: a powerful, husky voice, a capacity for irony and showmanship, and a penchant for playing cat and mouse with authorities, singing about the grayness of East Berlin with a mischievous smirk while producing a smash hit single for the state media. All were talents that she would bring to punk. The song even was a hit in West Berlin—an important boon for East German performers who could use the lure of foreign currency to placate skeptical officials.

The fateful moment in Hagen's conversion to punk took place in late 1976 (just weeks before the Sex Pistols burst into the headlines). Her stepfather Biermann was expatriated: he would not be allowed to return to East Germany from his tour in the West. Hagen had already been considering leaving to tour with the rock band Omega in Hungary; now an even greater opportunity presented itself. In a powerful statement written in a letter, she renounced her citizenship, affirmed her support for Biermann, and declared that she would follow him into exile. Her letter left no doubt that if anyone tried to stop her, she would use her powerful voice to speak out against injustice just as Biermann had.[33] Authorities wisely backed down, and Hagen was on her way, first to Hamburg and then to London, just in time for the punk revolution of 1976.

Nina took up residence in a squat and enrolled in the National Film and Television school, where she met the creator of the soon to be famous Sex Pistols documentary, *The Great Rock and Roll Swindle*.[34] When she went to a Sex Pistols concert with classmate (and burgeoning Sex Pistols documentarian) Julien Temple, she met fellow German immigrant Nora Forster, heiress to the German periodical *Der Spiegel* and host to many London punks, including Joe Strummer and also John Lydon of the Sex Pistols (a fellow quasi-outsider, as he suggests wryly in the title of his autobiography, *Rotten: No Irish, No Blacks, No Dogs*—Irish in London, and working-class without a working-class job).[35] Shortly after, Nora took Nina to see her daughter Ariane's band at the squat at 101 Wallerton—where Nina met Ari Up and the Slits.

Even if Nina seemed to Ari like she came from another planet (wearing a plain summer dress, a simple short haircut, and little makeup), right from the beginning, they identified with one another. Ari (along with Slits drummer Paloma Romero) was a fellow immigrant, and Nina and Ari shared German as a first language. They also shared an interest in testing and subverting gendered rules and expectations for appearance and behavior, like many early punks. Nina brought with her a fascinating alternative version of femininity that combined communist East Germany's reconceptualization of gender roles with the international blend of cultural influences from her childhood. Nina's "natural" appearance appealed to the Slits, who became known for refusing to adjust their bodies to expectations of the modern capitalist world, letting the hair under their arms grow naturally and displaying it with pride. For their part, the Slits offered Nina an alternative to the restrictive version of femininity demanded by the Western entertainment industry, as well as a refreshing contrast from the paternalistic relationship between state and citizens in the East. Nina found herself powerfully drawn to the Slits' "womanliness," "independence," and "emancipation"—characteristics equally suited for rebellion in the West and the East.[36]

Indeed, the Slits got attention almost immediately—even before they had played any shows—as outspoken women unwilling to conform to societal expectations. As a group of four young female punks, they provoked alarm among those who could dismiss the Sex Pistols as just "boys being boys." While the Slits insisted they weren't a "girl band" or a feminist group, they embodied their own variety of feminism by defying society's sharply gendered rules and expectations. The Slits provoked genuine rage; their name alone made it difficult for the band to book a show or even to get transportation or lodging (one hotel employee read the band name on a guitar case and sent them packing).[37]

Between their immigrant connections and their radical approach to femininity, the Slits and Nina shared the ability to view contemporary London from the vantage point of outsiders. Ari and Nina in particular quickly became friends, and Ari introduced her not only to the Slits but to the rest of the London punk scene. Nina described their relationship as that of schoolmates—with the school being the new music of the streets, punk. But, a few years older, Hagen was also like an older sibling to Ari. At one point, after Ari had been arrested on marijuana charges, Hagen picked up Ari on her release —delivering a lecture to the guards in the process. Nina had ample experience dealing with the forces of an obnoxious state, so when the Slits ran afoul of the law, she wasn't shy about coming to help.

A fellow outsider, the Slits' manager Donovan Letts could relate as well. Letts recalled, "The British establishment had managed to alienate its own white youth. . . . As a first generation British-born black of Jamaican descent, I was already well pissed off, so it was inevitable that we shared a sense of disillusionment."[38] Reggae and dub also spoke to many others in the First and Second Worlds who were just as disillusioned with Cold War ideologies, geopolitics, and the self-righteous, smug, soulless, and boring modern systems they were born into. Letts and Ari Up in particular formed a close relationship, attending reggae and punk shows together.

Ari Up might have been a German living in London, but her new spiritual home was Jamaica (Anglo-Caribbean reggae producer Dennis Bovell, also the producer of the Slits' first album, deemed her "Germaican"), and indeed, she would eventually permanently settle there. She embraced reggae, grew dreadlocks, and even attended a 12 Tribes meeting (getting thrown out for playing drums, deemed unsuitable for a woman).[39] Nina Hagen shared in the inspiration, co-writing a reggae song in German with Ari, "Like a Fish in Water" ("Wie ein Fisch im wasser"). The metaphor worked on multiple levels: besides the reference to Mao's famous philosophy of insurgency, it described Nina and Ari, two Germans at home as punks in London, and also immersed in the worlds of punk and reggae. Like Letts, Hagen augmented her attraction to the blues, soul, and rock and roll with a deep fascination with reggae; she would write a song called "Spiritual Reggae" upon her return to West Germany in mid-1977, where an incipient punk scene was already forming.[40]

John Porter and Walek Dzedzej

A punk revolution would soon be underway in Warsaw as well, thanks especially to the international repertoire of itinerant musicians Lesław Danicki and John Porter—two émigrés whose paths briefly converged in Warsaw as they crossed the Iron Curtain from opposite directions. As Nina Hagen headed for the West in 1976, John Porter was in England looking back to the East with just as much curiosity. Like Anglo-Irish John Lydon and Anglo-Jamaican Letts, he was also a bit of an outsider as a Welshman raised in England, never feeling a strong connection to either identity. He was uninterested in the predictable life that awaited him in capitalist Britain—perhaps becoming a lawyer as his parents hoped. Instead, he was interested in music and a radical alternative to life in the West.[41]

Like Strummer (who was two years his junior), Porter came to punk as an adult after having experienced the countercultural boom of the 1960s. He was particularly fascinated by the powerful student movement in West Germany, which, by the late 1970s, had degenerated from a popular movement into a conspiratorial, violent underground. The most extreme was a militant left-wing group called the Rote Armee Fraktion (also known as Baader-Meinhof), which viewed the capitalist, US-friendly West German government as right-wing and oppressive. When their actions peaked in late 1977, Joe Strummer caused a stir in the United Kingdom by wearing their name on a T-shirt at performances.[42] Porter's curiosity extended beyond mere wardrobe choices, however; he packed his bags and headed to West Berlin. Curiosity unsated, he then traveled to

Moscow and, finally, to Warsaw, where he unpacked his guitar and moved in with a Polish woman.

When Porter played the latest sound coming from London on his guitar in the living room salons his wife introduced him to, it was clear that he had brought a new and different musical culture. His reputation spread quickly, eventually reaching the band Przysnic Elektryczny (Electric Shower), a rock group whose aesthetic was as firmly rooted in 1960s psychedelia as its name. As it happened, the band was looking for a new guitarist and to update its sound; it found Porter and punk. Within a couple of years, with some assistance from the Polish Jazz Union, they would rise to the top of Polish hits charts as the punk-pop band Maanam. In the meantime, Porter played his guitar at the nearby club Pod Kurantem, inspiring young Poles with a repertoire fresh out of London, including the Sex Pistols' "Pretty Vacant."[43]

Poles who missed seeing Porter could instead hear a sample of punk courtesy of Lesław Danicki. An internationally minded student of multiple languages, Danicki had recently returned from East Berlin, where he had spent a year avoiding military service in Poland. While there, he had become acquainted with Nina Hagen's stepfather, folk legend Wolf Biermann, and his circle of dissident folk poets, impressing them with his idiosyncratic, raw, and gritty music and poetry.[44] By the time Danicki returned to Warsaw, the rock and roll boom that Nina Hagen had so thoroughly enjoyed a few years earlier had peaked and begun to stagnate. Erstwhile countercultural icon Niemen was on television with a backup choir singing nineteenth-century romantic poetry. The professionalization of rock and roll allowed for its expanded presence in the media, but for some fans, it sapped the vitality of the music and threatened its authenticity and allure. A few superstar bands like SBB (analogous to Omega in Hungary) were thoroughly entrenched and becoming increasingly accomplished, honing various hyphenated progressive rock genres like jazz-rock and symphonic-rock.

Lesław Danicki came to the Polish scene offering something completely different. He returned to Warsaw with an idiosyncratic guitar style, making rounds at cafes, on street corners, and in underground pedestrian passages. Like his New York and London punk counterparts, Lesław rechristened himself, opting for the name Walek Dzedzej; eventually, he formed the Walek Dzedzej "Pank Bend" ("Punk Band" adjusted phonetically for Polish). He toured between what would become the two early centers of punk in Poland, Gdańsk and Warsaw, intriguing people with his new unusual sound. "I'm not what you are" ("Nie jestem tym czym ty"), Dzedzej proclaimed in his nasal monotone, guttural voice, accompanied by harmonica and acoustic guitar, in unremarkable dress that was as suitable for a folk music concert as for punk. Aesthetically, he could be the Eastern European missing link between Bob Dylan and punk—but Dzedzej lacked Dylan's interest in metaphor, groaning plainly that he didn't belong anywhere in his society, be it the communist youth unions or the opposition.

By 1978, wandering bard Walek Dzedzej was once again ready to travel beyond the Eastern bloc. Having thoroughly canvassed the streets and cafes of Warsaw, Dzedzej secured a visa to study language and culture in Spain, and left his "pank bend" for Slits percussionist Paloma Romero's homeland. He arrived at the peak of La Movida Madrileña, the Spanish new wave movement that had been overtaking the streets of Madrid since dictator Francisco Franco's death in 1975. Next, he traveled to Paris, where he played in cafes and on the street, meeting French punks (including his eventual fiancée). Then, he returned to Berlin—this time its Western half—where the American sector radio station (once beloved by young Nina Hagen) recorded some of his songs, including "The Wall Must Come Down" (subtlety was never one of punk's arts). When a warrant was issued for Dzedzej's arrest in East Germany for his provocative musical statement, Radio Free Europe whisked him off to Vienna, where he shared his idiosyncratic folk-punk on a TV broadcast under the title, "My Songs Are Forbidden in Poland."[45] Having garnered the attention of the East German security service (much more efficient than their Polish counterparts, as Nina Hagen had discovered), Dzedzej filed with Amnesty International for asylum.

Walek Dzedzej's punk connections got him a place to stay in London among Clash groupies who helped him get a visa to the United States. There, he would spend the rest of his life on New York's Lower East Side, playing once again on street corners, in the subway, and at an occasional show back at the birthplace of punk, CBGB. Analogous to Johnny Rotten at the Berlin Wall, but drawing a comparison across the Iron Curtain from the opposite direction, Dzedzej was astonished by the similarity between postindustrial New York and his hometown, Warsaw. From the familiar viewpoint of an underground tunnel system—now the New York subway rather than Warsaw's subterranean street passages—he marveled at how similar the atomized, downcast people mired in their routines looked to the people he remembered from back home in the communist East.[46]

With Walek Dzedzej's move to New York, punk had come full circle— emerging from the diverse ethnoscapes of New York, transforming in London, infused with Kingston, and mixing with Berlin and Warsaw before finally returning to New York. As Dzedzej and countless others crossed the borders of the late Cold War world, punk scenes sprouted in their paths. Deadlock, Kryzys, and KSU formed in Poland by 1979. In East Berlin, Alternative 13 formed in 1978, followed by many others over the next two years. In Hungary, the Spions and the Galloping Coroners formed in 1977 and 1978, followed by Beatrice and others. Punk bubbled up from underground in Czechoslovakia in the late 1970s, with groups like Hlavy 2000, Energie G, and Jasna Paka forming as officials harassed professional bands like the Plastic People of the Universe.[47] In communist but nonaligned Yugoslavia, Branimir Štulić in Zagreb took up the name of his English punk counterpart, "Johnny," and converted his band Azra to punk, becoming part of a growing Yugoslav punk scene in the late 1970s.[48]

Even the Soviet Union soon showed signs of punk's influence, particularly in the Soviet western periphery, Ukraine, and the Baltic republics, where links to the West were strongest.[49] By 1979, though, punk could also be heard in Leningrad from punk bands like Awtomaticzeeskije Udowljetworitjeli, and the influence of punk and reggae permeated the sound of new wave band Kino and eclectic rock band Akvarium. The USSR made its contribution to the global punk scene too: besides the influence of Soviet imagery on the Ramones, Clash bassist and style guru Paul Simonon returned from his visit to the USSR with Soviet paraphernalia that would become part of the Clash's visual repertoire.[50] Meanwhile, his bandmates Strummer and Jones headed south to Jamaica (as did Sex Pistol John Lydon, following his band's acrimonious breakup) in search of inspiration.

Jamaicans soon began hearing about punk too, courtesy of world travelers and immigrants like Bob Marley and Donovan Letts. When "those nasty punks" (and the sight of Letts's bondage trousers) caught Bob Marley by surprise in London, Letts explained, "Dem crazy baldheads are my mates." Eventually Marley became convinced and was moved to record "Punky Reggae Party," a shout-out to the shared spirit of punk and reggae in the First and Third Worlds. In an early version, Marley referenced the Slits; later, they were replaced with the Clash, which got Marley's attention by covering Junior Murvin's Jamaican hit "Police and Thieves," a wry look at street violence and law enforcement that fit London as well as Kingston. Punk-reggae connections also formed in New York, where Patti Smith took up the cause of one of Letts's favorites, Tappa Zukie, whose "MPLA Dub" proclaimed solidarity with anti-imperialist forces in the Angolan civil war, placing them solidly in the camp of opposition to US Cold War policy. Smith introduced Zukie to the local music scene, bringing him onstage and releasing his album on her label, helping him take a stab at the First World—the colonizer—from within its heart.[51] Over the next decade, the sympathetic punk-reggae connection would expand to greater proportions, with Rock Against Racism and 2 Tone in the United Kingdom and United States. Punks in Poland recognized the shared connection as well: pioneering punk band Deadlock included Marley's "Get Up, Stand Up" in its early repertoire. The connection between Second World and Third World, punk and reggae, would come to full fruition over the next decade—a connection that will be explored in chapter 6.

None of this is to say that punks were prophets of an idyllic multicultural society. Punk scenes around the world would have tortured relationships with race over the next decades, ranging from collaboration and identification to tension and outright hostility.[52] However, the varied nature of this relationship should not obscure that punk's roots emerged from the ethnoscapes of the late Cold War world, bringing together people who had different backgrounds yet shared a sense of disillusionment with the late Cold War world and its limited possibilities. At a time of economic crisis, industrial decline in the First and

Second Worlds, and expansion of capital and communication, punk spoke to the conditions of young people in the cities of the East and West alike. They communicated regularly with one another across the boundaries of the late Cold War world, sharing their disenchantment and longing for something vital and engaging. Despite punks' shared connections, however, punk only achieved a lasting, high-profile presence in the places where it found institutional support. That's precisely what it would find in the established networks of the avant-garde art world, deeper even than those of the ethnoscapes that supported punk.

2

Prophets of Postmodern Provocation

In 1974, on the cusp of punk's New York debut, Henryk Gajewski announced that he was hosting New York Pop Art guru Andy Warhol at his art gallery and student club in Warsaw, Poland. Gajewski invited a television crew, journalists, and celebrities. The "Evening with Warhol," as he called it, would underscore Gajewski's work for the previous half decade directing the gallery and would also be a publicity coup d'état, enhancing the international prestige of arts in Poland and the Eastern bloc. On the evening of the event, more than three hundred people showed up at the studio, with many more crowded outside the door. They waited patiently for Warhol's appearance, eagerly anticipating meeting the renowned art celebrity. Warhol was fashionably late, it seemed, but that was to be expected of an international art icon. About thirty minutes past the scheduled appearance time, a few skeptics began to doubt that Warhol was coming. Others maintained their optimism for hours.

In fact, it was all a ruse. Andy Warhol hadn't even been invited. Instead, the whole event was a performance art provocation set up in the space created by the absence of a central figure, with Warhol filling a role analogous to Samuel Beckett's Godot. The crowd itself became the exhibit—a living complex organism that gathered, rose, swirled, and fell over the course of the evening. In the end, the writer of the student newspaper noted, those in attendance had created "their own happening."[1] Gajewski's Warhol exhibit was reminiscent of soon-to-be UK punk impresario Malcolm McLaren's first foray into the art of provocation. McLaren's 1967 exhibition at the Kingly Street Gallery in London directed visitors into an enclosed structure with high cardboard walls. Instead of finding art, however, they found themselves trapped in a maze of white cardboard.[2] They came to passively consume only to be transformed unwittingly into the exhibit.

Despite coming from different worlds, Gajewski and McLaren arrived at a similar place in the mid-1970s. They shared an interest in the twentieth-century avant-garde, an urge to rework the antiestablishment spirit from their youth in the 1960s, irreverence toward artistic convention, and curiosity about interfacing the worlds of art and mass culture. A gallery director and an art student-turned-provocateur, each turned art around, redirecting the act of creation at the audience to convert passive crowds into subjects. Their art was both participatory and irreverent; it exemplified the art of provocation that segued into punk. Within a year of Gajewski's exhibit, McLaren would launch the Sex Pistols—and, with them, punk—into the spotlight. Soon after, Gajewski was making similar maneuvers in the Eastern bloc.

The first chapter of this book traced punk's origins in the diverse, interconnected ethnoscapes of the first and second Cold War worlds. This chapter presents punk's second, parallel genealogy in the networks of the avant-garde art world. In one of the best-known accounts of punk, Greil Marcus ruminated on the aesthetic origins of punk in the twentieth-century European avant-garde.[3] Despite the important linkages his account draws out, however, it leaves the Second and Third Worlds out of the story. In fact, overlapping networks connected avant-garde art circles in Western Europe, Eastern Europe, and the rest of the world. Malcolm McLaren, Henryk Gajewski, and many others involved in punk were immersed in a world of radical, provocative art with roots reaching back more than half a century, to Dadaism, Surrealism, and Situationism—and, more important, to Pop Art and Fluxus. The international influence of these movements created a common cultural landscape and vocabulary that reached across the boundaries of the late Cold War world.

Scholars of globalization use the term "third cultures" to refer to hybrid cultures that develop among groups of people working together across national boundaries.[4] Over long periods of time, these groups form a shared vocabulary, practices, and codes that differ from those of the national cultures of their members. Most often, the term refers to the international organizations and institutions that proliferated with the globalization of the late Cold War era—multinational businesses, diplomats, and lawyers, for instance. The avant-garde art circle in which McLaren, Gajewski, and many others operated formed a third culture of its own, however, communicating similar ideas and forming shared codes and practices across the boundaries of the late Cold War world.

Rather than conforming to the contours of global capitalism, participants in the third culture of the avant-garde often experimented with avoiding, subverting, or co-opting the networks of global capital, distancing themselves from and sometimes ridiculing the emerging global economic and political order. Thus, to combine the terminology of global studies and cultural studies, punk might be described as a "third subculture," developed through transnational contacts but with networks, purposes, and attributes that were in tension with the predominant forces of globalization. In place of boardrooms and office buildings, its deterritorialized spaces were international exhibitions, galleries, journals, fashion, and mail art—and as the connection with punk developed, concerts, music venues, and fanzines. The heterogeneous shared language of the third culture from which punk emerged facilitated a radical approach to the aesthetics of everyday life, expressed in the overlapping spheres of art, lifestyle, and fashion. This culture challenged the boundaries that separated art from life, the masses, and the culture industry. In short, punk's emergence was intertwined with the rise of the heterogeneous culture of postmodernism, the defining cultural-aesthetic phenomenon of the late Cold War era.

While punks drew inspiration from networks spanning all three worlds, punk only became widespread in societies around the world where modernity had taken root—it only made sense as a *post*modern phenomenon. Here, the term "postmodern" is used to indicate two central tendencies. First, it suggests a blurring of boundaries between high and low culture and between genres, and the practice of recombining formerly incompatible domains and styles in a process called "bricolage." Second, it indicates the rejection of privileged, universal vantage points for understanding reality—that is, metanarratives that impose totalizing frameworks for conceptualizing the world, whether science, humanism, the notion of progress, or Marxism. In both of these respects, punk and the postmodern developed in tandem, transgressing the boundaries of the late Cold War, drawing and blending elements from its "worlds," and defying the metanarratives that structured and justified the existence of each—including core values like modernity, hierarchy, progress, tradition, family, religion, morality, order, and beauty.

As with the concept of postmodernism in general, there has been considerable debate about punk's postmodern status. In a pioneering empirical study, David Muggleton finds partial evidence for deeming punk as postmodern in the subjective realities of its participants, who seem postmodern in some respects but not others (such as their affirmation of depth and permanence of identity, and their affirmation of authenticity as a value).[5] In a more recent account, scholar of punk fashion Monica Sklar likewise notes the enigmatic tension between punk's apparent coherence and its seemingly postmodern eclecticism.[6] We need not be troubled by punk's uneasy fit with categories, however. As the recent collection from the Subcultures Networks argues, punk is best understood in terms of the tensions on which it hinges: between the avant-garde and the populist, creativity and negation, the artificial and the realistic, between symbols with conflicting meanings, and between individual and collective.[7]

The concept of the postmodern is useful for thinking about punk not because punks rigidly adhered to a postmodern doctrine but because they engaged with many of the same tensions that lay at the crux of postmodernism. Punks were preoccupied with the challenges of being an individual (within a community of punks), forming connections with others outside "the system" (often through the networks of the music industry), and nonconformity (like other punks). As Ivan Gololubov's recent work confirms, the simultaneous existence of punk's postmodern and anti-postmodern elements is less paradoxical than it initially seems. Immigrant punk in particular, Gololubov argues, uses the postmodern techniques of deconstruction and bricolage to critique the postmodern condition; it is simultaneously inspired by and critical of the postmodern moment in which it arose.[8] Rather than interpreting punk and postmodernism as ready-made doctrines, it is more fruitful to see them as related interrogative practices, questioning the boundaries between elite and mass culture, the separation of art and everyday life, and the status of the artist as a genius creator. Both punks and postmodern artists questioned the defining political fault lines of the modern world, the politics of class and of nation, and often, the importance of politics altogether (at least in the traditional sense of the term). Finally, and perhaps most important, both developed an acute but ambivalent self-awareness with respect to art's relationship with market forces.

This chapter shows how punk arose through transnational conversations that emerged in tandem with postmodernism along avant-garde artistic networks that stretched across the Iron Curtain and the equator. A decade before "postmodern" became a buzzword in the 1980s, impresarios McLaren and Gajewski and the punks around them followed the current of international avant-garde art networks away from high art and 1960s counterculture and toward the postmodernism of the late Cold War world. They abandoned conventional stylistic categories and any pretense of ideology, transgressed the boundaries between high and low art, and assaulted the dominant metanarratives of the day—whether progress, Marxism, or the idea of Western civilization. While McLaren and Gajewski differed in their respective preferences for utilizing and avoiding the structures of the music industry—each following a different branch of the twentieth-century avant-garde—they shared common inspiration and contacts in the East, the West, and the South. They inspired performance art groups to embrace punk and brought punks into contact with contemporary avant-garde artistic movements like Pop Art and Fluxus. They also exposed punks to the avant-garde aesthetic world, following the trajectory of Dada, Surrealism, and Situationism. It is that world where our examination begins.

Origins: Dada, Situationism, Pop Art, Fluxus

Malcolm McLaren's and Henryk Gajewski's provocative performance art exhibits may have struck onlookers as little more than pranks, but both men had extensive avant-garde art pedigrees. Like many of the burgeoning punks with art school backgrounds, McLaren was unimpressed by most of what he learned in art school—or, more precisely, across the three art schools he attended before dropping out. However, he was delighted by Dadaism, an art movement (or rather, anti-art anti-movement) from the first decades of the twentieth century. "Dada" was an intentionally nonsensical term coined by founding artist Tristan

Tzara, who traversed the European continent from east to west, moving between Paris, Zurich, and Bucharest in his native Romania. Spurred by disillusionment with Western civilization that had just devoured itself in the Great War, Dada tore down the conventions of great Western art: it infringed on the boundaries between artist and audience, challenged the definitions of what counted as art, blended elite and mass, and upheld the ordinary and ugly over the unique and beautiful. Among the most iconic Dada-inspired works were Marcel Duchamp's readymades (favorites of McLaren)—objects that desacralized art by grounding it in the banal and removing its aura.[9] Famously, Duchamp took a urinal, scrawled the label "fountain" on it, and submitted it as art. A few years later, McLaren would make an analogous gesture, selling bondage gear as "fashion" and presenting the Sex Pistols as "music."

Dada remained a cornerstone for twentieth-century modernism, and avant-garde art in general, for decades. Its spirit resonated with that of Surrealism, whose founder, André Breton, declared, "In the bad taste of my time I go further than anyone else." By the time of the post–World War II generation of punk impresarios, however, Dada's influence was most spectacularly visible in the combination of radical politics and art emerging from the 1968 student strikes in Paris (one of many dramatic outbursts of rebellion that year) and from a group of radical artists calling themselves the Situationist International. Seeking the intersection between radical politics, everyday life, and performance art (one of their ideas was to float corpses and red dye down the Seine to protest the Vietnam War), they distributed posters, flyers, and pamphlets. The transnational connection of art extended across the English Channel, giving rise to a third culture of radical art and rebellion: Malcolm McLaren was among the students around the world who were inspired to follow the lead of their French counterparts, joining a student strike at his own school, Croydon College. He made it to Paris in August; he may have been too late to participate himself, but he was fascinated enough to seek out a group of Situationists in England going by the name King Mob. Jamie Reid, who would later work with McLaren on posters for the Sex Pistols, recounted, "There was a genuine contact between the Sorbonne, Croydon and Hornsey. . . . I went from a student worrying about his little niche into being someone who was very aware of what was happening in other parts of the world—what was taking place in Paris, the riots in Watts."[10]

McLaren was never content to exist solely at the intersection of avant-garde art and radical politics, though—a quality he shared with most punks. In 1969, he organized an enormous free festival at his next school, Goldsmiths College. The festival nudged McLaren from the world of high art into popular culture. One final ingredient would take him right out of art school altogether, into the world of style, mass culture, and consumption. That ingredient was the absent subject of Henryk Gajewski's exhibition in Warsaw, Pop Art and its guru, Andy Warhol.

Pop Art explored the nexus between art, life, and consumption, and between high culture and mass culture. Adapting some of the iconoclastic impulses of Dadaism to the sleek consumerism of the postwar Western world, Pop Art challenged boundaries between mass culture and high art, consumers and art connoisseurs. Warhol took icons of pop culture and everyday consumption—Marilyn Monroe or a Campbell's soup can—and committed them to canvas. At the historical moment where the boundaries between high art and mass culture were dissolving, Pop Art struck them down with delight, ushering in the era of postmodernism in which genres, boundaries, and master narratives all collapsed.

Pop Art cleared a path for punk—a musical genre and style based on the mass cultural forms of pop and R & B, and blurring boundaries between trash, fashion, consumption, and art. Like Pop Art, punk was immediate, electrifying, and accessible as it tore down musical and stylistic conventions; it managed to work through both irony and genuine expressiveness at the same time. These characteristics had piqued the interest not just of McLaren and Gajewski but also of Joe Strummer when he was still an art school student called Woody Mellor: he submitted a sketch of a horse smoking a cigarette for a school art competition, a gesture in equal parts slacker and a nod to Pop Art. Like McLaren and many punks in the East and West alike, he was interested in aesthetics but scoffed at aesthetic convention (he once suggested that art school trained people to act like artists producing things that look like art).[11]

The fascination between punk and Pop Art was mutual. The crowd from Warhol's Factory art studio in New York were punk fellow travelers from the beginning. They shared the hangout Max's Kansas City, just around the corner from the Factory, with the New York Dolls, Douglas Colvin of the Ramones, and aspiring poet and performance artist Patti Smith. Several of the members of the cast from Warhol's 1971 production *Pork* participated in punk's internationalization on their journeys back and forth between New York and London. Among them was Wayne County—later Jayne County—who started a punk band called the Electric Chairs and became a regular fixture at the Roxy in London, befriending DJ Donovan Letts.[12] Punk pioneer Patti Smith also got a heavy dose of Warhol via her close friend, avant-garde artist Robert Mapplethorpe: "It was as close to hero worship as [Robert] ever got," she would later write.[13]

McLaren was drawn in as well. Warhol's claim that "being good in business is the most fascinating kind of art" was offensive to artists and incomprehensible to businessmen. It was perfectly suited for McLaren, though, fascinated as he was with art and provocation, consumption, and manipulation. He took Warhol at his word and dramatically shifted directions from studying art to marketing iconoclastic pop culture.[14] In 1971, he left Goldsmiths College and opened up a Teddy boy fashion apparel shop called Let It Rock with his partner, designer Vivienne Westwood. For them as for Warhol, "Selling things became an art in itself. The idea was provocation."[15] McLaren's aesthetic upbringing primed him for his experience two years later, when he would attend the National Boutique fashion show in New York, along with Andy Warhol, Patti Smith, and New York Dolls Sil Sylvain and Johnny Thunders.

The New York Dolls were the final phase of McLaren's pre-punk upbringing. The Dolls and McLaren were acquainted through their participation in the New York–London fashion circuit (the Dolls had visited McLaren's King's Road fashion shop and would later join him on a trip to peruse the fashion scene in Paris).[16] When he followed them back to New York for a second visit in 1974, he and Westwood tried out a new look for the band: skintight red patent leather costumes, a giant communist flag as a backdrop, a Situationist-inspired press announcing their foray into the "politics of boredom," as the "People's Information Collective" collaborating with the "Red Guard" of the People's Republic of China. McLaren instructed the Dolls to mention the word "red" at least six times per song, and (lest the metaphor get lost on the partying crowd) had them carry Mao Zedong's little red book. They had cobbled together the artistic influences of the previous century into one performance—the absurdity of Dada, the performance art provocation of Situationism, the penchant for fame and glitter from Pop Art, and the leftist fascination of 1960s counterculture.

The introduction of radical leftist politics to a rock concert, while suitable perhaps for the late 1960s, was passé in mid-1970s New York for the audience and the band alike; in fact, the Dolls would break up not long after. McLaren soon found new inspiration that played to his artistic interests but jettisoned the ideological elements of 1960s counterculture in the young, fierce, and decidedly less glittery scene coalescing at CBGB: Patti Smith, the Ramones, and Television. Television's Richard Hell in particular stood out to McLaren, with his "Please Kill Me" shirt with a bullseye on the front. McLaren decided, "I'd take this guy, this spiky hair, everything about it . . . I'd take it back to London."[17]

After his experience in New York, McLaren's penchant for provocation went in a postmodern direction. He abandoned the preoccupation with radical politics inherited from 1960s counterculture and instead embraced style and image as ends in themselves—a key turn from ideology and politics toward identity and culture that was central to punk. When he returned to London, he and Westwood changed their store's name to Sex and focused on provocative, bondage-inspired fashion and taboo sexual behavior. Westwood suggested in an interview, "If there is one thing that frightens the Establishment, it's sex. Religion you can knock, but sex gives them the horrors."[18] Rather than using red leather as a symbol for radical leftist politics as they had with the Dolls, McLaren and Westwood would use a similar look as an end in itself, shifting toward the personalistic, style-centered approach of punk and of the postmodern era. They decorated the store with slogans lifted from novels by Alex Trocchi—former member of the Situationist International who used the perception of his sexual deviance for provocation.[19] The slogans themselves were reminiscent of the ideals of free love from the previous decade, and certainly alternative style was nothing new to counterculture. However, there were two crucial differences: first, punk made no claim to be natural; second, unlike counterculture of the 1960s, style was not just a marker for alternative content; rather, it was an end in itself.

The biggest gun in McLaren's arsenal, though, would turn out to be the house band, the Sex Pistols. While he had been away, a few local kids—employee Glen Matlock and would-be customers (or shoplifters) Steve Jones and Paul Cook—had started a band called the Swankers. The new band became complete when its fourth member, a green-haired, stooped hooligan in a Pink Floyd shirt (with "I hate" scrawled above the band logo) slinked into the store. John Lydon made an impression, between his "rotten" look that earned him the nickname "Johnny Rotten" and his excruciating but passionate mauling of the Alice Cooper and Rolling Stones songs the band was rehearsing. For his part, Lydon was equally repulsed by McLaren's sex shop. It was a perfect punk match, cemented by mutual revulsion.[20] Drawing inspiration from New York's punk scene, the Sex Pistols wrote the song "Pretty Vacant"—the band's equivalent to Television's "Blank Generation." McLaren was never particularly concerned about plagiarism—good news, since the Sex Pistols and their "No Future" slogan would soon become a model for punks in Eastern Europe.

As McLaren transformed from a countercultural artist to a postmodern provocateur, Henryk Gajewski was developing his Warsaw gallery as the hub of a new variety of avant-garde art in the Eastern bloc. Gajewski had spent his early adult life as a photographer in the city of Białystok in the eastern borderlands of Poland. In the late 1960s, when the First, Second, and Third Worlds erupted in simultaneous rebellion, he headed for the action, moving to Warsaw in 1969, three years before Nina Hagen and in plenty of time for the flurry of counterculture in the late 1960s and early 1970s. He got a position as the director of an art gallery connected to Warsaw Polytechnic called Remont and made a name for himself among students and authorities alike for his atypical approach to art, emphasizing the avant-garde and international over the traditional and local.

Despite residing in a country where any invitation would be scrutinized by authorities, Gajewski established international connections through uncanny persistence. He corresponded tirelessly with artists around the world and printed one of his many publications, *Art Texts*, in both Polish and English to reach a broader audience.[21] His vision for his Warsaw gallery wasn't popular with everyone; he was nearly removed from the post in 1973. But he hung on, and over the next few years, Remont became an avant-garde and performance art center linking Warsaw to other cities in Poland, Eastern and Western Europe, and overseas. By 1978, when Gajewski brought punk over from the United Kingdom, the Remont gallery had become one of the most important performance art hubs in Central and Eastern Europe.[22]

Gajewski's inspiration came from many of the same sources as McLaren's—Warhol, Dadaism, and Situationism. However, his vast networks in the performance art world were largely courtesy of Pop Art's austere underground cousin, a movement called Fluxus. Like Pop Art, Fluxus had roots in the early twentieth-century avant-garde and sought to eliminate the boundaries between art and life and to shatter the aura of prestige around the aesthetic. Unlike Pop Art, Fluxus artists kept a critical distance from commercialism and media, preferring the role of underground saboteurs to that of art celebrities. The founder and organizational linchpin of Fluxus was George Maciunas, a Lithuanian-born immigrant who came to the United States by way of Germany just after World War II. Finding his place along fellow world citizens in the ethnoscape of New York City, Maciunas curated a gallery called AG for several years, attracting performance art and avant-garde elites like John Cage and Yoko Ono. In 1962, the gallery went bankrupt, and Maciunas returned to Germany to proclaim he was founding a neo-Dada movement. When the leading Dadaists informed him that no such thing could exist, he coined the term "Fluxus."[23]

True to its name, Fluxus—suggesting "flow" or "current"—spawned remarkable networks. Created in Germany, headquartered in New York, and with hubs in the Netherlands, France, Czechoslovakia, and Japan, Fluxus attracted avant-garde artists from New York to East Asia. From the beginning, it was Maciunas's goal to break down the boundary not just between art and life but between the parts of the world that were separated by Cold War boundaries. To do so, Fluxus artists utilized a preexisting global network—the world's interconnected postal services—to create lively exchanges of mail art between artists across borders. Maciunas also pursued collaboration on a larger scale, writing to Soviet general secretary Nikita Khrushchev for permission to introduce Fluxus to the USSR. Although he received no response from Khrushchev, Maciunas had better luck connecting with the Baltic republics and the satellite states of Eastern Europe. In Kaunas, Lithuania, professor and future president Vytautas Landsbergis cautiously integrated Fluxus into his lectures and university events. In 1964, several western artists took a Fluxus tour across the Eastern bloc, visiting Poland, Czechoslovakia, Hungary, and the USSR, performing at private apartments and jazz clubs, distributing the art kits from their car's trunk, and making connections with local avant-garde artists.

Maciunas selected Prague, Czechoslovakia, to become the Eastern European center for Fluxus. In the 1960s, Prague was already a center for international avant-garde and countercultural activity; its festivals drew artists from around the globe, including New York counterculture icon (and punk fellow traveler) Allen Ginsberg in 1965. The Plastic People of the Universe, a literary Beatles-inspired rock band directed by internationally connected art critic Ivan Jirous, were also active participants in the festival scene (they would become even more thoroughly transnational when Canadian vocalist Paul Wilson joined the band in 1970). Maciunas corresponded with Milan Knížák, artist and founder of the performance art group Aktual umění, inviting him to visit Fluxus headquarters in New York and then to serve as director of Fluxus East. In 1966, Knížák organized a Fluxus festival in Prague, attracting American and Eastern bloc artists alike.[24]

The lively festival atmosphere of Prague gradually subsided by the end of the 1960s, however, as the Warsaw Pact invasion put an end to the reforms and gradually forced the counterculture underground. The Plastic People lost their official status in 1970 and sought out a place in a new underground scene that formed at the junction of popular culture and avant-garde art. They made connections with Fluxus and performed with Knížák's avant-garde rock group, Aktual. Their activity peaked in lively underground festivals of the "second culture," as it was called, in 1974 and 1976.[25] These festivals inhabited the terrain between performance art and rock, high culture and popular culture, and 1960s counterculture and something new soon to come.

While the underground scene in Prague was vibrant, it was less amenable to the freely flowing circulation of art that defined Fluxus. In place of Prague, Poland and particularly Warsaw arose as the center of avant-garde activity in Eastern Europe in the first half of the 1970s—precisely as Henryk Gajewski was setting up his new gallery and tapping into global avant-garde art networks. Aided by the networks already in place through Fluxus, Gajewski hosted artists from Mexico, Holland, the United States, Croatia, the United States, West Germany, the Czechoslovakia, and Hungary in the early 1970s. When he announced in 1974 that Warhol would join the impressive international slate of visitors, the credulity of Warsaw's art elite was perhaps understandable.

By the mid-1970s, McLaren and Gajewski were immersed in the currents of the international artistic avant-garde. They had learned to question dominant assumptions about rationality and aesthetics from Dada. They had experienced provocative performance art through Situationism. Pop Art and Fluxus took them still closer to what would become the postmodern moment—and toward engaging with punk—by turning from ideological content to the free play of form, and collapsing the boundary between elite and mass culture. Pop Art fused the fame and glitter of popular culture and the media with art, taking an enthusiastic last step away from the world of art as the preserve of a cultured elite, abandoning authenticity and embracing the market and the new world of popular culture. Fluxus, on the other hand, embraced the austere and ordinary, using its own networks as an alternative to market-based proliferation of culture. Both models—one embracing the popular, celebrating inauthenticity, and reveling in the market, and the other positing an alternative version of popular culture and avoiding the market—would influence punk, forming an explosive tension that would shape the world's punks scenes for years to come.

When punk emerged in the East and West, it was (among other things) a continuation of a trajectory these artists were already following. Before punk, the avant-garde's blending of elite and popular was still an aesthetic gesture—using everyday objects and mass culture, but without breaking free from galleries and studios to become popular culture itself. The closest the avant-garde came to mass media was Warhol's factory, but even Warhol was mostly a cult figure celebrated by elites and bohemians in New York and London. Punk, in contrast, was actually popular culture itself. It didn't merely gesture toward collapsing art/life, elite/masses, authentic/inauthentic, high culture/popular culture boundaries; rather, its very existence defied those boundaries.

Punk's Postmodern Connections: West, East, and South

As was true with the ethnoscapes in which punk emerged among young, mobile populations in New York, London, Warsaw, and other cities, there were specific connections and experiences that brought punks into contact with artistic elites. Perhaps the most frequent contact zone was art school. A surprising number of punks had art school backgrounds that brought them into contact with radical art (before they dropped out, like Strummer and McLaren). Each band and each individual has its own story, however. This section will examine just a few, exploring the interconnected web of punk and avant-garde art in the East and the West—and also placing them in conversation with the global South.

Art schools and galleries were not just a demographic background and aesthetic primer for punks; they also served as concert venues, particularly before punk achieved mainstream success in the East and West. As the Sex Pistols made their rounds in the United Kingdom's art college circuit before they invaded the airwaves in late 1976, they caught the attention of the artistic avant-garde—and particularly artists connected to the Fluxus movement, which by the mid-1970s had expanded from its headquarters in New York and Prague to attract adherents in London and Warsaw. An affinity between Fluxus and punk was natural; both challenged elite conceptions of art, and both sought to combine the realms of aesthetics and lifestyle. Punk's musical toolkit—a few instruments and a few chords—was the sonic equivalent of the set of tools that arrived in the mail in a Fluxus art kit, ready for assembly by anyone interested.

The 1960s generation of Fluxus artists tended to avoid the bombast of popular culture, pursuing innovations to the aesthetics of everyday life within their own circles. The 1970s generation of Fluxus was different—particularly the Fluxus-inspired groups that formed connections to punk. Rather than creating an enclave of alternative culture untouched by mainstream society, they actively sought confrontation through provocation, interfacing with popular culture and mass media when necessary. The result was some of the most influential groups to come out of punk's artistic contacts—Crass and Throbbing Gristle in London, and Tilt and Kryzys in Warsaw. Each would influence punk and art simultaneously through a web of connections that extended across the Iron Curtain.

Among the first to embrace the art-punk connection in the West was a group called COUM, a radical performance art group that was taking part in a traveling Fluxus exhibit in the United Kingdom. COUM pushed Fluxus to new boundaries, embracing an extreme variety of performance art with a potential for provocation that matched punk's. The first formal contact occurred when COUM members Peter Christopherson convinced Malcolm McLaren to authorize a photo shoot with the Pistols. Initially, Christopherson was interested in using the band to create his own provocation, toying with the idea of homosexuality in photos that were too controversial even for McLaren.[26] Over time, though, COUM came to realize that there was something in punk's mass appeal that was part of the art itself, as Warhol had once suggested. Sick of the elitism of the art world, as punk arose in London, COUM formed an experimental band called Throbbing Gristle—the visceral metaphorical synonym for "Sex Pistol."[27]

Another avant-garde artist, Jeremy John Ratter (soon to be rechristened Penny Rimbaud) transitioned from Fluxus to punk in a similar manner. He studied in art school but struggled with art's self-important, hermetically sealed universe (he was as put off when his wisecracking image juxtaposing a nuclear explosion, flatulence, and a bikini-clad woman entitled "Modern (F)art" received praise from faculty). After trying his hand in the worlds of art and of manual labor (he got a brief job as a collier), he founded an artistic commune. As the wave of Fluxus swept the United Kingdom in the early 1970s, Ratter joined the London performance art group Exit, making a name for himself by pounding on bags of offal and reciting verse by beat poet Ginsberg in the nude.[28] When the Sex Pistols came over the airwaves in late 1976 promising "anarchy in the UK," Ratter took their words seriously. A young punk arrived at the commune shortly after, and Jeremy John Ratter the hippy became Penny Rimbaud the punk—named in true Dada fashion after a combination of the slang for a public toilet and the French poet. With fellow commune residents Steve Ignorant, Eve Libertine, and Joy de Vivre, Rimbaud formed Crass and assailed not just mainstream society but also the ideological foundation of their former hippy counterculture. One of the songs they performed included the lines "Alternative values were a fucking con. . . . They formed little groups like rich men's ghettos . . . tending their goats and organic tomatoes / while the world was being fucked by fascist regimes."[29]

Punk gave avant-garde groups like COUM and Crass a connection to the masses via popular culture, providing an audience far beyond that of a typical performance art group. In late 1976, just before the Sex Pistols (and, with them, punk) became a media phenomenon, COUM invited the punk band Chelsea (managed by Andy Czezowski, the Anglo-Polish accountant for McLaren and future Roxy proprietor) to play at the opening of their exhibit entitled *Prostitution*—and invited more punks to attend as audience members. The mix of punk and avant-garde art was a volatile combination, bringing art created by professionally trained provocateurs from the cloistered back alleys of the artistic intelligentsia to the broad avenues of popular culture. The show set off a storm in Parliament that famously earned COUM the label "wreckers of civilization" from a Tory MP and hastened the end of state support for avant-garde art. It was a harbinger of the firestorm and subsequent sociopolitical transformation with which punk would become intertwined in the decade ahead.

The art-punk fusion that swept London in the late 1970s developed in other cities as well, thanks to the global networks of Fluxus and punk. In fact, just days before COUM's art-punk gallery exhibition in London that propelled it to the headlines and floors of Parliament, the group was featured in an exhibition on the other side of the Iron Curtain in Poznań, Poland (COUM and Throbbing Gristle cofounder Genesis P-Orridge would eventually return for an extended stay, having a love affair, writing some new music for the band, and visiting Auschwitz concentration camp—a site of Western civilization's corruption that also held macabre fascination for Penny Rimbaud and Crass). COUM's exhibit was housed at the gallery Akumulatory 2, the first important Fluxus hub in Poland.

Fluxus and other performance and mail art initiatives had been growing in Poland over the 1970s much as they had in the United Kingdom, and they were extending their networks around Europe and the world. About a year before the exhibition, Akumulatory 2 proprietor Jarosław Kozlowski had circulated a mail and performance art manifesto entitled "NET" ("SIEĆ"), defining an international art movement that was open, noncommercial, diffuse, and uncoordinated; like a net, intersections between the strands occurred across its entire expanse. Kozlowski, who disavowed any claim to authorship or originality, encouraged copying and redistributing artistic works.[30] By the mid-1970s, the network included about fifty active participants from both inside and beyond the Eastern bloc.[31] In 1977, Akumulatory 2 hosted its first international Fluxus festival, including instructions and kits sent by founder George Maciunas from New York.

Unlike in the United Kingdom, the COUM exhibition in Poznań went off without major controversy—no doubt thanks in part to Akumulatory 2's connection to the SZSP socialist youth union, which (as with Gajewski's Remont) provided some protection from local authorities. Also key was that—unlike in the United Kingdom—the exhibition was not accompanied by punk bands bringing radical art into contact with the masses. That would change the next year, as the momentum of Fluxus headed for Warsaw, where Henryk Gajewski was quietly joining the ranks of Poland's leading facilitators of performance art.

While Kozlowski was hosting the international Fluxus festival in Poznan, Gajewski was in Warsaw preparing for his own international performance art festival under the title International Artists Meeting (subtitled "I AM"), which included works by US Fluxus stalwart Alison Knowles and many others. When he hosted the second International Artists Meeting the next year, he widened his scope even further, using the networks Fluxus had established. Leading performance artists around the world, including Yoko Ono, sent in RSVPs.[32] But Gajewski had his finger on the pulse of the international performance art scene, and he knew that the most dramatic and vital form of performance art was a new phenomenon called punk.

Crucially, like Malcolm McLaren, COUM, and Crass (and unlike many other avant-garde artists in East and West alike), Gajewski was able to recognize the value of engaging with mass culture to reach a wider audience. Despite his loathing for state-sponsored mass culture, he believed in the possibility of an alternative popular culture, created by individuals forming their own networks allowing for creative exchange that bypassed the culture industry or the state. As he designed his performance art exhibition, Gajewski reached out to his art contacts abroad and sought a way to bring a punk band from London to Warsaw.

Meanwhile, in London, the Raincoats had formed just weeks earlier when art students Ana da Silva (a recent immigrant from Lisbon, Portugal) and Gina Birch saw the Sex Pistols on the art college circuit and, like so many others, decided to form their own band.[33] Soon, the band would be joined by two members of Joe Strummer's circle, Paloma Romero (formerly of the Slits) and Richard Dudanski (a drummer with a self-assigned pseudo-Polish surname), who would help the Raincoats reach international popularity. When they played their first gig at their art school, they were just getting started; by their own accounts, their art professors were not impressed. However, they did get the attention of a Polish visitor scoping out performance artists to bring over for Gajewski's impending International Artists Meeting. Gajewski invited the Raincoats to Poland, and they accepted.[34]

It would be another year before the Raincoats became a leading force in UK punk, but they made an impression on Warsaw's incipient punk scene right from their first performance in April 1978. Besides Gajewski, several young Poles who had been desperately clinging to the sensational stories about the international punk phenomenon that appeared in the press now had the chance to see a live punk performance. Among those in attendance were Robert Brylewski and Tomasz Lipiński, who assiduously noted the outfits and hairstyles, marveling at the reckless freedom with which the band played. Each would form his own punk band in the coming months.

In the meantime, Gajewski cultivated a fruitful environment for a local punk scene, converting his gallery into a headquarters reminiscent of McLaren's Sex and Czezowski's Roxy. In his 1979 manifesto entitled "Punk," Gajewski positioned himself as the Polish equivalent of an international cast of punk band managers, including Bernie Rhodes and Malcolm McLaren, whom he credited with innovations to punk fashion and the "anarchic values" of the Sex Pistols.[35] Like McLaren, Gajewski decorated the walls with posters and slogans, including a sign demanding that visitors refuse to have their tastes dictated by "dilettantes from the radio and discotheques," or the "idiocy" of Polish record presses. Instead, he demanded that they take culture into their own hands. He posted: "WRITE A TEXT, FORM A MELODY, START A BAND, ORGANIZE A CONCERT, BUY 100 CASSETTES AND REPRODUCE YOUR RECORDING!"[36] It was a restatement of the philosophy Gajewski had long embraced as an advocate of Fluxus and mail art—but it was also the Second World equivalent of the classic early US punk slogan, "This is a chord, this is another, this is a third. Now form a band." Gajewski arranged a screening of footage from punk concerts in England and a three-hour film about the Sex Pistols that, he claimed, hadn't even been shown in theaters in the West. He also organized weekly musical meetings on Mondays under the title "Sound Club," during which Warsaw residents could come listen to DJ Andrzej "Amok" Turczynowicz present punk, new wave, and reggae—serving as the Polish counterpart to Roxy DJ Donovan Letts.[37]

As with Akumulatory 2, Remont's affiliation with the state-sanctioned SZSP youth union afforded it leeway in authoritarian communist Poland. By any standard, though, Gajewski and Turczynowicz pushed the bounds of what was possible. Indeed, before long, Remont's supervisors put an end to the Sound Club, ostensibly because "dancing to that type of music was bringing down the ceiling."[38] It wasn't the first time Gajewski had faced pressure from his superiors, and it certainly wouldn't be the last. For the moment, though, he took the ban on recorded punk as an opportunity to seek out local live acts to perform. Fortunately, a Warsaw punk scene had started to coalesce in the wake of the Raincoats concert. With a venue and impresario ready to get them going it didn't take Warsaw's burgeoning punks long to start bands—even for those without a background in music. By 1979, Remont became home base for the bands Kryzys and Tilt, and a regular performance venue for others.

Kryzys (Crisis) was among the first bands to take advantage of the resources Gajewski and Remont provided. The drummer, Maciej "Magura" Góralski, was already experienced with punk, having toured with Walek Dzedzej's Pank Bend the year before. The driving force of Kryzys, though, was guitarist Robert Brylewski. Born in 1961, Brylewski was the child of two performers in a traveling folk dance troupe—just the sort of group that socialist governments delighted in sending abroad in cultural exchange programs. The experience was enough to whet his father's tastes for travel; he emigrated to the United States, maintaining his relationship with Robert by mailing him cassettes of the music he encountered, including recordings from New York's pre-punk scene. Young Robert complemented his diet of Western rock with occasional performances by live rock bands from the Eastern bloc, attending shows by Yugoslavia's Bijelo Dugme and Poland's SBB—rock and roll bands like those that pre-punk Nina Hagen had idolized when she visited Warsaw. Like many punks his age, Brylewski looked at 1960s rock bands with a mixture of awe, envy, and contempt. He went to the shows "because there wasn't much else to do" but grew tired of the same unattainable look and sound from his parents' generation—the long hair, the fanciful dress, and the complex, polished progressive rock and roll routine.[39]

Instead, like many early Polish would-be punks, Brylewski opted for a look and sound that were simple and attainable, with as much in common with folk music and dress as with later punk musical and stylistic tropes (like the fast-paced sound of hardcore and the accompanying mohawks and studded leather). Initially, Warsaw punks typically dressed in straight pants and wore short hair, experimenting with playing simple rock and rolls songs, often pared-down covers of rock classics, with whatever instruments were available. Soon, though, Warsaw's punk vocabulary shifted (and eventually hardened), as sensational news about punk circulated in the wake of the Sex Pistols scandal and subsequent punk explosion in the United Kingdom in 1977.

Brylewski developed a sense of himself as part of a wider punk movement when he read about it in a report in the Warsaw daily paper *Zycie Warszawy*. Seeing language so scathing, he knew he had discovered something noteworthy. Inspired, he put fifteen safety pins in his clothes and nervously went out to a nearby traffic circle, looking for others. At first it seemed as if his plan had backfired: he saw a man in a trench coat—classic secret police attire—and got ready to run. Just in time, though, the man opened his coat, unfurling his own display of safety pins.[40] Warsaw was forming a punk community of its own.

When Brylewski discovered punk, he felt "like the doors opened and something fresh came through—music about what is really happening, and not about the imagined problems of rich stars."[41] He sought out the Clash, the Sex Pistols, and later the Buzzcocks. Then he started a band of his own, relying on a band member's mother's job at a local community center that doubled as a performance venue. When he attended the Raincoats show, he knew he had found a new home. He got to know Gajewski and formed the punk band Kryzys, choosing the name as the word "crisis" grew ubiquitous in the press over the late 1970s, first in reference to the economic crisis in the West, but increasingly to refer to the economic and political struggles at home.

Alongside Kryzys, Warsaw's second influential art-influenced punk band was Tilt. Tilt came together when art school dropout Jacek "Luter" Lenartowicz and some of his punk brethren headed to Warsaw from Gdańsk—Poland's major port and second early punk center—to survey the punk mecca that was reputedly arising around Remont gallery. Remont and Gajewski provided the infrastructure for punk to succeed that his Gdańsk band Deadlock had lacked. Luter moved in with Robert Brylewski from Kryzys and joined Tilt as the drummer and songwriter, composing punk songs in English as fellow art school dropout Tomasz "Franz" Lipiński worked out tunes on his guitar.

Luter took his name from the iconoclastic priest who defied the power of the church hierarchy—and for the irony of a diminutive, delicately featured Jewish punk naming himself after a blustery Christian judeophobe. Of the tiny portion of the Jewish community that had survived the annihilation of the Holocaust, most had left with the Communist Party's anti-Semitic anti-Zionist campaign of 1968—including Jacek's father. As part of an ethnic group seen by many Poles as foreign, Luter was a natural candidate for punk. Fortunately, his self-education gave him access to a community outside his native land. Luter's outstanding command of English allowed him to reach across the artificial boundaries of the late Cold War world, and his background in art and literature connected him to the networks of the international avant-garde (the same was true for his bandmate Franz, whose father was an internationally renowned caricature artist). As punk arose, Luter relentlessly sought out connections that would allow him to communicate with punk bands from the West, including striking up a correspondence with Generation X (formerly Chelsea)—the band managed by Anglo-Polish Andy Czezowski that had played for COUM's gallery opening in 1976.[42] Luter also had the connections of Fluxus at his disposal: along with Gajewski, Tilt's manager, Piotr Rypson, was an active mail artist and Fluxus participant.[43]

Luter immediately fit in with the avant-garde artistic side of punk at Remont, fashioning performance art provocations of his own: he developed a reputation for wearing a bloody suit on the bus around town. His enduring contribution, though, was his array of fanzines, which blended punk with Dadaist inspiration over several titles, creating a medium that can only be described as punk in visual form. *The White Volcano Paper*, for instance, defied the rationalist conventions of modern journalism by mocking anyone who tried to understand it. "What exactly is a white volcano?" Luter asked in the first issue. For an answer, he conjured Professor Lisol McWhite, an expert in White Volcano Therapy, who offered an absurdist response: "White is white, and the volcano is simply a volcano."[44]

Luter did not simply represent or describe punk in his 'zines; rather, he engaged in punk by creating them. Like Dada, Luter's 'zines eschewed the modern convention that a text ought to be constructed and read for meaning. Instead, they followed the postmodern practice of placing disparate images and symbols into play, irrevocably detached from their original source. One page is devoted entirely to a small picture and a lengthy caption in an unidentified non-Latin script. Other pages simply contain photographs or drawings, either without captions or with captions that only increase the confusion about the source of the image and the reason for its inclusion—such as a drawing signed by either an obscure or fictitious artist, captioned, "and then a scream rang out . . . AH!"[45] One section takes stories from the mainstream Polish press but rearranges the sentences to form alternative, often nonsensical meanings. As Matt Grimes and

Tim Wall argue about punk fanzines in the West, Luter's 'zines are best understood as a discursive practice.[46] Their pages are filled with signifiers that are intentionally left opaque as to what is being signified. This flexibility accounts for part of why punk was so amenable to travel across various national and local contexts of the late Cold War world. As Jonathyne Briggs has observed, as long as the symbols were aesthetically identified with punk, the specific meaning was adaptable across multiple local contexts.[47]

While Luter and Brylewski had global connections through their family networks and correspondence, Gajewski plugged them into the interconnecting worlds of avant-garde art and punk. In Paris, Gajewski found inspiration in his nearest French equivalent, Marc Zermati. Zermati had sought to build a French outpost of alternative musical culture, establishing the Open Market in Paris in 1972 and Skydog Records, which provided France access to pre-punk stalwarts like the Stooges and MC5.[48] When punk arrived in France via artists who had visited New York—and, more dramatically, with the media sensation of the Sex Pistols—Zermati promoted French punk singles, downplaying the Britishness of the Sex Pistols and encouraging a particularly French variety of punk through bands like Stinky Toys. In Gajewski's view, Zermati had succeeded in cultivating a uniquely French variant of punk—albeit one that he found frivolous and excessively preoccupied by fashion in comparison to the austere (in the tradition of Fluxus) Polish scene. Even so, Polish punks would profit from the French punk connection: even as Gajewski wrote, the French punk label Barclay was pressing copies of an album by Kryzys, smuggled to France from bootleg recordings, and released soon after in the United Kingdom.

However, the most direct connection between East and West for Gajewski proved to be Amsterdam (in fact, within a few years, he would move there permanently—as would Luter). Amsterdam was a punk outpost that attracted visitors from both sides of the Iron Curtain. The Pistols had come seeking refuge in early 1977 at the peak of their notoriety in the United Kingdom, and in 1979, Nina Hagen did the same after setting off a media scandal of her own (miming masturbation on Austrian television). Shortly after, Gajewski arrived to document the scene in photographs and get to know the people behind it. He quickly got to know the founders of the vibrant punk scene that had developed over the previous two years.

As in Warsaw, London, and New York, punk and avant-garde art circles overlapped considerably in late 1970s Amsterdam. At the heart of the linkage was an art school dropout named Diana Groenveld, who took the punk name Ozon (ozone), opened a gallery called Anus, and started an art punk fanzine called *Koecrandt*. With the help of half-Latvian graffiti artist Ivar Vičs (better known by his punk name, Dr. Rat), she also opened founded the punk club DDT666, blending together the catastrophic destructive forces of industrial science and biblical prophecy in a mere six characters.[49]

When Gajewski and Ozon met in 1979, they found that they had more in common than they had anticipated. Amsterdam might have seemed like a refuge to those like Hagen and Gajewski visiting from the East, but to Ozon, as for John Lydon a few years earlier at the Berlin Wall, the West was just another prison camp, perhaps slightly better disguised than the East. Referencing George Orwell's Eastern-looking dystopian novel, Ozon told Gajewski that 1984 had arrived in the Netherlands, and Western civilization was collapsing. It was a sentiment she shared with punks in the East, who had long believed the same about their own homeland.[50]

Ozon and Gajewski's connection extended across the Iron Curtain, but it also reached across the equator, drawing inspiration from the global South as was true for many other punks. Hearkening back to the modernist artists of the early twentieth century, their shared suspicion of modern Western (be it capitalist or communist) civilization prompted them to look to the global South as an enclave resisting contamination. Ozon explained to Gajewski that her life had changed when she had traveled to Mali in West Africa. For one, she found creative inspiration when she and her crew observed the use of stencil art in Africa. They would bring this art form back to make Amsterdam a hub for graffiti art, with Dr. Rat becoming the most celebrated (or notorious) of the pack, joining a transnational surge in graffiti art that intersected with punk scenes in Amsterdam and New York. However, Ozon also returned from Africa unsettled existentially, skeptical of her own life and her society's tendency to alternate between periods of war and "consumerist happiness." "We are a lost generation," she suggested.[51] Ozon developed a critique of her own society when she stepped outside it. Much as it did for punks in the United Kingdom who drew inspiration from the reggae and dub played by Donovan Letts, the culture of the Third World provided inspiration to the art-inspired punks of Amsterdam and Warsaw—a connection that would grow to fruition by the middle of the 1980s in Poland, as chapter 6 will demonstrate.

Gajewski's visit to Amsterdam was also creatively productive. When he returned, he shared his experience with Warsaw's punk scene. In one of the first native punk shows in the Eastern bloc, he arranged for Tilt and Kryzys to perform at the Gallery Art Studio in the Palace of Culture in Warsaw, the site of annual Communist Party congresses—and the Rolling Stones' legendary show in 1967. This time around, the Palace showcased Gajewski's collection of graffiti from Amsterdam and a photography exhibit called *Children of Punk*, while the band showed up dressed like the punks in the pictures.

The show lived up to its billing. Those who attended early punk shows, West or East, often had experiences that they described as life-changing in a way that art galleries seldom were, not just because those in attendance had never seen or heard anything like punk but because they could participate in it—by adopting punk attire, finding a circle of punk friends, and, for some, even starting punk bands of their own. Many young Poles underwent a conversion experience when Kryzys and Tilt performed: Lipinski recalled that crowds experienced shock followed by ecstasy when they experienced punk rock. "We gave them energy—by the third song, everyone was out of their chairs, going crazy. Two uncompromising brothers came after the concert and demanded pins in their ears. And I did it."[52]

The worlds of avant-garde art and young punks grew by feeding off of one another—the former contributing established networks, venues, patrons, and an endless supply of creative inspiration, and the latter providing energy, a young audience, and a critical connection to popular and mass culture. The intimate circles where art and punk first came together gradually grew and interconnected, forming scenes in cities like New York, LA, San Francisco, London, and Warsaw. But once the media caught on—first the music press, then television and tabloids, and finally record companies and a flurry of punk fashion and novelty stores—those networks intersected with the networks of globalizing capitalism, changing the basic character of punk in the East and West alike.

3

Subcultural Capital

In 1978, as Henryk Gajewski was building an art-inspired punk scene in Warsaw around his gallery Remont, a small circle of entertainment industry professionals hatched a plan to create what they called a "rock market" in communist Poland. Wojciech Korzeniewski, Marcin Jacobson, Jacek Sylwin, Piotr Nagłowski, and Walter Chełstowski sketched a "system of promotion, concert tours, and festivals" that would serve to promote new music to youth under the banner "MMG," for Music of the Young Generation (Muzyka Młodej Generacji).[1] Over the next two years, they would give punk bands access to the machinery of the mass culture industry in communist Poland.

They knew what they were doing. Jacobson had been a radio worker and rock promoter in the 1960s, Nagłowski was a disc jockey for Polish Radio, and Chełstowski worked for Polish Television. Much as for the rock impresarios of the previous generation, their challenge was creating something that both audiences and cultural authorities would embrace. Their first experiment took place at the international Pop Session festival in the summer of 1978, when MMG's promoters announced a "fantastic spectacle" that would showcase "young bands beginning their stage careers," "without compromises . . . fresh, modern, with a future . . . and GOOD!!!"[2] The language they sent via the Baltic Artistic Agency to the Ministry of Culture and Art's Department of Cultural Cooperation Abroad to get permission for the event was decidedly different. Organizers carefully chose language emphasizing that the concert would meet the cultural needs of Polish citizens and edify them in the process. The festival, they affirmed, would offer youth "attractive entertainment responding to their authentic interests" but would also stimulate "worthwhile thoughts, experiences, and cultural inspiration."[3] Even the name Music of the Young Generation served this purpose—much as "big beat" had two decades earlier—avoiding the controversial term "rock" and certainly "punk" while still suggesting the music's popularity with youth.

The overture worked perfectly. MMG's organizers were granted use of the theater; all they had to do was put together the concert and wait for the crowds to show up. That turned out to be the catch: so few people showed up that the organizers eventually had to let them in for free. One journalist blamed this on the high cost of tickets, but there was a more fundamental issue.[4] The five bands that performed, Drive, Exodus, Heam, Kombi, and Krzak, all played a variety of hyphenated rock—art-rock, symphonic-rock, or jazz-rock—a clear indication of their progressive rock backgrounds. It was just the kind of show that would appeal to someone who came of age in the 1960s—a solid rock and roll concert. Indeed, among the few audience members who were impressed were the main festival programmers: Krzak, Kombi, and Exodus would receive invitations to play at the main festival at Sopot the next year, not just the MMG rock showcase.

After the fiasco, MMG's promoters knew they needed something new to add to their stale progressive rock routine. They found a ready-made shot of adrenaline that could be injected into the foundations of MMG in the small circle of punk bands forming in Warsaw. Over the next few years, Music of the Young Generation mixed in punk bands, styles, and mannerisms, presenting punk-rock shows under the MMG title. Not everyone was pleased: that summer, at a "musical camping" festival near the small town of Lubań, crowds demanded "real" punk bands rather than the MMG bands—Music of Young Degeneration, they mockingly called it—leading to a clash with security forces.[5] Yet, the outcry from a handful of punks was no match for the forces of the entrepreneurs behind MMG. Within a couple of years, they would have not only a rock market but also, some would complain, a near monopoly on popular music in Poland.

Under the moniker of MMG, punk rapidly made headway into the national music scene in Poland. In the United Kingdom, punk had already collided with the mass culture industry. In 1977, record labels famously rushed to sign bands around the country, hoping to capitalize on the hype around punk. It took a bit longer to integrate punk into the music industry in Poland, where it had to penetrate the labyrinthine bureaucracy of the communist culture industry. As for record companies in the United Kingdom and the United States that scoured the punk scene for marketable bands (using the term "new wave"), the key for MMG's promoters would be finding the perfect balance between pop accessibility and punk subcultural allure. By 1980, the band Maanam—the punk incarnation of the rock band Przysnic Elektryczny we encountered in chapter 1—was at the forefront of a new set of punk-inspired bands that attracted festival invitations and mass audiences, got radio and television play, and had albums pressed on state record labels.

Arguably, punk's penetration of the media was a sign of success. However, much as in the West, punks' reaction to commercial success was far from universally positive. Neil Nehring has argued that the preoccupation with purity from commercial forces is a holdover from nineteenth-century romanticism and its celebration of individual freedom.[6] However, rightly or wrongly, for many punks in the East and West alike, the ability to claim and maintain their punk identity hinged on their ability to present themselves as unfettered by the forces of the music industry. *Sniffin' Glue* fanzine founder Mark Perry wrote that "punk died" when the Clash signed to a major label; when a similar trend took place in Poland, Henryk Gajewski made the same claim. Over the next few years, with the help of enterprising managers, promoters, and impresarios, bands like Maanam would bring punk to the masses, attracting huge audiences—but also the scorn of many punks, who accused Maanam and others of trading in their subcultural credibility in order to collaborate with the music industry—and, by proxy, with the whole "system."

As we saw in the previous chapter, punk's appeal to the artistic avant-garde derived from its ability to repackage the postmodern influences of the performance art tradition for a popular audience. However, this blend of aesthetic innovation and mass appeal also led to tensions within punk scenes as punks negotiated between reaching audiences and maintaining an aura of independence. This tug of war set the tone of punk, shaping the behavior of people involved in both punk scenes and the music industry (and everyone in between) in the places it intersected with the forces of modern capitalism—including communist Eastern Europe. East and West, each punk scene's development was shaped by the strategy it adopted for coping with the tensions in the relationship between punk and the mass culture industry.

Bands needed to reach an audience, and that meant working with the industry to find performance venues, make a record, or get radio or TV play. Yet, punks often eschewed the cash and fame associated with rock stars and the mainstream media. Instead, they privileged the characteristics most central to their status as punks: individuality, authenticity, uncompromising ideals, and independence. Analogous to "cultural capital," sociologist Pierre Bourdieu's term for nonmaterial resources like prestige, these characteristics were sources of an alternative form of capital for punks—a currency that increased their status within their respective punk scenes.[7] This "subcultural capital" became increasingly important in the punk scene as bands proliferated and evidence of "selling out" (i.e., cooperating with the music industry) abounded, leading punk bands and fans to root out imposters tainted by cooperating with "the system." Yet, at the same time, bands faced the constant pressure to leverage this capital in order to book a concert venue, make a record, or get radio play—thereby exchanging their subcultural capital for a contract, or actual capital.

Pioneered by Sarah Thornton's study of UK dance club culture, the concept of "subcultural capital" emerged as an effort to update and improve cultural studies. Theories of "subcultures"—style-based youth communities defined by their social connection to their working-class parent culture and their symbolic opposition to the dominant bourgeois order—have been debated, challenged, and revised over the past decades.[8] Critiques of cultural studies came from two interrelated directions. First, a methodological critique emphasized the lack of empirical research behind the CCCS approach, which was accused of focusing on the most spectacular examples, relying on media coverage, and producing accounts that often had little to do with how "subculturalists" saw themselves. A second, theoretical critique also developed as feminist, critical race, poststructuralist, and postmodern theory all challenged the primacy of class as the natural organizing principle of society and of scholarly analysis alike.

A period of "post-subcultural studies" approaches followed, replacing sweeping narratives and structural analysis with focused, micro-level, empirically driven sociology and anthropology, inspired less by the CCCS than by the Chicago School's empirical approach to youth and deviance in the 1950s. The progression of titles of some of the most important studies is telling: Thornton's *Club Cultures* in 1996, David Muggleton's *Inside Subculture* in 2000, and Rupa Huq's *Beyond Subculture* in 2006. By a decade into the twenty-first century, scholars were abandoning the term "subculture" altogether, favoring terms like "neo-tribes" and "scenes" in the West and "current" or "phenomenon" in the East.[9] These terms tended to favor viewing punks through the lens of microhistories and ethnographies, compiling empirical data on small groups of punks.

However, despite some attempts to supplant broad theories of "subculture" with less theoretically laden alternatives, focusing on cataloging empirical data left post-subcultural studies unable to address popular culture's broader significance, its relationship to major social, economic, and political trends. The most fruitful approaches have been those that have retained some of the theoretical ambition of the CCCS, strengthening its empirical foundation while jettisoning its less effective aspects. Hilary Pilkington—one of the few scholars to bridge the gulf between First and Second World studies of popular culture—has, for instance, sought to broaden the CCCS approach from its class orientation, acknowledging the shifting, diverse nature of subcultures while retaining the CCCS commitment to understanding micro-cultural practice in relation to historically rooted social structures.[10] This tactic has also proved effective in the recent collection *Fight Back* from the Subcultures Network, which selectively rehabilitates terminology and concepts from the CCCS, and in Kevin Dunn's *Global Punk*, which combines a close examination of the lived experience of punks with an insistence on punk's global social significance.

This chapter continues this trend by connecting practices among punks in various scenes to global structural and economic developments. It introduces the paradoxical relationship between punk scenes and capital, particularly with respect to the music industry—a relationship that continued to play out over the late 1970s and the 1980s, as the subsequent chapters will demonstrate. Further, it places the punk scenes and music industries of the West and East side by side, facilitating a revealing comparative approach to punk.

In fact, as punk arose, the music industries of the East and West were also undergoing a major transition, forming an emergent global "third culture" of their own. While some basic conditions of the music industry differed between the East and West, there were also some surprising similarities, including a fundamental clash between innate conservative tendencies and the allure of a popular new cultural product that could be sold for a profit. This chapter will explore how, contrary to the rhetoric of ideologues on both sides of the Iron Curtain, the music industry was not driven by free-market economics in the capitalist West or by communist ideology in the East. Rather, both systems were governed by complex mixtures of financial, political, structural, and personal motivations. The declining relevance of Cold War categories and convergence in a global capitalist marketplace did not mean a universal punk experience, however.

The two contradictory aspects of punk scenes—their connection to the mass culture industry and the value they placed on individuality and authenticity—were locked in a complex struggle that was central to the development of punk in the East and the West. Turning punk into a commodity was like burning a candle from both ends. Exchanging subcultural capital for regular capital damaged a band's credibility in the punk scene, where it was perceived as "selling out." Yet, this exchange was also essential, since cooperation with the music industry—capitalist or communist—was inevitable for anyone who wished to move beyond playing in a garage or living room. Each scene and each band within it had its own set of strategies for negotiating these contradictory necessities, creating a continuous tension by which punk thrived and (for some) died.

Capitalism and Subcultural Capital

In the capitalist West, punk was in some respects a businessman's dream. Its simplicity meant it was cheap and fast to record. The workers—musicians—were plentiful, enthusiastic, relatively unskilled, and often inexperienced and uninterested in the subtleties of negotiating contracts. Because the technical barriers to playing punk were low, there were plenty of bands to choose from. And, of course, the Sex Pistols' chart appearance in late 1976 proved punk could sell.

However, the music industry had changed considerably since the first wave of rock and roll in the 1950s. In place of enterprising hucksters searching for an exciting new act, the industry had come to be oriented around what the contemporary music scholar Simon Frith called the "platinum strategy."[11] Simply put, the platinum strategy applied economies of scale to the music industry. Record producers typically based their production decisions on the assumption of a platinum-selling album—one million copies in the United States—and anything that sold fewer than that was not worth the effort. Even with expensive contracts, extended recording timetables, and massive investments of capital for equipment, recording, and advertising, selling a platinum album was still more profitable than a dozen cheap performers selling one twelfth as many records each.

Progressive rock was the perfect fit for the platinum system, characterized by virtuoso star performers who could take the time and afford the equipment to create the level of sound quality audiences came to expect, and guarantee the volume of sales that record companies came to demand. By the late 1970s, the average cost of an album from production to promotion was between $350,000 and $500,000.[12] With the considerable amount of money invested, rock businessmen became risk-averse. Signing a new band with a new sound that might or might not generate a large number of sales might be a justifiable risk if simply turning a profit was the main goal, but in a market characterized by platinum albums and superstars, it was simply foolish.

In this context, anyone who dreamed of being a rock star had to find a way in. From the perspective of punks—and even some sympathetic industry insiders—the music industry had created a rock pantheon, producing bloated, grandiose records by the same aging bands. Punk was less a rebellion against rock and roll per se than against the ethos and gatekeepers that blocked the way for aspiring rock bands. Punk offered an alternative path to that which led through the music industry, which in turn became identified as part of "the system"—the whole structure responsible for their lame, boring, oppressive society. Punks' subcultural capital came in part from the creative strategies each scene developed to bypass, infiltrate, or otherwise frustrate the capitalist music industry. Yet, punk bands everywhere still needed a way to get their music to audiences. The strategies they chose to negotiate these tensions varied from scene to scene.

The New York punk scene started up in the negative space left untouched by the music industry, cobbled together from personal networks rather than market demographics. The scene coalesced around the bohemian crowds hanging out in clubs like Max's Kansas City and then, arguably the birthplace of punk, CBGB, which opened in 1974. Performing shows on Sunday afternoons when the stage was unused, the first wave of punk performances by Television, the Ramones, Blondie, and Patti Smith took place for audiences who paid just one dollar for admission.[13]

The punk scene at CBGB offered an alternative structure for the capitalist entertainment industry—it was no longer about exchanging money for entertainment as a commodity, or about bands exchanging their labor for money. Instead of making a profit, the one-dollar admission was sufficient to run the venue; it ensured that punk was about an experience and a community rather than turning a profit. This structure gave the scene a unique flavor that would not have been possible otherwise. Audiences didn't come with the expectation of getting good entertainment for their money, freeing bands and musicians (or nonmusicians, for that matter) to experiment with music. In stark contrast to the mass music industry, whose preferred scenario was virtuosos playing ten feet above the stadium-sized crowd, at CBGB, the often untrained musicians weren't substantially different from the listeners (some of whom in fact occasionally came onstage to join them). The thin, permeable barrier between performer and audience member was part of what helped punk expand so rapidly: many a punk band formed from audience members who were empowered by shows they attended. Punks often avoided the major sites of performance or recording—by choice or by exclusion—instead using their own alternative media. Together, they created a global network of homemade punk communication that rivaled that of the industry rock magazines that sought to maximize their market shares.

Not every aspect of modern media could be reproduced by using an empty club, a Xerox machine, glue, and scissors, however. If punk bands wanted to reach an audience wider than the local scene—for instance, producing an album or broadcasting a song—they had to work with the music industry. By the late 1970s, producing an album meant making a multitrack recording with specialized equipment and a professional mixer, pressing a record, promoting it, and distributing it to retailers that would sell it to the public. It wasn't the kind of thing most punks could do on their own.

Because major labels weren't likely to take a gamble on punk, bands looked for back entrances to the music industry—independent record labels. Independent labels and punk enjoyed a mutual sympathy from the beginning. Like punk, independent record companies existed in the shadows left by the major record companies. This insulated them somewhat from punks' animosity toward the music business and, in return, made some independents more willing to experiment with punk bands—like the Ramones, who signed with Sire records (after the owner's wife personally saw them at CBGB). They recorded their album in a week for $6,400, a fraction of the industry standard. What would have been considered a waste of time for most major labels turned out to be a great deal for an independent.[14]

However, the line between independent and major record labels was blurry. The Ramones had help getting their record deal from their manager, Danny Fields, who was not just a punk fan but also a "company freak" for Warner Brothers—a position created to liaison between the record industry and the local music scenes. Fields did precisely that: he hung out, went to shows, and partied in the same circles as everyone else in the scene but also provided industry contacts (for punk bands) and business opportunities (for the music industry). Independent record labels existed in a similar space, both apart from and a part of the music industry. For anyone wanting more work in the studio than the Ramones, an independent would likely need a loan, most often obtained through cooperation with a major label. Then, to market and distribute the record on anything more than a local scale, a distribution deal with a major label was necessary. Sire, for instance, had a distribution deal with ABC; before the end of the decade, Warner Brothers would acquire the distribution rights from ABC, and then the label itself.[15]

Sire might have been a great asset for the Ramones, but the label increasingly resembled the rest of the industry in its approach to punk. According to employee Greg Shaw, after Warner Brothers bought out Sire, it promoted the bands that could be marketed as "new wave"—the term used in the United States for market-friendly punkish bands like the Cars—and promptly dropped the rest of its punk roster.[16] Meanwhile, Shaw left Sire to found his own fanzine and record label, Bomp, which became the first of a flurry of independent record labels to rise along with punk in Los Angeles.[17]

Punk bands in the United States also faced challenges working with mass broadcast media, the radio and television. In part, this was simply due to economics. Because commercial radio relied on advertising for its income, maximizing profit meant being able to attract a large audience, justifying a high price for advertising time. Industry market analyses predicted what kind of demographics various types of music would attract—and thus determined the price of advertisements and a station's income. Even more important than building an audience, though, was avoiding alienating one. The bestseller charts offered guidance less for what radio DJs should play than for what they ought to avoid: if they played anything off the charts, they risked losing audience members, and thus ad revenues. The most important task of a radio DJ was thus to avoid anything that could make a listener change the station.[18]

For many DJs, this included punk. Commercial radio had a built-in conservative tendency that made it an unlikely medium for promoting an unfamiliar, unusual musical form. Only music at the margins of punk—the most accessible Blondie songs, Patti Smith's collaboration with Bruce Springsteen, and, by 1978, the post-punk band Talking Heads—made radio charts and got significant play time. The exceptions to this rule were stations in areas that had both vibrant punk scenes and adventuresome DJs willing to take a risk on punk, like KROQ in Los Angeles (which employed Rodney Bingheimer, former proprietor of LA's glam club), or KSAN in San Francisco.[19] Beyond these few exceptions, noncommercial radio was the best bet, such as Georgetown University's WGTB, which managed to slip broadcasts from CBGB under the noses of conservative school officials thanks to the antics of punk-friendly DJ Steve Lorber.[20]

Even with some inroads to the industry, though, punk never took off in the US national market the way it did in the United Kingdom. Even a major punk band like the Clash was unable to duplicate its contract with CBS in the United Kingdom with the label's US office. Industry executives in the United States were slow to invest in marketing punk—which required more capital than in the United Kingdom, making it a greater risk. It was safer to wait until bands became stars with a guaranteed audience, and by that point, it was often too late. That was certainly true for New York's Television, whose album on Elektra came out in 1977, when New York's scene had been eclipsed by the spectacular antics of the Sex Pistols in the United Kingdom.

Like the various local punk scenes of the United States, London also had a small, intimate punk scene, made up of personal networks and out-of-the-way venues such as art schools up until late 1976. Analogous to New York's *Punk*, London had its own independent, self-produced punk 'zine, *Sniffin' Glue*. Even the venues and shops associated with punk—Czezowski's Roxy, Letts's Acme apparel, and McLaren and Westwood's Sex—were only quasi-capitalist ventures. Much like CBGB, the Roxy charged only one pound for admission. This nominal fee was insufficient even to cover the venue's operating costs (despite the fact that it was run by an accountant), and the Roxy closed down for lack of funds after a year. At Acme, Letts operated the register out of his pocket and would sometimes give merchandise away to customers. Profit was simply not the primary objective.

This was just as well, because the UK industry was, at least initially, as conservative as in the United States. For record companies, maximizing sales meant aiming at the widest market. A typical strategy was that used by RSO Records, which produced albums with an eye to "the widest demographics possible."[21] The situation with the broadcast media was no more promising for punk. As in the United States, commercial radio stations in the United Kingdom—preoccupied with maintaining a demographic that would draw in ad money and, above all, avoiding alienating listeners—had little to gain by playing punk. As one station director observed, "Punk records are bought by people under 20 and they don't have the money to spend or the interest in the consumer durables we advertise—unless of course, we start advertising safety-pins. The last thing I want is for a listener to hear a record he doesn't like and say 'What the hell is that?'"[22]

Yet, there were a few places for punk to play. Analogous to CBGB in New York, the Roxy became London's most important punk venue when it opened at the end of 1976, just as the Pistols' scandal on the *Today* show fortuitously made it one of the few places open to punk. There were also a few independent record labels willing to deal in punk—most notably, the independent record store Rough Trade and the like-minded retailers and distributors (including Crass's first label, Small Wonder) grouped under the ironic-yet-apt name Cartel.[23] Finally, punk found an unexpected partner in the United Kingdom's state-run broadcast media. The BBC was governed by a subtly but significantly different objective than commercial radio, reminiscent of state-run media in the communist East: listeners were viewed as constituents whose varied tastes and entertainment needs had to be considered rather than as broad demographic groups that they had to avoid alienating.[24] This encouraged a comparatively diverse range of programming. Most important, though, BBC-1 had a DJ whose adventuresome spirit was matched by his producer's tenacity in carving out an independent space in the station bureaucracy.

John Peel had been a cult icon in the 1960s for his show *The Perfumed Garden*—a favorite of young Woody Mellor that played the psychedelic poetry and music of 1960s counterculture. Like Don Letts, Peel had discovered counterculture via the United States: while visiting in the 1960s, he discovered the black blues and got involved in opposition to the Vietnam War.[25] Upon Peel's return to the United Kingdom, he brought his experience back with him to his radio show. When the United Kingdom decided to shut down private "pirate" stations, BBC-1 brought Peel on board, perhaps hoping to recapture young listeners.[26] Peel added some excitement by bringing reggae over from Jamaica, inviting Bob Marley on his show in 1973 before he was an international superstar or punk fellow traveler. In the summer of 1976, when the Ramones released their first album, Peel played "Judy Is a Punk" on his radio show. A few months later, he was among the first to play the Sex Pistols' first single, "Anarchy in the UK."

Peel became one of the champions of punk in the United Kingdom. He not only played punk on the airwaves but also brought bands in and recorded them—including the Slits.[27] Peel's influence extended well beyond London, the English Channel, or even the Iron Curtain: his show was broadcast from the British sector's radio station into East Berlin, where it was picked up whenever possible by eager prospective punks. Once the BBC recognized that an international market existed for its broadcasts, it began sending records by airmail to buyers around the world. Peel had fans at least as far away as Moscow, as he would discover on a visit to the East shortly after the fall of communism. His recorded broadcasts—along with Radio Luxembourg and Radio Free Europe—became a link between Western and Eastern punk scenes.

As Peel found out, operating within "free markets" did not mean greater choice than under state direction. Peel found that public radio gave him leeway to promote unusual music like punk that would not have been possible at a commercial station (he would know, having been fired from several). Even so, some producers at the station complained that he was wasting airtime on "unlistenable" bands like the Slits—a concern that was compounded when scandal erupted over punk in the media, courtesy of the Sex Pistols. While Malcolm McLaren reveled in the explosions that resulted when subcultural capital and capital collided, the strategy was highly volatile. Following the band's scandalous exchange with host Bill Grundy on the *Today* show, the aftermath reached Peel and his producer John Walters, who received a call from the Radio 1 controller to verify that he wasn't behind any of punk's "filth." Fortunately, Peel was actually ahead of it; Walters could reply that they had already played several records and, in fact, had recorded punk band the Damned the previous week.[28]

The private sector was also often intertwined with politics in the capitalist West. Music industry elites showed that they were willing to collude with political elites when provoked—even against punk bands on their own label. In response to the antics of the Sex Pistols, MP Sir Robert Adley struck up a correspondence with EMI records chairman Sir John Reed, after which Reed denounced the band's "attack on society."[29] EMI dropped the Pistols soon after. Their next label, A&M, went even further, destroying its inventory of the Sex Pistols' single "God Save the Queen" after the scandal at the queen's Silver Jubilee. While several major retailers refused to stock the record, it was still popular enough to sell 150,000 copies in just five days. To avoid the collective embarrassment of the Sex Pistols rising to the top on the back of the music industry, the British Market Research Bureau reportedly fudged its own figures, cherry-picking data to keep the Sex Pistols' numbers low enough to keep them out of number one.[30]

The coordinated reaction between the state and capital against the Sex Pistols showed that in the capitalist West, the lines between the music industry, semi-official institutions, and the state were blurry. The Independent Broadcasting Authority (IBA) instructed all commercial radio and television stations not to broadcast "God Save the Queen" because it was in contravention of Section 4 (10) (A) of the IBA act, being "against good taste or decency, likely to encourage or incite to crime, or lead to disorder." The BBC joined commercial broadcasters in banning the song on June 6 for its "gross bad taste." DJ John Peel, again ahead of the curve, managed to play "God Save the Queen" in the weeks before—and again when the fury died down four months later. Evidently, not everyone was impressed. The next month, he found his show had been replaced with the progressive rock *Friday Rock Show*. Peel was left to rebuild his audience and continue his struggle from another slot.

As a few industry renegades like Peel kept punk visible amid the panics it provoked in early 1977 and again that summer, record companies weathered the storm, surveying the scene for potential business opportunities. Major and independent labels alike scoured the punk scene for bands to sign; EMI returned to punk after dropping the Pistols, signing Sham 69, while the Pistols found a new home with Virgin. Most astounding was the Clash, which signed with the enormous multinational firm CBS. Yet, other bands like the Slits had trouble finding and negotiating record deals—in part because they were hesitant about working with the record industry, which they knew perfectly well was built with the purpose of selling (to them, exploiting) music for profit.[31] As some bands were dropped, banned, and ignored even as others succeeded in working with the industry, the conclusion among many punks in London was that some bands must be more compromising than others.

The Sex Pistols' strategy of using the mainstream media as a Trojan Horse for their music also helped set the tone of the London scene. London punk developed a vitriolic, charged character as punk's two sides—its subcultural and popular aspects—were set against each other. Punks sought out signs of collaboration with capital, or proof that bands were maintaining their subcultural credibility. Even independent record companies were connected to major labels in one way or another, and all were connected to capital and the market.

Even more alarming, some of the biggest names in punk (the Sex Pistols, the Ramones, and the Buzzcocks) made it on major national television shows like *Top of the Pops*—a feat that punks hadn't been able to manage on US airwaves. In contrast, the Clash pointedly refused to appear—using the show as a line in the sand that marked their subcultural space. Yet, their contract with CBS—the death of punk, according to Mark Perry from *Sniffin' Glue*—meant their subcultural credibility was also seriously jeopardized.

The journey of the Clash from humble roots to a contract with CBS, to triple albums, to playing arenas captures the tension between capital and subcultural capital supremely. To some fans, they started to look like they had become just another rock group; they had "sold out." The group that suffered the most, however, was the Sex Pistols themselves. While McLaren's strategy had gotten the Pistols plenty of cash and subcultural capital, he eventually ran out of opportunities to reinvest it as the Pistols disintegrated amid the constant chaos. London punk thrived and died on edge of contradiction between subcultural and capital, and the space between the two was incredibly thin. By the beginning of 1978, two staples of the London scene—the Roxy and the Sex Pistols—would both be counted among the deceased.

Subcultural Capital without Capitalism

If punk emerged in the space between capital and subcultural capital in New York, and out of the explosive interaction between them in London, what could it possibly mean in the communist Second World, where capitalism ostensibly did not exist? Journalists, cultural authorities, and politicians asked precisely this question as punk rose up from the underground in parts of Eastern Europe in the early 1980s. The communist music industries of Eastern Europe offered a particular set of challenges, and occasionally opportunities, for the punk bands of the Second World. The conditions of punk in the East were shaped by each state's unique combination of capital, cultural politics, and administrative complexity, all of which contributed to an environment of conservatism.[32] However, punk economics around the Eastern bloc were also shaped by the struggle between capital and subcultural capital, much as they were in the West.

Contrary to the myth of politics driving cultural decisions in the communist world, earning money was a major concern for the music industries of the Eastern bloc. With the late Cold War era communist state deriving its authority from distributing resources to its citizenry, recouping some of its outlays through citizens' voluntary spending on leisure and entertainment was essential. Financial incentives were particularly powerful in states that had undertaken reforms in the direction of a market economy, such as Poland and Hungary.

As the vice director of the Department of Theater and Estrada in Poland noted in a 1981 interview, the industries he oversaw functioned as both artistic institutions and revenue generators, unlike other areas of the arts.[33] This was also true in Hungary, where the New Economic Mechanism introduced limited market forces to the economy in 1968. The imperative to generate income became even more powerful around the Eastern bloc by the mid-1970s, when economies slowed due to the global recession.

The need to make money had practical consequences. As in the West, the most efficient way to make a profit was to generate the maximum number of record purchases and concert ticket sales from the fewest possible recordings and performances. These incentives toward conservative repertoire choices were compounded by the scarcity of materials and outdated machinery for recording and producing records across 1970s Eastern Europe. The safest way to meet quotas and collect income was by working with a handful of established major performers.

Most states in the Eastern bloc had their own superstar progressive rock bands: SBB in Poland, Omega in Hungary, and Time Machine in the USSR. Other guaranteed big sellers came from abroad: the Beatles were pressed even in the most culturally cautious states of the East, the USSR and East Germany. Meanwhile, Poland and Hungary had much of the Western Top 40 available on records and broadcast media (albeit months or years behind their appearance on charts in the West). Bands from the East and West were also in contact with each other, traveling on tours in both directions. There were incentives to encourage bands to tour outside the Eastern bloc—not only as a reward for good work and as cultural diplomacy but as a chance to bring in valuable foreign currency to the East. East European bands toured Western Europe, the United States, and much of the Third World in the 1970s and 1980s. However, this privilege was generally reserved for the bands most likely to attract large audiences (and positive press) in the West—not punk bands.[34]

Broadcast media in the East were potentially more amenable to punk than the record industry. Unlike commercial radio in the West, state-run media did not rely on advertising for their revenue. Like the BBC in England, part of the mission of broadcast media was to cater to a spectrum of listener tastes. Yet, at least initially, decisionmakers saw punk as too marginal to even be on the spectrum—at least until the early 1980s. As one of the directors at Polish Radio explained in 1980, "new recordings cost so much, we try to risk as little as possible. . . . We want to meet the tastes of the widest range of listeners, including old, middle-aged, and young."[35] Television had even stricter standards for what it was willing to present, since the resources required to produce a video segment—a director, a set, and film—were even greater than those for making an audio recording. In short, like the platinum strategy in the West, the structure of the music industry in the East tended to privilege established musical acts over experimentation and risk-taking.

Of course, the necessity of earning money coexisted with ideological and political imperatives placed on the industry by the state. Industry executives constantly worked to balance financial incentives with cultural politics when selecting a repertoire for recording, performance and broadcasting. However, by the 1970s and 1980s, the ideological imperatives of the Second World were not necessarily Marxist. Rather, as the fourth chapter will demonstrate, by the late 1970s, the main cultural imperative trumpeted by the ministries of culture and communist parties of the Second World with respect to music was disseminating "serious music" (i.e., "classical") that would elevate the population toward socialism. The second priority was providing "recreational music" to soothe and entertain the masses (both, needless to say, were valued above any music that might be deemed harmful to socialism or the party/state).

A tension resulted from the fact that low-priority recreational music was much more popular than high-priority serious music. Economics favored recreational music, while politics favored serious music. There were ways to mitigate the dilemma, such as using proceeds from recreational music to fund "serious music" in order to claim that financial gains were in service of cultural objectives. Similarly, industry elites sometimes argued that the media's cultural-political objective of uplift could only be achieved if citizens were willing to "tune in"—requiring attracting listeners and earning their goodwill by playing the latest music trends that would interest them.[36]

Youth and cultural organizations were sometimes willing to work with punk in order to attract young people. Across the Eastern bloc, local cultural centers known as houses of culture, jazz unions, and youth union clubs provided essential equipment, exposure, and performance space for bands. Even so, some elites fretted that these endeavors interfered with efforts to expose youth to "true culture." In 1980s Poland, for instance, rumors abounded that young people were buying up classical tapes and recording popular music over them—a somewhat different concern from that of their Western counterparts, who were distressed by the financial implications of cassettes (giving consumers the ability to record music on their own, bypassing the industry).

Financial and political imperatives each shaped the music industries of the East. However, the most ubiquitous characteristic of the music industry in the Eastern bloc was its complex, disorganized structure. Contrary to the impression given by terms like "planned," "command," or "centralized" economy, the music industries of the East were organized haphazardly. In Poland, for example, there were multiple record presses, distributors, retailers, broadcast media, recording studios, regional concert agencies, unions, and concert venues—all under different management and seldom aware of what others were doing. Some were overseen by various state ministries, and some by divisions of the

Communist Party. The different branches of the industry seldom coordinated their operations and often were left on their own in making day-to-day decisions. This diffusion of responsibility might sound similar to capitalist countries, but the crucial difference was that the music industry in the Second World lacked the professional market research and consumer polling that informed production decisions in the West. The information available to record presses was typically limited to lists of what retailers had previously ordered (rather than what they were actually selling). Without reliable information, music industry officials in the Second World were left to rely on gut feelings or personal preference.

What looked complex in theory was often even more chaotic in practice. While a labyrinth of regulations shaped the structure of each state's music landscape, they were not always followed. As was the case across Eastern European economic life dating to the Stalin era, second-economy ("black market") conditions affected the music industry. The most popular bands, for instance, sometimes earned extra payment "on the side" in exchange for performing at a show in order to boost ticket sales (while band members in Poland did not benefit from large audiences, concert organizers—and the state, which shared in profits—certainly did). This created the impression that few industry executives and bands were getting rich at the expense of others, and amplified the accusations directed at bands that presented themselves as subcultural but seemed to be working with the system.

Each of these conditions—capital, cultural politics, and complex, chaotic structure—had significant effects on the punk scenes of Eastern Europe. The need for guaranteed sellers and predictable reactions from authorities conspired to make it very difficult for a new, amateur band to secure a recording, a show, or even musical instruments to play. The need for income and scarcity of materials contributed to an extremely restrictive policy for licensing bands to record—one that did not favor new punk bands without established audiences. Moreover, punk didn't seem to fit either definition of music offered for cultural politics. Unlike progressive rock, it was difficult to make the argument that punk was "serious music," or even a gateway to it, yet it wasn't relaxing or soothing like "recreational music" was supposed to be either. Economic and cultural-political incentives both discouraged risk-taking, and punk seemed risky.

While some basic characteristics were shared across the Second World, each of the music industries of the Eastern bloc had its own peculiarities, since each developed according to local policies, proclivities, and contingencies.[37] For example, in Hungary, bands earned royalties on records and a portion of proceeds from concerts, as was true in the West—making large-scale recordings and concerts a viable financial option for some bands. In Poland, however, bands were paid according to a table of rates by minutes recorded in the studio, or by the concert for live shows. This meant a band's financial interest was to perform as frequently as possible, without regard to the size of audience. This favored a dynamic, intimate live music scene.

Perhaps the most important characteristic shaping each state's music scene, though, was whether that state distinguished between "official" and "unofficial" bands. In the USSR, Czechoslovakia, and East Germany, cultural policy divided bands into official/professional and amateur bands—with only the former licensed by the state to make income from performances or recordings. Punk scenes with this distinction tended to have a rigid boundary between subcultural and mainstream bands. Bands had to explicitly choose between official or unofficial status, and whether to exist above ground or underground. Each option came with serious consequences.

Submitting to state verification for official status placed bands under the microscope of the state. These bands were vulnerable to interference, since the state could revoke their status at any time (as became clear when East Germany and Czechoslovakia cracked down on popular musicians in 1976). However, without official status, bands had no access to scarce resources like equipment, practice spaces, and performance venues. As in the West, some bands developed creative methods for exploiting the dynamic between subcultural capital and access to the music industry. This could be achieved by strategically switching categories periodically—as did the Plastic People of the Universe in Czechoslovakia and Akvarium in the USSR. However, since punk bands were unlikely to submit to (or pass) a verification exam for official status, punk bands in these states typically remained underground, staying out of the sights of authorities and rarely breaking through to popular consciousness. In the Soviet Union in 1983, for instance, the Ministry of Culture's Moscow Research Centre on the Arts suggested that 40,000 out of 70,000 bands were unregistered amateur groups; a mere 145 were professional bands.[38]

For the most part, it was in states like Hungary and Poland, whose cultural policy did not legally distinguish between official and unofficial bands, that punk had the greatest impact. The reason for this is twofold. First, since any group could be invited to perform anywhere, concert organizers could book the bands they deemed most likely to bring in audiences (and revenue) rather than having to choose an official licensed performer. Second, these states tended to have more visible mechanisms for promotion. In turn, they also often had large, popular progressive rock bands that dominated the national scene—a precondition for the most powerful punk insurrections in the West and the East. In 1976, as East Germany and Czechoslovakia cracked down on rock, Hungary's premier progressive rock band, Omega, entertained the nation with concerts featuring fireworks, professional dancers, balloons, and banners, all topped off with a tour around Western Europe. The only band that could compete, Lokomotiv GT, even traveled to the United States for a tour. While punk arose in the unofficial space outside rigid regulations on popular music in the USSR, Czechoslovakia, and East Germany, it arose in Hungary and Poland as a reaction against the domination of established rock bands—much as it did in the United Kingdom and the United States.

By the 1980s, though, even states that distinguished official bands from amateur groups began to occasionally allow punk bands to make use of official institutions. In Czechoslovakia, some relatively polished punk-pop bands, akin to Poland's MMG bands, performed at Prague's Jazz Days, inspiring other punk bands to form.[39] In the Soviet Union, by the 1980s, Leningrad created venues at which even upstart new wave groups could start a band and eventually get exposure. In 1981, the Leningrad Rock Club created an institutionalized space for rock and punk using classic cultural-political language in its slogan, voicing goals of "attracting youth to a wide range of creative activities," "raising the cultural level of visual presentation and ideological artistic content," and "portraying and propagandizing the best examples of national and international music in the given genre."[40] There, groups like Kino and its Soviet-Korean leader, Viktor Tsoi, would bring a playful punk sensibility to their music. The close connection between punk groups and official youth organizations was particularly evident in Yugoslavia, the pariah of the Eastern bloc, where the youth magazine *Polet* set off a punk explosion as it sought out new topics to attract young readers in the wake of the Tito regime. A flurry of punk bands arose in Ljubljana, Zagreb, and Belgrade, where they would flourish until 1981.

Meanwhile, in the states with the most visible punk scenes, Hungary and Poland, punk bands were soon playing at concerts and festivals, recording albums, and even making music videos for state television. The thinner and more permeable the boundary between amateur and professional band was, the more visible and dynamic the punk scene became. However, the exposure came at a price. Bands struggled to maintain their credibility as subcultural bands when they had no "unofficial" or "amateur" category to attest to their independence. Bands that prized their subcultural capital were left to decide the extent to which they would work with the state-controlled music industry and how they would justify it to their fans—with serious consequences either way. Industry conditions heightened the tensions between the music industry and punk bands—and between punk bands that managed to get media access and those that did not. The structure of the industry meant that countless gates had to be passed (and palms greased), and each link in the chain was capable of capriciously putting an end to a band's quest for a record deal or performance space. At the same time, these conditions allowed for occasional loopholes that savvy impresarios or band managers could exploit. For those who were able to understand the industry's needs, speak the language, and make use of connections, opportunities arose—at the expense of other bands, it seemed to some punks.

Adding to the tension between capital and subcultural capital, in the East, capital was not just connected to the music industry but also was ostensibly controlled by the state. As uncool as international music conglomerates were in the United States and the United Kingdom, the state-run music industry in Eastern Europe was still less popular. Anyone working with it was seen not only as "selling out" but also as collaborating with the system. Those who weren't willing or able to work with the media were restricted to local networks like student unions (such as Gajewski's club, Remont) and houses of culture. Yet, these institutions—connected to the Communist Party and the state, respectively—were also vulnerable to accusations of collaboration. These characteristics of the music industries of the Second World gave rise to massive tension within the punk scenes of the East. Consequently, the clash between capital and subcultural capital would be even more bitter than in the West when punk and the mainstream media collided—which is precisely what happened in Poland in the summer of 1980.

That summer, Poland's prestigious song festival in Opole brought new wave band Maanam and punk to national attention. By then, Welsh-English émigré John Porter had left the group to form his own band, but Maanam's singer, Kora Jackowska, had enough verve to fill the stage on her own. Like other professional singers at the festival, Jackowska showed up onstage without her band, which performed from the wings. Unlike others, though, she wore short cropped hair, androgynous black pants and a shirt, and fingerless gloves—directing attention to her white sneakers. It was a stark contrast with the permed hair and formal evening wear of other women performing at the festival. Stranded on the stage alone, she made the best of the situation, moving around enough to give the spotlight operator fits. The biggest surprise for the festival audience, though, was the performance itself, which took an unremarkable pop song about Buenos Aires and turned it into punk with Jackowska's confrontational, intense performance, ranging from gruff, gravelly growls to rapid vibrato and high-pitched squeals—all delivered while staring down the festival audience members, left squirming in their seats.[41]

From the perspective of most punks, Maanam's performance may have seemed unremarkable, or even tame. However, like the panic-inspiring bombshell dropped by the Sex Pistols' Steve Jones on the *Today* show, it was televised—and, in this case, nationally. Consequently, it marked the beginning of punk's rapid rise into popular consciousness in Poland. The same summer, Kryzys (Crisis), Robert Brylewski's pioneer punk band from Warsaw, showed up at Pop Session, the premier international festival in Poland. A new wave band like Maanam was one thing, but audiences, critics, and punks were all taken aback when a full-blooded punk band like Kryzys showed up onstage. One journalist marveled at witnessing the performance of "punk-reagge [sic]", a form of music so new and different that it evidently exceeded his vocabulary.[42]

Within a year or two, those new words would become common parlance in discussions of popular culture and youth in Poland. Thanks to the efforts of MMG promoters, new albums by Maanam and John Porter's Porter Band were produced by state firms in respectable (by Polish standards) runs of 67,000 and 27,000, respectively. Yet, as in the United Kingdom, the success of some bands stood in contrast to the underground followings of others. As some groups rose into the national spotlight thanks to the socialist music industry, it set into action an intense struggle over subcultural capital between bands that were willing and able to cooperate with the music industry and those that were not.

From the moment punks started trading their subcultural capital for actual capital, pioneering punk impresario Henryk Gajewski worried about the interaction between punk and "the system." In September 1980, as new wave was errupting into popular consciousness, he fretted, "New wave in Poland awaits certain death. The spontaneous bands playing the newest music do not have a chance."[43] Punk and MMG had grown simultaneously, feeding off of each other for the right combination of maintaining their subcultural capital and capitalizing on it. The dynamic was fruitful for some bands like Maanam, but poisonous to Gajewski. After all, his motto was "To play well, you just follow rules. To play badly, you need to create every second of every song." As the previous chapter showed, unlike Malcolm McLaren, Gajewski saw the Polish music industry as something to bypass rather than a vehicle for punk's infiltration. Gajewski eschewed existing clubs, festivals, and performance networks, urging others to "support other bands who are independent of Intervision [festival] and [Polish Television's] Studio-2."

Punk's encounter with Music of the Young Generation threatened precisely the opposite. Gajewski felt much like Mark Perry of *Sniffin' Glue*, who declared punk dead the day that the Clash signed to Capitol: punk had traded its subcultural capital for actual capital, and through its spectacular success it had become part of what it was against. By the end of the year, Gajewski wrote, "Musical rebellion against the system started, but it adjusted to the system because the system wouldn't adjust. . . . First there was punk in the late 1970s . . . then the new wave of 1980. Now both are dead."[44]

Fortunately, a few weeks later Gajewski found an antidote to his depression—and to the corruption of the Polish scene—when he got his hands on the latest album from UK punk band Crass. Penny Rimbaud and Crass had already weathered the storm of punk's commercialization in the United Kingdom, watching uneasily as punk went "from being a force for change, to becoming just another element in the grand media circus."[45] Where Malcolm McLaren and the Sex Pistols dealt with the media on its terms, through contracts, Crass avoided the standard mechanism of the market. The band's first album, *The Feeding of the 5000* (named for the size of the press run), was sold at a loss. Not surprisingly, Crass had trouble getting someone to press the album until finding Small Wonder, an independent record company that was part of Rough Trade's Cartel. To avoid the taint of capital, Crass directed the proceeds to criminal defense of anarchists on trial, an anarchist center, and the Campaign for Nuclear Disarmament. In place of cash, the band earned subcultural capital, amassing a loyal following and rising up the United Kingdom's alternative record charts. Even so, Crass ran into trouble at the few places it inevitably brushed against the mechanisms of the music industry. When the band was unable to find a printer or distributor willing to handle the record with the first track on organized religion, it had to substitute a blank track titled "The Sound of Free Speech," revealing the oppressive operation of censorship and contradiction with liberal promises of the United Kingdom.[46] It was a bold response to censorship that resonated with Gajewski and punk bands on the other side of the Iron Curtain. Crass's second album, *Stations of the Crass*, went further still. It was deemed so offensive that even Small Wonder refused to produce it. Small wonder the label refused: the band's harsh, grating style compounded by the insistence on selling the album at half price made it a challenging business proposition. Crass decided to self-release the record instead.

Whether or not Gajewski was aware of Rimbaud's shared roots in Fluxus, *Stations of the Crass* rejuvenated Gajewski's hope for punk. He was particularly impressed with the way Crass managed to avoid the mechanisms of capitalism—producing music without profits, remaining financially independent and uncompromising. He translated Crass's assault on punk bands that cooperated with the capitalist system into the terminology of the Polish music industry and redirected it at punk in the Second World: "Crass hates recreational music [*rozrywka*]," he wrote, and "especially hates punk bands that start out with ideals but go on to prostitute themselves."[47] Rather than relying on authorities, Crass showed how to rely on yourself and a community of like-minded people—all embodied in the phrase "do-it-yourself," translated into Polish as *rób swoje* (make your own). It was much like the Fluxus movement both he and Rimbaud had participated in—but adapted to punk.[48]

In Gajewski's view, Crass's principles applied perfectly to the People's Republic of Poland, from the band's advocacy of anarchy to its opposition to aggression, force, violence, the army, and bureaucracy. Even in oppressive systems where "cultural institutions are manipulated by the state," Gajewski wrote, Crass showed "how freedom is possible." Gajewski translated "Big Man, Big M.A.N," into Polish: "Oh yes, oh yes, oh yes, what a wonderful life, / God, queen, country, colour telly, car and wife."[49] Crass's attack on consumerist, patriotic patriarchy worked just as well as a critique of the paternalistic, nationalist, consumerist bureaucracy of Poland as of the conservative suburban businessmen of the capitalist West.

Perhaps Crass would have been surprised to learn that *Stations of the Crass* became a manifesto for a Polish man a thousand miles away, on the other side of the Iron Curtain. Yet, when the band had created the album the previous summer, it had also drawn comparisons with the authoritarian East. On another track, "The Gasman Cometh," Crass twisted a playful postwar comedic song about a handyman into a portent of apocalypse, examining modern civilization through the eyes of Auschwitz concentration camp in Poland. Auschwitz, "now a tourist spot for the goggle eyed to pry," was the quintessence of corruption, inhumanity, and self-destruction of modern civilization. Now, the gasman was on his way over from the East, Crass warned, as the violent "Southall coshes" wielded by police a few months earlier at the rally attended by an alliance of punks and antifascists made clear. Nodding in agreement across the Iron Curtain, Gajewski and Crass saw the violent, authoritarian regimes of the East and West as evil twins. The apocalyptic vision turned out to be prophetic: punk's intersection with the mass media brought it to the attention of new audiences—including the political elites of the Eastern bloc.

4

The Politics of Aesthetics

Punk in the East and West

Widespread concern about punk began building in Poland the moment MMG and the media propelled it into the national spotlight. Against a backdrop of crisis, punk's notorious slogan of "no future" exacerbated elites' preoccupation with the nation and the socialization of youth. In February 1981, the upper echelon of the Communist Party decided it was time to consult the leading experts about punk. The Central Committee's Division of Culture reviewed a brief pamphlet, "Social Aspects of Rock Music: The Meaning of Youth Culture in Society," authored by sociologist and rock enthusiast Jerzy Wertenstein-Żuławski, who was inspired by British cultural studies (in fact, he would translate an excerpt of Dick Hebdige's *Subculture: The Meaning of Style* two years later for a Polish music industry trade journal).[1] The Division of Culture knew little about punk, but party elites were largely amenable to the CCCS-inspired approach—particularly the idea of subculture as a protest against inequality in capitalist society. Punk, Wertenstein-Żuławski suggested, arose in the 1970s as a rebellion against the capitalist recording industry and a reassertion of rock's folk roots. Essentially, punk was mass culture returning to the people.

From the perspective of the People's Republic of Poland, interpreting punk as a rebellion against capitalism was appealing. The problem arose in applying that interpretation to punk in a socialist country like Poland, which ostensibly had no capitalist music industry or society to rebel against. Wertenstein-Żuławski entered trickier territory translating the account of punk in the West to conditions in the East. He observed that music in Poland faced "limits of an administrative nature" and lacked a social base due to the "paternalistic" relationship of Polish society to youth and—most damning—the "less democratic" nature of Polish society compared with the United States and England. Needless to say, the Division of Culture underlined "less democratic" for correction. After all, it pointed out (with some justification), punk and rock had been suppressed by the capitalist establishment, demonstrating antidemocratic tendencies in the West.

In a curious turn of analysis, the Division of Culture implicitly accepted the argument that suppressing punk was antidemocratic—something that capitalist countries, not socialist ones, were prone to do. Even so, the proper response to punk for a state like Poland remained uncertain.

The Division of Culture's ambiguous approach to punk wasn't unique to Poland. At nearly the same moment in Hungary, authorities responded to the proliferation of punk and new wave by inviting several rock bands to advise the state at a three-day conference in March 1981. More surprising still, the initiative yielded a seemingly workable strategy: negotiating with Janos Brody from the band Illes, authorities proposed a three-pronged approach, "ban the dangerous, tolerate the objectionable, promote the acceptable."[2] For two more years, the Hungarian punk scene would flourish, evidently viewed as no worse than objectionable.

Meanwhile, in the Soviet Union, the editors and journalists of the Ukrainian socialist youth periodical *Rovesnik* had also been eyeing UK punk, and especially Rock Against Racism, with interest from their home base in Moscow. In their view, punk groups like the Clash had recaptured the flagging spirit of anti-imperialism and antiracism that had inspired the radical left in the West (and in the East) in decades past. Between 1978 and 1980, *Rovesnik* included multiple favorable reviews of the Clash and its struggle with racism in the West; in 1982 and 1983, the magazine even reprinted the lyrics from "Guns of Brixton" and "Know Your Rights."[3] Local Komsomol youth union discos joined in the celebration of punk, playing "Heart of Glass" by the New York punk scene's Blondie in Soviet Ukraine in 1979.[4] Punk shows were one of the few bright spots in the otherwise dismal ability of youth unions to attract youth.

Meanwhile, back in Poland, the Division of Culture concluded its analysis, thanking Wertenstein-Żuławski for his "interesting account" and ordering four hundred copies—once the "political errors" were corrected, of course. The pamphlet then could serve as a guide for lower-level officials in deciding what to do with punk as they encountered it on an ever more frequent basis. Whether that information would make a local official more or less likely to, say, allow a punk festival was anyone's guess, however. The central party apparatus had a chance to lay down an official line with respect to punk, but it demurred, leaving the door open for local authorities to embrace or combat punk as they saw fit.

As this example indicates, when punk intersected with popular consciousness through the mechanisms of the modern media, political elites in the East and West felt compelled to address it. Yet, as they did so, they found that punk refused to fit neatly within the contemporary ideological frameworks they used to make sense of the world. In part, this was due to punk's ideological ambiguity (if not agnosticism). However, it was also because punk arose in societies undergoing a massive transition in the East and West alike. While the global upheavals of the 1960s have typically overshadowed the decade that followed, historians of the United States, the United Kingdom, the USSR, and Eastern Europe, and most recently, of globalization, have begun to acknowledge the 1970s as a watershed in its own right. In *The Seventies*, Bruce Schulman shows how the decade ushered in a momentous shift in American politics, society, and culture marked by a decline of trust in government, renewed faith in the market, and a retreat from the public sphere to the private.[5] Similarly, scholars identify the 1970s in the United Kingdom as the end of the era of "consensus politics," when the postwar settlement between the Right and Left to accept a capitalist system with substantial social programs came under attack, dissolving by the end of the decade.[6]

The 1970s were arguably a time of even greater change in the Second World. The austere self-sacrifice of Stalinism had been discredited across the Eastern bloc by the mid-1950s, but efforts to find humane socialist alternatives had been suppressed by force in 1956 in Hungary and 1968 in Czechoslovakia. Khrushchev's attempts to reinvigorate communism in the USSR through mass participation were firmly rebuked in the mid-1960s as well. By the 1970s, once-potent communist ideology had dwindled to little more than rote quotations from Lenin and Marx. In the absence of ideological justification, the state increasingly based its legitimacy on its firm hold on the production and, more important, distribution of goods in what James Millar calls the "Little Deal"—a new form of acquisitive socialism in the Brezhnev era.[7] At the same time, new social and political movements besides the Communist Party arose in states around the Eastern bloc, provoking vociferous debates both within and beyond their respective governing structures.

Alongside scholarship examining the 1970s in various national and regional contexts, scholars of globalization identify the decade as a moment of global transition. Following years of postwar overproduction and an energy crisis in 1973–1974, the mid-1970s marked the onset of a global economic downturn followed by a series of economic assistance—and readjustment—plans brokered by the International Monetary Fund (IMF). Drawing states from all three worlds—places as diverse as Peru, Poland, and the United Kingdom—into a global capitalist order, the result has been described as a third wave of globalization, a transition as significant as the transatlantic exchanges of the late fifteenth century and the age of imperialism in the nineteenth century. To draw from the terminology of world historian Eric Hobsbawm and cultural studies scholar Michael Denning, the 1970s were "crisis decades" that brought an end to the "age of three worlds."[8]

This chapter will show how punk was an important part of the massive changes taking place in societies on both sides of the Iron Curtain. While journalists noted a correlation between punk and domestic crisis in the East and West from the beginning, punk's relationship with the global transformations of the 1970s was deeper and more significant than most imagined. The rise of punk was intertwined with an international transition from a sociopolitical worldview toward a cultural-aesthetic worldview. Around the world, punk encountered societies where class- and ideology-based political and social demarcations were gradually losing their dominance. In the realm of politics, the transition began in the late 1960s, with the rise of a "new left," based more on a progressive and globally minded worldview than on working-class credentials, and the subsequent rise in the 1970s of an equally culturally based new right in response. This sociopolitical transition intertwined with an aesthetic transformation. After decades of challenge from the artistic avant-garde, the high-low distinction that was central to modern understandings of culture began to crumble in the face of postmodernism. The Arnoldian model of culture that had dominated since the nineteenth century in the West—and that had made a miraculous recovery in the communist Eastern bloc—began to face serious challenges from relativistic consumerism and postmodernist skepticism. As punk became intertwined with this societal shift, it resulted in a series of moral panics that unfolded in the media and expanded into the realm of politics, pushing politicians to respond even as punk eluded their political sensibilities.[9]

Punk made such a significant impact on the societies in which it arose because it overlapped with and exacerbated these emergent fissures. Besides disrupting postwar consensus between the Right and Left, punk provoked growing tensions within each of these sociopolitical groupings. As Andrew Hartman has shown in *A War for the Soul of America*, the intense debates that emerged from the upheavals of the 1960s scrambled political identities on the Right and Left in the decade that followed.[10] Over the course of the 1970s, many erstwhile leftists struggled to incorporate the radical cultural changes that came out of the 1960s, and they found their cultural sensibilities overcoming their economic-political allegiance to the Left. Punk dramatically amplified this tendency, forcing them to choose between a class-based political allegiance to the Left and a traditionalist cultural identity increasingly connected to an emergent cultural Right. Punk's effect on the political spectrum was just as significant in the United Kingdom, where, as Matthew Worley has shown, punk eluded traditional right and left categories, bringing out generational fault lines as it defied overtures from parties across the spectrum.[11] However, perhaps the most dramatic transformation took place in the Eastern bloc, where punk played a key role in fracturing the main political categories of the postwar era, the communist government and the nationalist opposition, spurring a major realignment.

Much like the debates between cultural studies versus postcultural studies approaches to popular culture, scholarly debates about the politics of punk are both contentious and inconclusive. Whether punk seems "right wing" or "left wing" depends on the example one chooses—varying not only by scene or band, but even within the same song text or stylistic convention.[12] The reasons for this ambiguity should by now be clear. Accounts of the politics of punk typically try to locate it on the political spectrum by testing it according to the standard political categories of the Right and Left—class, nation, race, gender. In other words, they attempt to define punk in terms of the political categories that punk was so effective at scrambling. Contrary to the common wisdom that punk in the West was about capitalism, race, and gender while punk in the East was about anticommunist politics, politicians in the East and West reacted to punk similarly. After all, both societies had long relied on surprisingly similar cultural models based on the tradition of Matthew Arnold, and both societies were undergoing similar socio-cultural-political transformations in the 1970s and 1980s. East and West, punk's assault worked on the level of style, aesthetics, identity, and moral sentiment rather than ideological content. While many politicians reacted strongly to punk on moral and cultural grounds, it didn't line up with their political sensibilities and thus eluded a political response—at least initially. This would change, however, by the 1980s. Even as punk resisted categorization along conventional lines, it fueled an emergent political formation based not on class, race, or gender ideology per se but, rather, on one's identity as socioculturally progressive and cosmopolitan, or conservative, traditionalist, and nationalistic. In the decades that followed, these new, culturally oriented political groupings would overtake the economic sociopolitical categories from the previous age in part thanks to the fracas that arose around punk.

The Politics of Punk in the West

The mixture of concern and confusion that punk evoked among officials in the Central Committee's Division of Culture in Poland was reminiscent of the initial reactions of politicians in the United Kingdom to the rise of punk into popular consciousness in 1977. There, too, the context was an atmosphere of national crisis. The recession of the mid-1970s was the immediate catalyst, but the roots ran much deeper. One factor was the collapse of consensus politics and the welfare state. Since the middle of the Second World War, politicians on the Left and Right had held to a tacit agreement to avoid chaos by compromise. The Right accepted a Keynesian policy of state-spurred economic growth, providing workers with a safety net of basic comforts and necessities, and the Left accepted the basic inequalities of capitalism. However, as growth slowed in the mid-1960s and was overtaken by inflation in the 1970s, holding up both sides of the bargain grew increasingly difficult.[13]

Prime Minister Callaghan's Labour government tried to maintain social services and salaries despite slowing growth and rampant inflation, but in 1976, Callaghan announced that cuts were the only way out. Further, the budget required a loan backed by the IMF, with additional cuts and austerity measures as its conditions. The benefits that formed the basis of the social contract were being revoked—and the Labour government would pay the price. A contemporary survey showed that public trust in the government fell to 39 percent, and just a quarter of citizens believed politicians generally spoke the truth.[14] Among the few factors on Labour's side was that the Conservative opposition under Edward Heath had also accepted the compromise-based approach of the consensus era; only a few renegades aligned with Margaret Thatcher on the party's right wing championed an alternative vision based on neoliberal economics and neoconservative social values. For the time, though, they remained the minority voice within the party.

The economic crisis was compounded by a crisis in British identity. Great Britain was an empire by definition, but it had been hemorrhaging its colonies since World War II. For some white English citizens accustomed to holding a clear place at the top of a global hierarchy, the whole world order seemed to be inverted. Instead of enterprising Britons conquering the world, they fretted over the influx of "colonials" from around the world—especially West Indians and South Asians—who had returned to the metropol in search of new opportunities. Some argued that English culture was threatened by these new residents, as Enoch Powell notoriously envisioned in a 1968 speech predicting an inevitable conflict between Britain's ethnicities, flowing in "rivers of blood." Powell was no longer active in politics by the mid-1970s, but amid growing doubts about national greatness, concern about immigrants posing a threat to law and order (including a mugging scare in 1972 that was tinged with racist imagery), and finally, the recession, radical right-wing nationalist groups like the National Front and the British Movement rose in popularity polls. Finally, the existential crisis facing the United Kingdom directed special attention toward English youth, the future standard-bearers of the nation.

In the context of ideological crisis, distress over declining greatness, and concern over youth, punk had the potential to arouse more than casual concern, even among elites who normally wouldn't deign to address popular culture. In this context, the scandal over the Sex Pistols' release of "God Save the Queen" and performance on the Thames during the queen's Silver Jubilee brought punk to the floors of Parliament in the summer of 1977. By taking on the monarchy, the Pistols transcended the realm of political debate, striking at a symbol at the heart of British pride, culture, and imperial potency. The debate that ensued was emphatically not about politics—at least not in the traditional sense. Rather, the Members of Parliament from across the political spectrum considered deeper issues like the youth, society, and culture as they struggled to align punk with their worldviews—much as their counterparts soon would in the communist East.

When Labour MP Bruce George addressed punk, he did so in the context of a genteel discussion of "public safety at pop concerts." His tone grew more ominous, though, as he mentioned punk by name, bringing the salacious tone of the tabloid press, present since the *Today* show scandal the previous December, into the halls of Parliament. Quoting a report from the *Sunday People*, he read, "It is sick. It is dangerous. It is sinister. And their findings are a warning to every family. Our investigation has uncovered a creed which glorifies violence, filth, sadism and rebellion." George admitted the article's tone was alarmist (he had once been a "pop fanatic" himself). Yet, he couldn't deny that there was something to the licentious report he read. "I have been to a couple of punk rock concerts and seen how even quite respectable youngsters respond to this phenomenon," he observed. "Despite the total opposition of the Press, a punk rock record by the Sex Pistols has shot to the top of the hit parade. Young people are listening to this new phenomenon and it is one about which we should be concerned."[15]

Punk pushed George to transform his pragmatic concern for public welfare toward a Manichaean view of order versus anarchy. Over the next few minutes of his speech, he argued that punk was not culture—indeed, it wasn't even proper entertainment. He warned, "With the 'new wave' of music, as it is euphemistically called, we have people who can deliberately provoke violence." In contrast to the responsible pop groups from George's youth, punk bands lacked the restraint to put a stop to the "rioting down below." Instead, punk gave free rein to the anarchic energy of the masses. Even at a time when consensus politics were under duress, George's interpretation of punk in terms of chaos versus order attracted support from across the floor. Conservative MP David Mudd offered a dubious helping hand, assuring Parliament that George was not being alarmist but was "merely drawing attention to the holocaust of death and destruction" that punk could generate. Mudd too linked punk to chaos—and called up the countervailing need for order to keep the masses in line—as he put it, "crowd control."

There were alternate interpretations of punk available besides the order-versus-anarchy model. For instance, MP Kenneth Marks briefly pondered punk as an expression of working-class resentment of the establishment—a sentiment that he, as a member of the Labour Party, could comprehend. Yet, most of his generation's radicals had trouble recognizing punk as a form of working-class culture. Marks noted from the floor that Joe Strummer had attended a public school—a sign of elite background and a major challenge to his working-class credibility. Punk might be understandable, but it was still part of the problem. As Marks noted, "The fans describe themselves as the 'blank generation', 'hate' and 'destroy' slogans are frequently used."

More often than not, like Bruce George and David Mudd, politicians on all sides initially struggled to accommodate punk to their political worldviews. Consequently, many responded to punk based on what had become a common-sense framework for understanding culture and society—a model of culture formulated more than a century earlier by cultural theorist, poet, and school inspector Matthew Arnold in the book *Culture and Anarchy*. Arnold equated culture with rationality, beauty, and order—"sweetness and light." The opposite of culture was chaos, the unrestrained impulses of the brawling, bawling masses who lack proper respect for order—in short, anarchy.[16] Because some of the first words most people heard from punk were Johnny Rotten snarling "I am an anarchist" over the radio, it was not difficult to imagine that was precisely where punk belonged.

On the Right, Arnold's view of culture resonated with the idea that cultured elites ought to be models for (if not rulers over) the unruly masses. However, it also spoke to leftist concerns, in the tradition of Frankfurt School theorists like Theodor Adorno, about mass culture turning people into mindless consumers rather than critical thinkers. Further, many traditional class-oriented leftists, already alarmed by the Left's growing association with the radical counterculture of the 1960s, found punk difficult to identify with. In an interview with the *New Musical Express*, seventy-seven-year-old Labour MP Marcus Lipton took exception to punk's commercial exploitation of sex and depravity, suggesting that if pop music like punk "was going to be used to destroy Britain's established institutions then it ought to be destroyed first."[17] In terms of culture, this position wasn't far from that of conservatives like MP Nicholas Scott, who likened "punk rocker syndrome" to other social diseases like socialism, fascism, and football hooliganism, or MP Eldon Griffiths, who argued, "Not every young punk is a victim of his environment. . . . There are and there always will be young villains, and they need to be dealt with as such."[18] Whether coming from the Right or the Left, the Arnoldian view of culture typically associated punk with anarchy. As a result, with the postwar political order shaking on its foundation, punk pushed Parliament together, at least briefly, in defense of the people, the queen, and the nation, solidifying a new consensus against punk, voiced in Arnoldian terms that MPs on both sides of the floor could understand.

As long as punk was the opposite of culture and either an indicator or cause of social problems, the main question was the proper strategy for intervention. Parliament technically stopped short of drafting legislation on punk; as Marks euphemistically noted, that would likely lead to "civil rights problems." He instead suggested leaving the initiative to local authorities, who could "use powers under the Public Health Act of 1890 to regulate places of music and dancing." Concerned about punk but unable to formulate an appropriate political response, Parliament left the initiative to local authorities—much like the Division of Culture in communist Poland would a few years later.

In the case of London, George suggested that authorities carefully peruse the "Code of Practice for Pop Concerts" drafted by the Greater London Council (GLC) the previous year (the flurry of restrictions that ensued have been detailed by Jon Savage in *England's Dreaming*).[19] More remarkable was the fact that George's call for applying the GLC concert pop code played right into the hands of his ostensible political opponent, Conservative Bernard Brook-Partridge, MP and chairman of the Greater London Council. While Brook-Partridge had none of George's circumspection in discussing punk (the *New Musical Express* quoted him as saying, "I think the Sex Pistols are absolutely bloody revolting. I think their whole attitude is calculated to incite people . . . to anti-social behavior and conduct"), he shared the interpretation of punk as a force of anarchy against order.[20]

The strange alliance that punk created between Conservative and Labour MPs reached outside the houses of Parliament as well, as ordinary working-class people joined conservative elites in opposition to punk. While punks and the working class might have shared a mutual skepticism about elites and the state in the United Kingdom, unions and punks generally kept their distance. The Sex Pistols' assault on national tradition was a major component of the tension: workers went on strike to protest the Pistols' first single after the *Today* show incident, and again in May 1977 in response to their second single, "God Save the Queen." The monarchy was a powerful symbol for many in the working class—and they were willing to use the weapons of the workers' movement to defend its image.[21] The month after the Jubilee, the working-class *Sunday Mirror* demanded, "punish the punks"—and people did. Teddy boys, the working-class subculture of the previous generation, still revered God, queen, and country and were willing to take up arms to defend those values from punks. Punk-Ted violence was sometimes inflated and sensationalized by the press, but punks also saw its serious side: John Lydon was injured by Teds shouting, "We love our queen" as they attacked him with a knife.[22]

As punk evoked panic, scorn, and rage across political and class lines, punks reciprocated, dispensing their vitriol without consideration of conventional boundaries. Even the Clash, which established a reputation for sympathizing with the Left, distanced itself from the Labour Party. In a January 1978 interview on the BBC2 youth program *Something Else*, Strummer explained to MP Joan Lestor, chairman of the Labour Party, "Most young people feel remote from the mechanics of government, they don't feel a part of it. It's just so boring, it doesn't interest anyone. All the parties look the same and it looks a big mess."[23] Punk band The Jam went even further to separate itself from a comfortable slot on the Left, claiming it would vote conservative in the next election. For the most part, though, mainstream politicians of all stripes had difficulty adapting to punk. This left an opening for creative thinkers on the margins of the political spectrum who showed greater flexibility in adapting punk to their interests.

In November 1977, the *National Review* published an article that sought to claim punk for the far right. Opening with a quotation from "God Save the Queen" ("the fascist regime" was now read as an acclamation rather than a critique), Edward Meadows characterized punk as the music of right-wing working-class rage against the failed welfare state.[24] Pointing to punk's animosity to hippies, its ability to elicit apoplectic fits from Labour politicians, its use of right-wing symbols, and its antifeminist chauvinism (with the Slits as an example!), Meadows sought to claim punk for the National Front and the far right. Meadows's argument was one-sided (he neglected to note that Conservatives also often opposed punk), misleading (the Slits redefined feminism rather than rejecting it), and just plain wrong (most new wave bands did not support the National Front). However, he was on target in one respect: punk did not seem to fit with the mainstream left. Its anti-hippy ethos, lack of respect for working-class culture, disregard for doctrinaire second-wave feminism, and willingness to use symbols from all over the political spectrum separated it from the political left of the previous decade. What Meadows missed was that punk didn't fit any better with the resurgent far right. It lacked the reverence for nation and race that formed the core of radical right-wing politics; the pomp and grandeur of the British Empire was part of the mythology that punk deflated.

The far right made other overtures as well—such as when the Young National Front newspaper, *Bulldog*, added a Rock Against Communism supplement. But when *Bulldog* tried to claim Johnny Rotten in 1978, Rotten made it clear that the feeling wasn't mutual—he told the Rock Against Racism fanzine *Temporary Hoarding* that he "despised" the National Front on the grounds of its inhumanity. Even more forthright in rejecting the far right was the Clash, which explicitly declared itself antifascist and antiracist. The members of the Clash might not be Labour supporters, but neither were they willing to be co-opted for the National Front. Within a few months, a core of punk groups including the Clash launched a massive counteroffensive—a litmus test for punk's potential for cooperation with the far left.

In April 1978, the Clash played in front of a hundred-thousand-strong crowd that had joined the Rock Against Racism (RAR) march to Victoria Park—the momentous gathering described in the first pages of this book. The Clash was part of an impressive lineup of punk and reggae bands, each with its own reasons for joining RAR. There was X-Ray Spex—fronted by Poly Styrene, a stylistically unique Afro-British punk famous for coining the Situationism-worthy catchphrase "Oh bondage, up yours." There was Steel Pulse—an Afro-Caribbean-English reggae band from Birmingham that used punk's networks and venues to perform when it struggled to find Caribbean-owned businesses open to Rastafarians. There was the Tom Robinson Band, which would soon rise to fame not only for a punk hit but also as crusaders for gay rights. And there was Jimmy Pursey from Sham 69, who was quickly becoming a symbol for the proletarian faction within punk. These bands were just a few of the key acts that would participate in RAR over the next year.

The idea for Rock Against Racism came in response to the dramatic growth of far right nationalist groups like the National Front and British Movement that sought to address the United Kingdom's existential crisis by lashing out at nonwhite immigrants. The immediate catalyst was when a drunken Eric Clapton called on his audience to "keep Britain white," prompting Red Saunders to write a letter on behalf of the Socialist Workers Party (SWP) calling for antiracist rock (wryly pointing out the irony of the comment from a man who had risen to fame on Bob Marley's "I Shot the Sheriff"). The initiative became even more urgent by August 1977, when a massive street battle took place between the National Front, police in riot gear, and a coalition of antiracists in Lewisham—all to the tune of Marley's "Get Up, Stand Up," blaring out of a window high above the fracas.[25]

In response, leftists including the SWP redoubled efforts to build a coalition against the far right, including RAR. Rather than making it an explicitly political event formally connected to the party, the SWP—distinguished from other socialist parties by its willingness to bend doctrine to adapt to the contemporary environment—decided to instead make it an open-ended concert series. This strategy opened the doors to collaborators who would otherwise have been turned off by politics—socialist or otherwise. Rock Against Racism started out simply with the idea of black and white bands performing together, but over the course of 1977, as organizers watched the impressive synergy between punk and reggae building at the Roxy (including a particularly memorable joint punk/reggae show by the Slits and Aswad), they realized they could build on the cross-racial connections that already existed in punk.[26]

It was also a good opportunity from the perspective of punks. There had been connections between punk and black (particularly West Indian) culture from punk's beginnings, as described in chapter 1. Rock Against Racism was an opportunity for punks to distance themselves from association with the far right. Just as important, though, it was an opportunity for punks to take action without sullying themselves in mainstream politics. The balance of voicing social critique while remaining safely alternative was a challenge: in February 1978, two months before the Victoria Park march and concert, Strummer of the Clash reported in a *New Musical Express* interview, "We always go on the defensive when confronted with this political stuff. We see it as a trap, a hole to get stuck in." Yet, he followed enigmatically with, "We wanna move in any direction we want, including a political direction."[27] Rock Against Racism offered bands like the Clash precisely that: the opportunity to move in a political direction without getting trapped in partisan politics. Bassist Paul Simonon (the reggae fanatic from multiracial Brixton) suggested as much, stating that the band challenged the status quo by playing reggae music to display solidarity with black people. Punks had no natural home in the political spectrum of the United Kingdom in the late 1970s—nor did they want one. Identifying themselves with the black immigrant community created a safely alternative space for sociopolitical activism and cultural inspiration.

Rock Against Racism bolstered punk's antifascist image, separating punk from the far right and forging important links with others opposed to racism across social and political divides. Even if it didn't necessarily convert the audiences in attendance into antiracists, it created a culture of integration, drawing cross-racial connections in a way that may seem unremarkable now but constituted a paradigm shift in the late 1970s. Gene October of the punk band Chelsea recalled, "Before Rock Against Racism got going, if you were white, there were parts of town you simply didn't go . . . after punk happened and Rock Against Racism got going, you could. . . . You'd get black kids at punk shows, punk kids at reggae shows. That simply couldn't have happened a year earlier."[28] Anglo-Jamaican dub poet Linton Kwesi Johnson concurred after initial skepticism, he agreed that Rock Against Racism did "an important job," bringing different groups "together under the same banner."[29]

However, there were limitations to the harmony between punk and the Socialist Workers Party, as there were with political parties of all stripes. Whenever SWP organizers tried to extend the scope of RAR beyond sharing a diverse set of music among a diverse crowd, the synergistic relationship between punk, reggae, and the SWP rapidly deteriorated. From the perspective of some SWP members, collaborating with punks was pointless if it neither brought people to the party nor contributed to socialist politics.[30] The Marxist intellectual tradition of associating popular culture with capitalism turned off many socialists to the idea of working with punk and reggae—even in the relatively flexible SWP.

For their part, punks' commitment was also limited. While RAR may have made some punks more sympathetic to the SWP, most were no more likely to join it than they were the National Front—or the Labour or Conservative parties, for that matter. The politics of Rock Against Racism were surprisingly open to interpretation, socialist sponsorship notwithstanding. The mere presence of white and black bands playing together was no guaranteed antidote to racism among audience members. Like punk itself, once it entered the public domain, RAR's symbols became just another signifier, ripe for appropriation—as demonstrated by fans wearing RAR pins alongside buttons for the racist National Front. Placed side by side, the only meaning that remained intact was the assertion of subcultural affiliation.

No one represented punk's ambiguous intersection with politics of class, race, and identity more fully than Jimmy Pursey of Sham 69. Sham 69 and its fans embraced football culture and sought to assert punk's working-class identity (often including unspoken "white" and "masculine" modifiers) against what they saw as the effete intellectualism of art school punks. In an interview in *Sounds*, Pursey empathized with white kids from places where "the black population is well over the limit"—but then took the same kids to task for failing to recognize that the white and black working class were in the same boat. A day later, Pursey appeared with the Clash—a band he criticized in the interview for becoming a "pop group"—at Rock Against Racism.³¹ Pursey and Sham 69 evinced all the complexity of love and theft in racial relations in the modern world—much like the skinhead subculture they helped revive in the late 1970s, which celebrated (or stole) black styles and provided inspiration to both antiracists and neo-Nazis.

Ultimately, politicians across the spectrum had trouble adapting to punk, including those who made the greatest effort on the far right and far left. As Matthew Worley has argued, both sides of the spectrum sought to understand and appropriate punk amid the socioeconomic and political crises they perceived in UK society. However, both sides found that focusing on punk and cultural expression cut across their foundations, fitting uneasily with the nationalist tradition of the Right or the traditional working-class culture of the Left.³² In fact, much the same would soon prove to be the case in Eastern Europe, which was undergoing its own effort to grapple with punk's meaning.

The Politics of Punk in the East

As in the West, punk in the East arose in societies undergoing an existential crisis. The economic challenges of the recession were serious in the United Kingdom, but they were harder still on the production-centered economies and distribution-centered governments of Eastern Europe. When the states of Eastern Europe found themselves forced to restrict the flow of goods and raise prices, they undercut their own unspoken social contracts with their citizenries. In response, a new wave of vibrant oppositional movements arose, such as Solidarity in Poland and Charter 77 in Czechoslovakia, that were prepared to challenge the shaky authority of their respective communist parties and states.

Nowhere was the challenge to party authority as dramatic as in Poland. Punk arrived at the end of Edward Gierek's tenure as first secretary of the Polish United Workers' Party (PZPR). Gierek had come to power in 1970 with the purpose of appeasing the population in the wake of his predecessor's nationalist but authoritarian brand of socialism. Besides capitalizing on his charming personality and youthful good looks (by party leadership standards, at least), Gierek eased cultural policy and travel restrictions, creating opportunities for culture (including punk) to flourish. Analogous to Brezhnev in the USSR, Honecker in East Germany, and the late Kadar regime in Hungary, Gierek shifted emphasis from the party's floundering ideological authority to a consumerist model of authority, based on the party's ability to provide goods and services for Poland's people.

It worked, for a while: borrowing from the West spurred increases in production (and political approval ratings).³³ When global recession hit in the mid-1970s, though, the state could no longer subsidize goods for its citizens. Because the regime's authority was based on providing for consumer needs, raising prices constituted more than simply an economic problem. Responding to the threat to affordable goods and secure jobs, the Solidarity labor union formed among striking workers at the shipyards in Gdańsk in the summer of 1980. Solidarity fought first for basic rights for workers, but gradually it also took up the cause of all citizens (and consumers). Soon, the movement encompassed a massive one third of Polish society (including many members of the PZPR), allowing it to use strikes in the summer of 1980 and again the following spring to bring the country to a near standstill.[34] Like the strikes that erupted in the United Kingdom in the winter of 1979 (the "Winter of Discontent"), Solidarity's strikes spelled the end for leadership (in this case by nondemocratic means). Gierek was replaced in the fall of 1980 by another party elite, Stanisław Kania. For many Poles, however, the real alternative to Gierek was Solidarity. Solidarity presented itself not only as the guardian of the rights of workers and their families but also as the savior of the Polish nation. As the recession set in, the PZPR and Solidarity engaged in a struggle over who could best lead Poland to a prosperous future, with a heavy emphasis on defending the Polish nation, culture, and youth.

At a moment of crisis and struggle between the party and newly formed opposition groups, enterprising political thinkers on both sides eyed punks as a potential source of support. Yet, as in the West, they ultimately found that punk cut across the foundation of the quasi-Marxist-Leninist (or, increasingly, simply conservative) culture of the Communist Party, and also that of the culturally conservative, nationalist opposition. Elites of all stripes often embraced a model of culture remarkably similar to the Arnoldian model in the West, identifying culture as a source of order and uplift, and its opposite as chaos and anarchy—casting punk as a symbol, symptom, and perhaps even a cause of the crises facing their societies.

Long before punk, discourse on popular culture in the Eastern bloc had an ambivalent and variable history. From the early days of the Soviet Union, popular culture was regarded as a critical component of the project of preparing the masses for communism. While Marx viewed culture as superstructure that would naturally fall in line with the proper economic base, communists in the relatively undeveloped Soviet Union had no such luxury. Instead, they used the state to ready the country and its citizens for communism through massive industrialization and cultural dissemination projects—creating a "new Soviet man" to construct a new socialist society.[35] This quasi-Marxist approach to culture developed in tandem with another conversation taking place about culture around the modernized world. Since the nineteenth century, elites in industrialized societies marveled and fretted over how culture was increasingly mass-produced by a growing culture industry for consumption by ordinary people. On one hand, mass production and distribution of culture could be embraced as a sign of modernity and progress, part of the benefits of industrialization accepted by capitalist and communist regimes alike. On the other hand, mass culture could be critiqued (in the tradition of Matthew Arnold) as a vulgar substitute for true culture, giving free rein to the anarchic instincts of the masses, or (in the tradition of the Frankfurt School) as a distraction, duping ordinary people into passively accepting their own oppression.

These two discourses on popular culture—one quasi-Marxist and the other modernist—intertwined in the communist world, fueling raucous, complex debates.[36] By the middle of the century, the Soviet Union brought Eastern Europe along on its path socialism, and one by one, Eastern European elites debated the popular cultural phenomena of their time—first jazz, then rock, and by the 1970s, punk.[37] As the ideological fervor of the Stalin era was overtaken by consumerist socialism, party elites were preoccupied with two goals with respect to culture: first, with providing culture to uplift the masses as part of the mission to prepare society for socialism, and second, to distribute culture for the population's entertainment and relaxation as a consumer good, much like sausages and bread.

These goals were interrelated, but as we saw in chapter three, they tended to privilege different types of culture. With respect to music, the mission of cultural dissemination and uplift placed the highest value on the European orchestral and chamber tradition (i.e., "classical" music), designated by the label "serious music" (*muzyka poważna* in Polish). By the mid-twentieth century, for instance, every communist state in the Second World held up Beethoven as a paragon of culture. "Serious music" was celebrated by cultural elites and the media as true culture—worthy of serious attention and imbued with the potential to improve its listeners by stimulating great thoughts.[38] The secondary goal of culture, entertainment and relaxation, allowed for a different type of music—"recreational music" (*muzyka rozrywkowa*). This music was seen as a benefit of the progress of modern society, providing pleasure for the working person after a day's labor. While elites agreed that recreational music was less desirable than serious music, in some cases it was viewed as a potential gateway to high culture. A classic example of this two-tiered understanding of music's function was Jerzy Waldorff's column in *Polityka*, running regularly since the late 1960s and entitled "Music Soothes the Manners"—capturing the idea of music as both ennobling and relaxing.

A few other genres of music managed to bridge these two categories by the 1970s—especially jazz, folk, and some of the music of the cabaret tradition (deemed "sung poetry" in Poland, affirming its place alongside high art). Some rock groups—especially the Beatles and progressive rock—began to gain traction in some circles as serious music as well, or at least were tolerated as recreation. Along these lines, the summer before punk began showing up at Warsaw's festival scene, an article in a youth periodical described the new popular youth music coming out of the MMG initiative as "a phenomenon from the realm of art," subject to taste rather than moral or political judgment: "You like it or you don't . . . that is all."[39]

Even so, when punk arrived in earnest in Eastern Europe in the late 1970s, it proved challenging to incorporate into dominant understandings of culture. It certainly didn't resemble the "serious music" from the classical tradition, yet it didn't quite fit as recreational music either. To some, it simply registered as noise and chaos. In late 1979, as punk was making its way into popular consciousness in Eastern Europe, prominent critic Andrzej "Ibis" Wróblewski addressed new popular music (haphazardly lumping together everything from rock to punk) in the sensationally titled article "Battering Ram of Sound" in the highbrow magazine *Literature*. Wróblewski raged that the popular youth music of the day "exceeds the boundaries of pain" as "synthesizers bore into the ears like needles," the bass guitar "pounds the diaphragm," and "The salvos of percussion force you to open your mouth, because it seems that the eardrums can't stand the atmospheric pressure."[40] For Wróblewski, as for some of his counterparts to the West, punk and rock (and everything in between) were noteworthy primarily because of the risk they posed to one's hearing and sensibility.

Even those cultural elites who normally defended popular culture had trouble embracing punk and new wave. In *Razem*, a general youth magazine that was often open to rock, popular music critic Marian Butrym interviewed Maanam's Kora Jackowska in an article entitled "The Phenomenon Called Maanam." Despite a generally cordial interview, near the end, Butrym launched into a tirade against punk, criticizing the "idiocy" of people piercing their skin with safety pins. While Jackowska defended her fans on the grounds of free choice ("it doesn't hurt anyone but themselves"), Butrym dismissed punk as "less a musical than a sociological phenomenon," altogether rejecting its status as culture.[41] As a defender of popular youth music, Butrym was obligated to protect the boundaries of rock and pop; for him, jettisoning punk from legitimate rock culture into the realm of sociology was the necessary price for defending rock's hard-earned musical status.

The conversation about punk and its status as a form of culture eventually caught the attention of political elites—particularly because they encountered it amid Solidarity's challenge to party authority. As the regimes of the Second World turned toward socialist consumerism, they found themselves vulnerable to anti-consumerist critiques, especially in the satellite states of Eastern Europe, whose nationalist elites often saw socialism as a Soviet foreign import. Eager to use concern over mass culture to discredit the socialist regime, the opposition sometimes accused communist leadership of advocating the mindless consumption of mass culture—and thereby failing as the steward of national culture. Solidarity leveled precisely this charge at the PZPR. It portrayed the party's culture as artificial, foreign, atheistic, ideologically constrained, and excessively focused on mass consumption—in contrast to its own culture, which was authentic, edifying, Polish, Catholic, individualistic, and humanitarian. In 1980, cultural workers presented a platform as part of the wider strikes in the union, declaring that culture ought to serve "the individual development of man and free thought," as well as bolster Polish national identity. They criticized the patronage of culture by the party, which was guilty of turning "Polish culture into that of thoughtless consumption." They also criticized the party's monopoly on cultural policy, calling for "democratization in access to culture" plus "tolerance for the creative freedom of individuals."[42] The critique was pointed and potent: it was a direct challenge to the ruling strategy introduced by the Gierek regime (and also through most of the rest of the Eastern bloc).

Yet, while Solidarity portrayed its model of culture as the opposite of that of the party, beneath the surface, they shared similar culturally conservative foundational assumptions—particularly the Arnoldian view of culture as a source of edification. In stark distinction to the feud between high art and socialist realism in decades past, by the 1970s, both communist and anticommunist elites openly celebrated high art and culture. Like Matthew Arnold, they agreed that the best culture ought to elevate the masses by stimulating higher thoughts and aspirations, providing uplift and order against the forces of anarchy. In fact, Solidarity's critique of the excessive domination of mass culture over the best national cultural traditions under the party's patronage was shared by many in the party—particularly by hardliners who wanted to take additional measures to privilege "serious music" over the recreational variety. Additionally, by the 1980s, both communist and anticommunist elites were comfortable using the language of nationalism. Facing resurgent anticommunist nationalists, communist elites struggled to recast themselves in the role of patrons and guardians of national culture, seeking to bolster their authority by taking up the language of patriotism.[43]

The Arnoldian and nationalist models of culture that were prominent among both the party and the opposition offered few footholds for embracing punk. Punk was unlikely to be interpreted as having ideological-artistic value, contributing to the spiritual value of man, or developing Polish national culture. Even so, there were a few loopholes available. The encounter with Solidarity unleashed substantial reformist forces within the PZPR, with the program for the IX Extraordinary Congress calling for openness and tolerance with respect to culture. Endorsing punk was certainly not what the framers had in mind: the program advocated culture that facilitated achievement of "the supreme spiritual value of man" (language nearly identical to that in the Solidarity platform from a few months earlier).[44] However, enterprising elites could use this language to court young people who were interested in punk. Similarly, for cultural progressives in the opposition, punk provided a potential opportunity to emphasize Solidarity's openness in comparison to the party—and bring in young people who might otherwise not be attuned to the union's interests.

Indeed, there was a powerful incentive to repurpose the party's and Solidarity's rhetoric of openness in order to justify engaging with punk. The two organizations were locked in a struggle over Polish culture and youth—a struggle that Solidarity was decisively winning. In 1981, the Division of Social Organizations, Sport, and Tourism determined that only 3.5 percent of youth surveyed in Warsaw saw the party as a positive influence on the current situation in the country, compared with nearly 50 percent who saw Solidarity this way. Solidarity had taken over the support of the working class and increasingly wide segments of Polish youth—and some party elites were beginning to acknowledge that fact. In 1981, the party division responsible for youth organizations acknowledged the widespread "dissatisfaction, frustration, and criticism" from youth, who had come to see youth unions as "a façade."[45] One possible solution was to adapt party policy to allow room for youth to set their own interests. A month later, the IX Extraordinary Congress Program Committee suggested as much, calling for "openness to the initiative and energy of young people" and for giving youth organizations "the right to independent activity and pursuits."[46] It was just the sort of language that an enterprising local youth union leader might interpret as allowing, or even encouraging, youth unions to form connections with popular youth culture like punk. In fact, that was precisely what student clubs (like Gajewski's Remont) were already cautiously doing. The clash between and within Solidarity and the party with respect to youth, the nation, and culture set up a particularly complex, tense relationship with Poland's punk scenes, as is illustrated by two major festivals that took place in the summer of 1981—one organized by the local government of the town of Jarocin, and the other by the Solidarity labor union.

The most ambitious initiative to integrate punk with youth and musical culture in Poland was the annual Jarocin festival. The small town of Jarocin in western Poland between Poznań and Kalisz had been the site of the Wielkopolska Youth Rhythms festival since 1970—a competition organized for amateur bands with the objective of improving their performance skills. When MMG cofounder Walter Chełstowski took over the festival in June 1980, it expanded dramatically in length (extending over three days) and popularity. Fifty-seven bands applied to perform in the amateur portion of the concert, with fifteen making it into the competition.[47] With help from Warsaw punk band Nocny Szczury (Night Rats), Jarocin immediately revamped its reputation from a hokey song festival to an edgy, punk-friendly youth mecca.

The next year, after Solidarity launched its massive challenge to party authority, and amid the growing debate over punk, still more punk bands applied to perform at the 1981 festival. Evidently, for the authorities and organizers in Jarocin, the need to attract youth (not to mention keep an eye on them) was potent enough to overcome any doubts about the cultural politics of punk: the festival not only was authorized and expanded but also was sponsored by the

Jarocin cultural center and the local party-affiliated youth union. It also received an enthusiastic endorsement from the town's mayor. The state and party were not alone, however: they shared credit in the Jarocin festival program with representatives of the local Solidarity chapter. The Solidarity chapter also served in the ambiguous capacity of the "order service" (*służba porządkowa*)—making a connection with local youth and simultaneously ready to respond if any of the unruly punks got out of line.[48]

In fact, Solidarity elites were preparing a more intimate and more ambitious attempt to integrate punk and new wave into their movement. As they planned the First Review of Genuine Song, "Forbidden Songs," to be held just weeks later in August 1981, Solidarity organizers extended an invitation to new wave band Maanam and to the new incarnation of Robert Brylewski's punk band Kryzys, which had brought in a few members from Tilt and updated its name to the equally controversial Brygada Kryzys (Crisis Brigade).[49] Along with Maanam and Brygada Kryzys, Solidarity lined up an impressive array of hosts and performers for the festival—including Solidarity leader Lech Wałęsa, premier actors, and leading cabaret and folk singers. It was the closest communist Poland could get to a red carpet event outside the auspices of the state. The tremendous investment in the festival was neither a fluke nor an aberration: Solidarity was deeply concerned with presenting itself as the guardian of Polish national culture. Yet, while punks and Solidarity activists shared a distaste for the PZPR, the Forbidden Songs festival was an awkward fit for punk (and even for new wave).[50]

The festival opened with a heartfelt, folksy acoustic "Sunrise Prayer" ("Modlitwa o wschodzie słońca"), immediately setting a tone of earnest reverence and calm solidarity in defiance of secular authorities. The song entreats God for protection from hatred and contempt of unspecified origin—but in the context of the Solidarity festival, the audience would no doubt have perceived the threat as coming from the party/state. In case there was any doubt, performers segued into songs about the Solidarity movement, referencing the difficult times of the strike the year before and persecution faced from the party/state. Performed in a style identical to opening prayers—heartfelt, reverential, folksy, and acoustic—the song's connection was clear. Solidarity presented itself in quasi-religious terms, as the martyr in a struggle of good against evil—symbolism with a long history in the romantic nationalist Polish literary tradition that would not have been lost on the audience.

Most of the songs from the festival upheld the tradition of "sung poetry"— complex, carefully constructed lyrics and music that fit the Arnoldian cultural uplift model, but complemented by Solidarity's trademark nationalist and religious accents. For instance, Jacek Kaczmarksi's "Rejtan" told an elaborate tale of an ambassador lamenting the partition of Poland by Russia (an obvious allusion to the contemporary Soviet dominance of Poland), derived from a nineteenth-century painting by Polish romantic artist Jan Matejko. The festival also had a few lighter moments: for example, Maciej Zembaty's "Brygadzista Albin" told a satirical story about Politburo member Albin Siwak, a bricklayer-turned-bureaucrat who is inspired to start his party career after coveting the superior food given to party officials at meetings. Overall, the festival focused on the singer-songwriter cabaret tradition and emphasized themes of truth, honor, anticommunism, Polish nationalism, and Catholic piety.

For their part, the members of Brygada Kryzys had something quite different in mind for their contribution to the festival. Their performance would begin "with the scream of a siren in complete darkness . . . a blonde woman would appear in the spotlight holding a child's hand, and carrying a machine gun in the other."[51] Then they would launch into their routine with the screaming, distorted guitar and staccato drumbeats of punk. It was to be a true punk onslaught, particularly when placed beside Zembaty's satirical sing-along, Kaczmarski's fifteen-verse acoustic historical narrative, or the "Sunrise Prayer" for God's protection from evil. A greater stylistic contrast could scarcely be imagined than that between the host of Solidarity-affiliated performers and punks.

The incongruity was not missed by Solidarity festival organizers: at the last minute, they asked Brygada Kryzys not to perform. Robert Brylewski blamed the festival organizers for caving in to party pressure, but this is unlikely. Solidarity was a greater threat than punk in the view of party officials, and Solidarity was quite bold about defying official directives. In fact, Zembaty's "Brygadzista Albin" was explicitly forbidden by the censors who reviewed the show program—yet he performed it anyways. Rather, the festival's organizers found Brygada Kryzys's performance distasteful and out of place. The objection was cultural, not political—a matter of style and identity, not ideology. Reminiscent of conservative critic Wróblewski's tirade against punk in the press (drilling into the audience's ears), the sound technician had told the band it couldn't play loud because "there would be many old people present."

Even relatively professional new wave band Maanam proved difficult to reconcile with Solidarity's cultural style. Saved for the last moments of the final day of the festival, Maanam stood out conspicuously from the litany of acoustic ballads. The next closest thing, also appearing on the final day, was the sixties-style rock group Pomorzanie performing the reverential "Mother Mary" ("Mario Matko")—still a far cry from punk or new wave. Perhaps not surprisingly, when recordings of the Forbidden Songs festival were released later that year, Maanam's contribution was left out (indeed, Maanam's performance was not included on any anthology of the festival until 2014).[52]

Punk and Solidarity's cabaret-style music were aesthetic opposites: the folksy acoustic guitar of Solidarity's favorite songs was suited for storytelling rather than assault like the distorted electric guitar of punk. Punk vocals were suited for provocation rather than conveying complex political ideals. Punk's irreverence stood in direct opposition to the religious piety of most of the performers.

While much has been made of the stark contrast between the ill-fitting suits of Communist Party officials and the rugged jeans and rolled-up sleeves of Solidarity members, punks' cropped hair (or mohawks), straight-legged pants, and leather (augmented with DIY writing and safety pins) presented an equally glaring divergence from Solidarity.[53] "They invited us not really knowing what they were doing," Brylewski recalled. "They just knew we were against the system."[54] Solidarity was an anticommunist organization, and most punks had no love for the Communist Party, but their differences in matters such as taste, style, and identity were substantial. Brylewski noted, "We didn't feel at home there. I was put off by the caricatures of Polish and Soviet officials on the walls. It wasn't our style." Reminiscent of the Clash's Joe Strummer's view of collaborating with the politics of the Labour Party as "a trap," Brylewski concluded, "They were too political for us. If you involve yourself in politics, you never know what you're becoming part of."[55] There was some solace: "We were sorry at the beginning, but with time, we felt validated by fact that we were so subversive we were even banned at a freedom festival."[56] Shortly after, he penned the song "I Don't Trust Politicians"—not after being arrested, censored, or banned by the government but shortly after being turned away from the Solidarity concert.

Indeed, from the vantage point of punks, the dominant cultural values of the party and Solidarity were actually not so far apart. Both were paternalistic and preoccupied with culture's potential for uplift. Both accepted a prominent role for nationalism and Catholicism in cultural life. By 1981, representatives at party congresses parroted Solidarity's model of culture nearly word for word. To be sure, there were differences between the party line and Solidarity—not the least of which was that the Communist Party relied on the coercive power of the state, while Solidarity was based on popular support. Yet, while both claimed to be democratic and open, they each actually had quite specific ideas about culture and what it should look or sound like. To put it simply, the party's idealized vision of culture was of patriotic folk singers and classical musicians who were skeptical of Solidarity and belonged to the party, and Solidarity's was of patriotic folk singers and classical musicians who were skeptical of the party and belonged to Solidarity. Punk, needless to say, was not an obvious fit for either.

Further, upon a closer look, in terms of aesthetics, the differences within each organization were at least as great as the differences between them. While some relatively progressive party members and Solidarity members alike sought out opportunities for collaboration with punks, their efforts exacerbated tensions within each organization. Analogous to punk in the United Kingdom, punk in Poland cut across the foundations of both the party and the opposition, dividing cultural progressives in each organization from cultural conservatives. The song festival in 1981 was the last passing effort to link punk to Solidarity. As in England, despite punk's distaste for privileged political authorities, it did not easily fit with the cultural frameworks of labor unions or the traditional left. It turned out that punk was at least as much a threat to pious romantic nationalists in Solidarity as it was to hardline communists.

If elites in the PZPR Division of Culture or the Ministry of Culture and Art derived any pleasure from the collapsed collaboration attempt between Solidarity and punks, archival documents show no evidence of it. They had their own problems to worry about. The years 1980–1981 saw the expansion of punk in Poland's festival scene and the recording industry alike, as detailed in chapter three. Punk's awkward fit with the Arnoldian cultural values of elites made it a cause for concern. Yet, there were still good reasons for providing leeway for local authorities to work with punk. In its report on the 1980–1981 season, the Department of Theater and Estrada noted that the year was dismal—in the midst of the economic crisis, the efforts to save money by offering inexpensive forms of entertainment had backfired. Compared with 1979, profits decreased by a staggering 50 percent due to problems training new performers, production difficulties, and the irrational structure of the entertainment industry. The result was a season of "weaknesses and shortcomings," from empty concert halls to incompetent performers.

The department also noticed a second major trend for the season, though: "spontaneously developing individuals, bands, and tendencies in rock music"—namely, new wave bands like Maanam. Here, the department's assessment was deeply ambivalent.[57] While new wave had roots in Western Europe, it lamented, it had nonetheless become "an original style of Polish youth music"—and thus was not wholly bad. The real problem was that the infrastructure of the entertainment industry was not able to support it, indicating the party's failure to promote culture, forcing new wave to develop spontaneously rather than through the patronage of the state. In other words, the problem was not punk per se but the Department's failure to incorporate it into the state cultural program. Despite mounting concern over punk in the media—and serious misgivings among political elites—politicians in the East ultimately found themselves divided over what punk was and how they ought to respond.

East and West, punk provoked alarm from elites as it rose into the public eye (and ear) via the media against the backdrop of crisis. It was provocative and divisive—yet it was difficult to categorize politically, and the reaction it provoked defied conventional political lines. While a few enterprising politicians sought to incorporate punk into their programs, few were able to do so. From the Sex Pistols to Brygada Kryzys, punks refused to neatly fit the category of the political right or left, or even the margins. However, between the late 1970s and early 1980s, a new constellation of political forces began to develop that did know precisely how to make sense of punk and other "deviant" sociocultural phenomena. As citizens of the East and West increasingly cried out against their governments' willingness to abandon the welfare system on which postwar society was based, the massive unrest caused by strikes and rioting became a concern in its own right. A new brand of politicians arose using this concern to turn political discourse around from a critique of inequality to a critique of disorder, calling for a return of standards, decency, order, tradition, and national strength. The proponents of this emergent political formation viewed punk as a threat to society, culture, nation, and youth; by opposing it, they would amass a powerful following that crossed traditional socioeconomic lines.

5

Thatcher, Reagan, Jaruzelski

In April 1979, one year after the Victoria Park Rock Against Racism march and concert described in the book's opening, an interracial crowd again assembled to protest racism in the United Kingdom. This time, the gathering was a response to a National Front meeting provocatively scheduled in Southall, an area with a large Asian population—and home to Rock Against Racism mainstay reggae band, Misty in Roots. When the Special Patrol Group (SPG), Britain's anti-riot police, showed up, it was like dousing a fire with gasoline. In the ensuing fracas, the equipment of Misty in Roots was destroyed, and band manager Clarence Baker's skull was fractured by an SPG truncheon—an experience that would enhance the resonance of his message when Baker visited martial law Poland a few years later. Still less fortunate was Blair Peach, a protester and antiracist activist from the British colony of New Zealand, who was killed by a blow to the head.

Punk band the Ruts responded to the events in Southall with "Jah War," a fierce reggae-style report on the "hot heads . . . in uniform" in "violent form" amid air "thick with the smell of oppression." On the French release of the single, the group affirmed its commitment to cross-racial alliances still more explicitly: the B-side, "SUS," was a cry of fury against the Suspicious Persons Act from nineteenth-century Britain, notorious for being directed at racial minorities.[1] After all, the Ruts had benefited enormously from collaborating with Misty in Roots, making their first recordings with the group's People Unite! record label. In a show of solidarity across the racial divide from the other direction, Anglo-Jamaican dub poet (and Slits labelmate) Linton Kwesi Johnson recorded "Reggae Fi Peach." No one was ever charged in the death, and the findings of an internal inquiry were never made public, but Johnson filled in the conspicuous silence, flatly calling the SPG murderers in a passionate poem in memory of his fallen comrade in arms. At the funeral, punks and reggae artists came together; as one participant described it, "Everyone had their fists up in the air as the police helicopters circled overhead."[2]

News of the violence in Southall spread quickly over punk's networks. The Clash organized a benefit gig for Misty in Roots to replace its destroyed equipment. On the other side of the Iron Curtain in Poland, the DJ at Henryk Gajewski's club Remont and punk fellow traveler Andrzej "Amok" Turczynowicz could also empathize: brutality from the anti-riot police squad was all too familiar in communist Poland. In the subsequent issue of his punk fanzine *Kanal Review*, Amok reached out in solidarity with the oppressed of the United Kingdom, including a full page of dub poet Linton Kwesi Johnson's ode to Blair Peach, with a superimposed image of Africa and a photograph of a black crowd, fists raised in the air like those gathered at Peach's funeral. No translation was provided, nor was one necessary: an oppressed people fighting against overwhelming force from the state required no explanation to make sense to Polish punks.[3]

The fracas in Southall took place amid a massive transition that was underway on both sides of the Iron Curtain. Just over a week afterward, in April 1979, the United Kingdom voted in a general election that sent Margaret Thatcher's Conservative Party into power. Southall was the latest in a line of crises facing UK society, the most spectacular of which was the 1979 "Winter of Discontent," which saw the largest work stoppage in half a century. Thatcher combined a neoconservative emphasis on strength, national pride, traditional values, and order with a neoliberal distaste for welfare, state subsidies, and organized labor. In January 1979, CCCS scholar Stuart Hall marveled at the Right's growing mastery over discourses of class, race, and law and order. Playing on concerns over mob rule and "handouts" (class) and the loss of English culture (race), both of which amplified the threat of chaos and anarchy (law and order), allowed Thatcher to speak with growing legitimacy in the name of "the people"—whom the Left had long claimed to represent.[4]

Ever a savvy observer, over the months that followed, Hall recognized that the massive changes taking place were intertwined with developments in popular culture, and specifically punk. In 1981, as the significance of class and culture shifted under his feet, he drafted "Notes on Deconstructing 'the Popular,'" arguing that culture's meaning derived from how people categorized themselves according to it, rather than from the content. Accordingly, Hall redirected his attention from the traditional working class to the progressive "Two Tone Sound" coming from punk-ska bands like the Specials. What mattered was not so much the content of culture but the continuously shifting way that culture divided society into sociopolitical constellations. Thatcher's combination of neoconservative sociocultural politics and neoliberal economics marked an important moment in a broader realignment from a class-oriented politics based on the distribution of wealth toward a culturally oriented politics based on identity and values—and local punk scenes were being drawn into the fray.

Simultanesouly with the unrest and realignment in the United Kingdom on the cusp of the 1980s, Poland underwent its own massive wave of strikes led by the Solidarity labor movement—eventually prompting General Wojciech Jaruzelski to declare martial law in late 1981. Jaruzelski didn't stage the coup to end punk—but he did come to stop the chaos, and there were few things that embodied chaos like Poland's proliferating punk scenes. For Henryk Gajewski, it was the final nail in the proverbial coffin. First, DJ Andrzej "Amok" Turcznynowicz's Sound Club was permanently discontinued; then, the store associated with Gajewski's Remont gallery was forced to close.[5] Gajewski himself had declared punk dead by the end of 1980, but just to be sure, in April 1982, a few months into martial law, authorities escorted him to the airport, accompanied by a group of punk and art co-conspirators he'd connected with during his years as Warsaw's punk guru. Gajewski left for Amsterdam to reunite with his punk connections there; he would never again live in the People's Republic of Poland.

As Poland transformed under Jaruzelski, punks in San Francisco were busy putting together the first issue of the politically aware, globally distributed punk fanzine *Maximum Rocknroll*. The 'zine's founders readily identified parallels between martial law Poland and the sociopolitical transformation taking place under Ronald Reagan. The issue included a small feature presenting an image of an "illegal Polish 'zine"—none other than Turczynowicz's *Kanal Review*. In fact, it was the same issue that featured Linton Kwesi Johnson's poem on the murder of Blair Peach by the SPG. Under the image, editors had scrawled the incredulous, mocking caption, "It won't happen here?"[6] Just as Turczynowicz had instinctively identified with the struggle of Blair Peach against the state oppressing its people, the staff at *Maximum Rocknroll* identified with Polish punks' fight against oppression from their state. Punk's network had circled the globe: a page from a Polish punk 'zine with a poem written by an Anglo-Jamaican immigrant about a New Zealand antiracist activist killed by the police in London had made it from Warsaw to San Francisco, where it was reprinted and redistributed globally in a sign of punk solidarity across the boundaries of the three worlds.

The previous chapter showed that while punk provoked concern about youth, culture, and morals in the East and the West, politicians struggled to incorporate it into their political worldviews, instead often defaulting to an Arnoldian cultural framework. Over the early 1980s, this would change, as a new brand of explicitly culturally oriented politics arose in the East and the West. In the West, a political formation emerged on the Right seeking to replace the postwar consensus framework with a new regime of neoliberal economics and neoconservative cultural politics. An analogous shift was taking place in the East, where nationalist, conservative cultural politics and a growing acceptance of the predominance of global market capitalism emerged amid party rule. This shift undermined older sociopolitical categories, evoking competing claims from both the opposition and the Communist Party as they vied to represent the Polish nation.

East and West, neoliberalism-inspired economic transformation intertwined with neoconservative governments in the early 1980s in a potent but volatile mixture—and punk scenes engaged in a complex interplay with this global transformation. It was no coincidence that the rise of punk was followed by the rise of Margaret Thatcher, Ronald Reagan, and Wojciech Jaruzelski. If punk seemed to mock the key moral and cultural values holding UK and US society together, Thatcher and Reagan arose promising to restore those values. Beneath superficial differences—the stern matriarch and the charismatic, populist movie star—Thatcher and Reagan shared a faith in the simple recipe of markets, morals, and military. As no less an authority than the Sex Pistols' Johnny Rotten observed, "The punks absolutely guaranteed that Margaret Thatcher would take over."[7]

Like punk, Thatcher and Reagan were successful in part because they operated in the realm of identity more than ideology. This enabled them to overcome the long-standing rift between workers and the Right, shifting the political landscape of the modern world. By the late 1970s, the Left had lost the near-guaranteed support of the working class it had enjoyed for decades (much as it had in the East). Rather than emphasizing policy, Thatcher and Reagan were able to attract support across class lines by appealing to common sense, old-fashioned values, tradition, piety, morals, hard work, and patriotism—all of which countered punks (and related subcultures) as dissolute, waifish, irreverent, immoral enemies of civilization. The Reagan and Thatcher revolutions redefined society, citizenship, and politics, co-opting identity politics—once a way for those disenfranchised by race or gender to defy the patriarchal, Eurocentric, modernizing metanarratives of the postwar world—for the Right. As Lauren Berlant put it, the slogan of 1970s radical feminists, "the personal is political," was "reversed and redeployed on behalf of a staged crisis in the legitimacy of the most traditional, apolitical, sentimental patriarchal family values." In the 1980s, in the wake of punk and then the conservative counterrevolution, the political and the personal were indeed increasingly intertwined, and the currency of policy became identity more than ideology—a regime of "national sentimentality" combated by the stylistic nonconformity of punks and other subcultures.[8]

As Thatcher and Reagan arose in the West, a political shift was also underway in Poland, where General Wojciech Jaruzelski declared martial law in an attempt to restore party authority. Backed by the Military Council for National Salvation, WRON (also Polish for "raven," to the amusement of its opponents), Jaruzelski came to power promising to restore order and to save the Polish nation. If punks in the West saw Thatcher and Reagan as the ultimate anti-punks, Jaruzelski was at least as good a candidate. A stony-faced retired general who fought in the Polish resistance to German occupation in World War II, Jaruzelski wore prescription shaded glasses that added delightful irony to his profound lack of charisma.

Jaruzelski—unlike Thatcher or Reagan—did not come to power by democratic means, and traditional Cold War politics would put him at the opposite end of the spectrum from either Western leader. Historians of Eastern Europe tend to view Jaruzelski as representing a resurgence of authoritarian communism in response to Solidarity, for instance. However, when re-evaluated from a global perspective according to the emergent political spectrum of the late Cold War era, Jaruzelski shared some key characteristics with his neoconservative/neoliberal Western counterparts, including the language of moral rebirth, emphasis on order, heavy use of police and military, and, perhaps most surprisingly for the new first secretary of the PZPR, an interest in market economics.[9] Ideological affiliations aside, the function of martial law—to enforce adjustments in pricing and imports to meet the demands of international finance and the IMF—was typical of many societies in the First, Second, and Third Worlds amid globalization and the economic crisis of the recession.

The rise of these new regimes developed in productive tension with the punk scenes of the East and West. In the West, many punks embraced their part, gleefully playing the antithesis of the conservative identity that Reagan and Thatcher promised to restore. However, the sociopolitical transformation had serious and unexpected consequences for punk scenes: in each country, scenes divided into unexpectedly antagonistic branches in response to the changes taking place around them. In the United Kingdom, Oi! and 2 Tone found that their different stylistic approaches placed them on opposite sides of the emergent political spectrum. In the United States, the "straightedge" and do-it-yourself subculture of Washington, DC, punks unexpectedly brushed up against the moralistic capitalism of the new right, even as their San Francisco brethren took the equally controversial path of explicitly resurrecting leftist politics, culminating in Rock Against Reagan.

In Poland, the tensions that emerged in the country's punk scenes were arguably still more spectacular. While Jaruzelski himself was the antithesis of punk, the growing forces of globalization combined with reforms in economic and cultural policies allowed for punk's unprecedented expansion during the period of martial law (and shortly after it concluded, in 1983). Punks in the East and West enjoyed more contact than ever before and even got some help from the local and global music industry. Hardcore punk may have captured the disgust and rage of martial law, but it was mostly media-friendly new wave bands that were able to take advantage of these new opportunities, propelling them into the national spotlight to a degree that exceeded even punk's exposure in the West (indeed, by the mid-1980s, Poland was exporting a few punk recordings to the United Kingdom and United States). This asymmetry created a tension between the independent ethos of punk and the lure of market success—a greater clash between capital and subcultural capital than ever before. This unprecedented level of exposure and the ensuing struggle to maintain subcultural capital would set the stage for a supreme cultural clash in the middle of the decade.

Thatcher's United Kingdom: 2 Tone and Oi!

Two new punk subgenres, Oi! and the ska-punk music of 2 Tone Records, captured and amplified the tensions of the United Kingdom on the cusp of the 1980s, particularly with respect to the changing political significance of class and cultural identity. Matthew Worley has shown how in the early 1980s, Oi!—initially interpreted as the music of working-class rage—was reframed as a "recruiting ground for fascism."[10] This change was representative of the broader shift away from class-based politics and toward the new cultural-political alignment that changed what it meant to be "right wing" or "left wing." Conversely, 2 Tone's multiracial cast and multicultural musical inspiration placed it in the camp of an incipient progressive formation. While Oi! and 2 Tone bands and fans shared roots in the skinhead tradition and the working-class milieu, their respective aesthetics of white working-class masculinity and multiracial multiculturalism unwittingly put them on opposite ends of the emergent cultural-political spectrum.

Oi! developed as a populist, working-class subgenre of punk. When popular working-class skinhead bands like Sham 69 and the Ruts dissolved in 1979 and 1980, respectively, their fans formed bands that would become iconic of Oi!—among them the 4-Skins and Cockney Rejects. Named after the stereotypically working-class Cockney greeting, Oi! bands and their followers rejected punk's reputation for scholasticism, avant-garde aesthetics, and leftist politics, instead embracing masculine virility, football fandom, and a cult of work—the antithesis of dissolute, waifish punks like Johnny Rotten. Oi!'s emphasis on masculinity sometimes came with a reputation for violence: the Cockney Rejects prided themselves on their willingness to join the scrum themselves to "settle" conflicts that broke out at their shows. Finally, Oi! was self-consciously white. Most Oi! bands declined to join Rock Against Racism, distinguishing them from their unabashedly antiracist predecessors, the Ruts, or even the complex populist views on race of Sham 69's Jimmy Pursey, who had struggled mightily to keep his band from being co-opted by politics or descending into violence.

There was nothing inherently right-wing about proletarian rage, at least initially. In fact, Oi! was probably the closest any punk scene came to fitting the CCCS theory that subcultures were attempts to recreate the vanishing working-class communities of their parents (and thus belonged on the Left). However, in the changing political landscape of the late 1970s United Kingdom, Oi! became associated not with the labor movement or socialism but with the resurgent far right. The first major Oi! compilation created a stir in 1981 less with its sound than its album cover, using the title *Strength through Oi*, an uneasy play on the "Strength through Joy" campaign in Nazi Germany. Punk had long toyed with Nazi imagery, but this time there was more than an empty symbol: the cover image featured an angry, belligerent skinhead who turned out to be the radical right-wing British Movement activist Nicky Crane. While producer (and music journalist) Gary Bushell fought against Oi!'s incorporation by right-wing politics, Oi!'s imagery suggested to many onlookers that it belonged on the right of the emergent political spectrum.

The yang to Oi!'s yin was 2 Tone. Where Oi! was conspicuously white, 2 Tone was self-consciously multiracial right down to its name. Jerry Dammers started 2 Tone Records in 1979 to take the antiracist spirit of solidarity inspired by Rock Against Racism to its logical conclusion. Inspired by Dammers's belief that UK society needed "an integrated kind of British music, rather than white people playing rock and black people playing their music," 2 Tone's name, bands, and the music were all racially integrated, offering a model of an alternative British identity that affirmed the diversity of the United Kingdom.[11] Like John Mellor before he became Joe Strummer, Dammers was thoroughly acquainted with imperialism from the side of the colonizer. He was born in India (his father served in the colonial administration) but returned to England and also witnessed the inequality within the capitalist metropol, spending his childhood in the steel and textile towns of Sheffield and Coventry. Punk was a natural fit for him, especially the combination of global scope and proletarian imagery embraced by the Clash. Dammers started a punk-reggae group, picked up the Clash's Bernie Rhodes as a manager, and opened for the Clash in January 1979.

The crucial innovation by Dammers's band, the Specials, and its 2 Tone labelmates was to harness the spirit of the punk-reggae collaboration, but to look back further down the Jamaican pop timeline for sonic inspiration, to ska rather than reggae. Ska was a natural fit with punk—both were relatively treble-focused (compared with bass-heavy reggae), and ska's upbeat tempo fit with punk's high energy level. The styles associated with 2 Tone Records were as self-consciously transcultural as the music, picking up the sharp, clean-cut gangster rude boy look of skinhead culture that some punks remembered from their youth. The label took up a fictitious character, Walt Jabsco, as its symbol—a cartoon sketch of a man in a black suit with pork-pie hat, shades, and hands in pockets. Dammers got the image from a record cover photo of Jamaican music icon Peter Tosh, but the black and white (two-tone) image was deliberately racially ambiguous like the music itself.

Certainly nothing was new about looking to black styles for coolness, but 2 Tone's participants also crossed racial, cultural, and national borders. Neville Staples (vocals) and Lynval Golding (guitar) for the Specials were both from Jamaica, a former British colony. When the Specials covered Dandy Livingstone's rude boy Jamaican rocksteady classic "Message to You Rudy," they permanently brought on Cuban-Jamaican Rico Rodriguez, the trombonist from Livingstone's original recording.[12] Nor was the cross-racial collaboration limited to the Specials: Pauline Black, front woman for 2 Tone band the Selecter, was born to a father from Nigeria (another former colony) and a half-English mother and was raised by an adoptive white family. As for Don Letts a few years earlier, Black's musical and political inspiration came from the US civil rights movement (she changed her name from the stereotypically English "Vickers" to the explicitly Afrocentric "Black").[13] The 2 Tone record label's multiculturalism set it on the progressive, outward-looking left side of the emerging political spectrum.

In terms of its roots, its class basis, and the demographics of its fans, 2 Tone shared much with Oi! However, in the changing political landscape of Britain under Thatcher, elements of working-class identity—gender roles, nationalism, traditional values—were being co-opted by the Right. So, too, was working-class racial animosity: in 1978, Thatcher had expressed sympathy for those who felt that the United Kingdom was "swamped" by immigrants, courting support from the far right National Front. It was more than rhetoric: in April 1981, operation "Swamp 81" stepped up the police presence in Brixton (the multicultural neighborhood of Don Letts and Paul Simonon of the Clash), ostensibly to bring law and order to the community but resulting in riots and a massive police response.[14] That summer, following budget cuts and the concomitant unemployment, riots exploded in nearly every major city in the United Kingdom. In fact, the only parts of government to not have their funds cut were the police and military—whose budgets grew at three to four times the rate of the overall budget.[15] The extra riot shields, plastic bullets, and truncheons would come in handy. While the Right under Thatcher co-opted cultural elements of the traditional working class, it accelerated the demise of its social and economic roots, facing down unions with state power through a combination of forceful strike-breaking and legislation like the Employment Acts of 1980 and 1982 and the Trade Union Act of 1984.[16]

This was the context in which the notorious incident at Hamborough Tavern (also in Southall) took place on July 4, 1981, when three Oi! bands were met by an angry crowd of the community's heavily Asian local residents. The ensuing fracas quickly became a full, three-way street fight between Asians, skins, and the police. In stark contrast to the solidarity between white punks and Anglo-Asian locals two years previously in Southall, this time the community fractured along racial lines. The incident solidified Oi!'s connection in the public imagination with the far right. Yet, at least one of the allegedly Nazi bands there, the Business, was actually outspokenly antiracist; it was already planning an appearance in the awkward but earnest "Oi Against Racism and Political Extremism but Still Against the System" tour. Treating the street fight as an isolated problem of two outsider groups—Nazi punks versus immigrants—conveniently absolved the forces in mainstream UK society and politics that set up the conflict. In fact, the clash in Southall was just one of many outbursts of frustration and rage around the country: the same night, a simultaneous riot took place on a much greater scale in Toxteth, Liverpool, and many others would follow around the country that summer.

As the United Kingdom erupted in flames, the Specials captured the mood in their hit "Ghost Town," which made it to number one on the radio charts when the government requested that both BBC and independent networks observe a media blackout on any future flashpoints to avoid attracting troublemakers to the scene. The Specials' Dammers reflected on the situation in the United Kingdom and noted, "Margaret Thatcher had apparently gone mad, she was closing down all the industries, throwing millions of people on the dole."[17] The situation was dire enough that fellow punk and Rock Against Racism mainstay Tom Robinson traveled east, heading for East Germany to escape crippling debt in the faltering economy of the capitalist United Kingdom. A year after the Solidarity strikes in Poland, the United Kingdom in the summer of 1981 was mired in a crisis of its own.

While punk initiatives like Rock Against Racism and 2 Tone brought together antiracists of all stripes, they also consolidated a powerful force on the Right. In terms of ideology, most punks were as indifferent to Thatcher's signature blend of neoliberal free-market capitalism and neoconservative Victorian values as they were to the faltering consensus politics of the Callaghan government. When it came to identity, however, punk fit the framework perfectly, proudly proclaiming itself to represent the anarchy, chaos, national decline, and cultural and moral collapse against which Thatcher's new right defined itself. In this way, it played into the hands of the resurgent right, which excelled at presenting itself as defender of "the people" (the nation, culture, and law and order) from the forces of anarchy ("the mob," hooligans, outsiders, misfits, and punks). At the same time, the 2 Tone and Oi! punk scenes were drawn, willingly or not, into the emergent culturally based political spectrum, divided into outward-looking progressives and inward-looking reactionary traditionalists, respectively.

Reagan's United States: HarDCore and Maximum Rocknroll

As punk and Thatcher transformed Britain in the early 1980s, hardcore punk and Ronald Reagan arose side by side in the United States like a Hegelian dialectic. There were also opposing forces at work within the world of hardcore punk, however—between the fiercely personalistic straightedge scene of Washington, DC, and the intensely political scene around the fanzine *Maximum Rocknroll* in San Francisco. By the mid-1980s, both would became wrapped up with the politicization of culture, identity, and morality in Reagan's United States.

Like the United Kingdom, the United States in the late 1970s was beset by signs of crisis. While the US economy was stronger than that of the United Kingdom, the country was plagued by inflation in the wake of the OPEC crisis and the global recession. Punk arose at a time already characterized by political cynicism after the Watergate scandal and the morass of Vietnam: national surveys revealed that the proportion of voters who could be defined as "politically cynical" increased dramatically from 6.4 to 50 percent between 1964 and 1978, while the proportion that was "trusting" dropped from 57.1 to 15.1 percent.[18] By the summer of 1979, Democratic president Jimmy Carter admitted on television that the nation faced "a crisis of the American spirit."[19]

Ronald Reagan rose into the national spotlight against a backdrop of national malaise in tandem with punk, making use of tensions punk created as it pressured the status quo. Reagan had been climbing the ranks as a renegade in his own Republican Party past the moderate Gerald Ford during the four years of Democrat Carter's presidency. Like Thatcher, Reagan turned dismantling the social contract from an unfortunate necessity into an ethos. Rather than redistributing wealth to ensure the needs of everyone were met, he flipped the postwar model upside down, emphasizing the supply side—that is, maximizing income for the rich, who would presumably pass down wealth, bypassing the redistributive efforts of the state. He also shared Thatcher's willingness to employ muscular police and military force. However, Reagan's charismatic, common-sense everyman speaking style gave him a populist appeal that Thatcher lacked, while his skillful incorporation of evangelical Christian themes into his rhetoric made Thatcher's Victorian traditional values seem quaint and subtle in comparison.[20] The Reagan administration's remarkable success at projecting itself as a bastion of traditional, conservative, patriotic Christian values was due in part to its connection to a group called Moral Majority, led by Jerry Falwell and Tim LaHaye. Moral Majority made a name for itself by linking the socially conservative Christian right to the Republican Party, cementing a bond that would redefine US politics over the next decades.[21]

When hardcore punk rose into the media spotlight, some onlookers saw it as the culture of an "immoral minority" and the antithesis of "traditional family values" that the Moral Majority and its supporters sought to defend. The day before president-elect Ronald Reagan was inaugurated in January 1981, the *Washington Post* marveled at the relatively new phenomenon of Washington, DC, hardcore punk—harDCore, as it became known—describing it as "atypical, apolitical, and seemingly amoral." "Atypical" was right (what punk scene is typical?), but each subsequent adjective fit increasingly poorly. The DC scene indeed eschewed partisan politics, but DC bands were deeply preoccupied with the politics of the personal, expressed in terms of identity. Peaking in an ascetic punk submovement known as straightedge, DC punk was also profoundly moralistic.

The straightedge movement in the DC punk scene was the punk mirror image of the ascetic zeal of the rising phenomenon of right-wing political Christianity. Rather than seeking to restore alleged "traditional" religious values and a Christian lifestyle, straightedge proclaimed sobriety—rejecting drugs, alcohol, and, for the truly committed, meat and sex—as a method for empowering the self and questioning the status quo. Straightedge punks identified themselves by "X" marks drawn on their hands, converting the system used to alert bartenders not to serve alcohol to minors at punk shows into an ethos. Like the hardcore punk music that defined the scene, straightedge was serious, intense, and focused, abandoning the playful artsy aesthetics of the first wave of punk along with the decadent indulgence of rock and roll. At times, it was also confrontational: reports of militant straightedge punks slapping beers out of people's hands circulated in the scene. While straightedge's militancy and asceticism may have rivaled those of the religious right, punks and the Moral Majority certainly never mistook each other for potential allies. Minor Threat's "Filler" described religion as another opiate of the masses alongside drugs and alcohol; Youth Brigade's "Moral Majority" was still less ambiguous.

Even so, like Oi! in the United Kingdom, straightedge did not fit neatly into the emerging culturally determined political spectrum in the United States. It self-consciously set itself apart from the style and culture of the religious right. Yet, its asceticism and moral zeal confused and alienated those who had grown out of the progressive, freewheeling left-wing counterculture of the 1960s. Hardcore's patent dance move—slam-dancing—replaced the self-contained vertical "pogo" dance of early punk shows with a pit of hardcore fans crashing into each other. In combination with the new interest among some hardcore punks in physical fitness, some observers found hardcore disturbingly reminiscent of fascism. An ad hoc "bent edge" movement popped up briefly, rejecting straightedge as just another set of rules that punk ought to be defying.[22]

Further, even punk sympathizers worried that hardcore transformed what had once been a relatively egalitarian enclave of punk into a male-centered microcosm of patriarchal society. Slam-dancing alienated women with its emphasis on physical confrontation; similarly, straightedge's rejection of sex could be read as associating women with weakness. Minor Threat's "Out of Step" (1982) in particular aroused the suspicion of punks, with the lines "Don't smoke / Don't drink / Don't fuck / At least I can fucking think." MacKaye, a lucid and prolific communicator, insisted the song was about individual choice, not rules; the "I" in the last phrase was intended to modify the three previous phrases. He clarified his stance on sex to be a rejection of the casual use of women in the scene, adding: "I am not anti-sex, I am anti-fucking, if you can understand the distinction."[23]

Yet, as society increasingly associated punk with immorality, disorder, and violence, many hardcore punks were as likely to embrace the reputation as to dispel it. As with Oi! in the United Kingdom, the link between punk—especially hardcore—and violence solidified in the social imagination, and punks everywhere in the United States noticed changes in their respective scenes over the early 1980s as outsiders came to punk shows looking to prove their hardcore credentials. Against the backdrop of the Moral Majority's campaign to restore tradition, order, and morality, hardcore set itself up as a natural antagonist in the media. Easily identified on television by their outrageous dress, rude, destructive behavior, and propensity for petty crime and violence, punks frequently appeared opposite the forces of law and order in shows like *CHiPs* and *Quincy*.[24] Even ostensibly factual and objective television presentations often sensationalized punk, presenting its fantastical dangers to outraged television audiences, as with the ABC special "We Destroy the Family" (1982), about the pioneering LA hardcore band Fear. These sensational accounts of punk had consequences: when LA hardcore band Black Flag tried to release its EP *Damaged* in the fall of 1981, it was told that the president of MCA had personally intervened to stop distribution of the EP, which he deemed to be an "anti-parent record," despite having already pressed twenty-five thousand copies.[25]

In the face of hostility or at best indifference from the mass media, punk scenes around the country sought out creative strategies to reach their audiences. While punks had often resorted to using independent labels to get their records pressed, DC punk Ian MacKaye transformed DIY from a survival tactic into a full-fledged ethos—much as Henryk Gajewski had in Poland, but on an even greater scale. In late 1980, MacKaye founded Dischord records to release an EP from his soon to be defunct band, Teen Idles. Living in the shadow of the national government, he sought to bypass the system rather than confront it. MacKaye recalled, "We didn't ask, we didn't get permission, we didn't get licenses, we didn't get copyrights, we didn't get trademarks, we didn't fill out any forms, we didn't get lawyers. We just rented rooms and put on shows, and we never formalized anything with the government whatsoever."[26] His motivation was not just practical but ideological: MacKaye described major labels as "the musical manifestations of the corporate culture that we exist in." One of his responses was to stamp Dischord records with "Don't pay more than $5" to prioritize access over profit.[27] Distribution was a challenge, so Dischord perfected the mail-order system and worked with local shops.

While MacKaye's independent distribution strategies emerged from the late Cold War world, they also portended an incipient antiglobalization movement that would come to define global politics in the subsequent era. MacKaye was able to make the independent label successful by adopting an alternative definition of success from that of the capitalist marketplace. He approached the label as a craft or hobby more than a growth-focused business, becoming part of a growing punk alternative network: Touch and Go in the Midwest, Black Flag's SST in LA, and the Dead Kennedys' Alternative Tentacles in the Northwest.[28] In an era of globalizing capitalism, punk's independent labels and the bands on them were self-righteously regionalist, insulated from the international music business but interconnected by punk's own growing networks.

None were as extensive, however, as the rapidly expanding subcultural empire of Maximum Rocknroll in San Francisco, where the punk scene was undergoing its own contentious transformation in the face of shifting global, national, and local politics. On a visit to San Francisco, Ian MacKaye ran into Dave Dictor of punk band MDC in a bookstore, where the latter was reading about the 1954 US-backed coup in Guatemala that replaced the democratically elected leftist president with a right-wing dictator. MDC had recently relocated from the Austin, Texas—an oasis for punks (including those who were openly homosexual like Dictor) in the Texas desert of conservatism. Taking up residence in a beer vat in an abandoned brewery with other local punks, MDC brought a ferocious political edge that fit perfectly with the increasingly political scene of San Francisco. MacKaye, like many punks everywhere, had intentionally avoided politics (in the traditional sense, at least). Yet, when presented with the history of US interventions in Latin America, he couldn't help but agree that the situation there was "a very fucked up thing." MacKaye admitted, "MDC are knowledgeable about what they're saying, they're not just a bunch of fucking kids getting onstage and shouting 'Fuck Reagan.'" He told MRR: "I choose to speak about one thing and [Dave] about another."[29] MacKaye focused on the local, personal side of rebellion, while Dictor and MDC specialized in the mix of global sociopolitics that were rapidly coming to define the punk scene in San Francisco.

Some quarters of San Francisco's scene had started transforming toward political engagement even before MDC arrived, with no example more glaring than the quintessential San Francisco punk band Dead Kennedys (whose leader, Jello Biafra, had run for mayor in 1979). As a resident of the US countercultural capital, Biafra directed his venomous sarcasm at mellowing hippies and moderate progressives in songs like "California Uber Alles." Biafra changed his tone with the onset of the presidential campaign in September 1980, however. The band's single "Kill the Poor" mocked the right-wing rhetoric praising the rich and industrious and chastising the undeserving poor with irony. When confronted with Reagan, Biafra's twisted sense of humor evaporated, turning from ironic critique to a blunt bludgeon.[30] The band's next EP, released at the end of 1981, took aim at the Right's co-optation of religion under the new regime. On the single "In God We Trust, Inc.," the Dead Kennedys included a new version of "California Uber Alles" called "We've Got a Bigger Problem Now."

The center of San Francisco's politicized punk scene, however, was Tim Yohannan—longtime punk DJ and local Rock Against Racism chapter organizer—and his new punk 'zine, *Maximum Rocknroll*. With the first issue of the new 'zine, Yohannan declared an end to the days of political apathy in a critique aimed squarely at the ex-radicals of San Francisco. He asked, "What has two legs, hangs out on street corners, panhandles, sells dope, says 'That's cool, man,' is apolitical, anti-historical, anti-intellectual, and just wants to get fucked-up and have a good time? A Hippie? Nope, a punk!" Much like Gajewski in Poland three years earlier when he believed punk's principles had been compromised, Yohannan released a history of punk as a manifesto, defining punk as a counterculture that redressed the "failures of the 60's kids" by choosing confrontation rather than mellowness. Punk was not just a look; it was about fighting mainstream ideologies of racism, sexism, ignorance, violence, and the fear of knowledge. Recognizing the reluctance of punks to engage in demonstrations—especially in a city where alternative politics were dominated by aging hippies—Yohannan called for the formation of punk factions to join protests. The accompanying image in the 'zine (including right-wing leaders and nuclear missiles labeled with the names of corporations) offered a glimpse of the message for those too impatient to get through the manifesto. The caption read simply: "KNOW WHO YOU'RE FIGHTING FOR. . . ."[31] Yohannan's editorial was followed by an equally militant interview with MDC, the perfect example of politicized punks from the perspective of *Maximum Rocknroll*: their debut interview in the 'zine likened the police to the Ku Klux Klan, since both wanted to "kick ass on the poor, minorities, women, [and] homosexuals."[32] Taking the most radical aspect of 1960s tradition, MDC's name stood for Millions of Dead Cops—although it would switch to the more ideologically precise Multi Death Corporations later.

Despite *Maximum Rocknroll*'s skepticism toward the legacy of the previous generation's radical tradition, politicized punks found willing allies among some of the radicals of that generation: the New York–based Yippie magazine *Overthrow* printed a positive review of MDC and extended the band an invitation for a nationwide tour. The collaboration between punks and Yippies was tenuous but meaningful: it extended even to the allegedly apolitical DC punk scene, where the Yippie commune Madame's Organ (a provocative play on the name of the neighborhood, Adams Morgan) sponsored regular punk gigs and became the heart of the local punk scene. In fact, in the mold of the SWP in the United Kingdom (and Yohannan in San Francisco), DC's punk-Yippie alliance established a local Rock Against Racism chapter and worked with black punk band Bad Brains to put on a show at the Valley Green housing project. New connections to international organizations and initiatives like the Yippies and Rock Against Racism spurred the development of a network of politically-engaged punks in DC and elsewhere. For the national tour punks and Yippies organized, they took the concept of Rock Against Racism a step further into the realm of politics, turning the RAR acronym into "Rock Against Reagan."[33] On the tour's stop in Washington, DC, the Dead Kennedys' Jello Biafra sought to solidify harDCore's political engagement right in the middle of the capital: staring up at the Washington Monument, he dubbed it the "great eternal klansman with two blinking red eyes" as police helicopters and buses filled with riot squads stood by, ready to confront the forces of anarchy.[34]

The increasingly politicized approach to punk taken by Rock Against Reagan and *Maximum Rocknroll* drew criticism from punks who preferred to remain apolitical. Yet, for Yohannan and his counterparts in other US punk scenes, the politicization of culture and emphasis on traditional morality in the early 1980s United States invested punk with an increasingly clear sociopolitical meaning. Just as punk provided a symbol of anarchy and disorder to politicians like Thatcher and Reagan, Thatcher and Reagan gave punks with any inclination toward activism a perfect symbolic enemy. If punk struck a sharp contrast with the Thatcher and Reagan administrations in the West, however, it stood in even sharper relief against the backdrop of martial law in communist Poland. By the time Yohannan and his crew at *Maximum Rocknroll* printed their issue that empathized with punks facing martial law in Poland, hardcore punk band SS-20—named for a Soviet ballistic missile—was about to explode in front of thousands of young Poles at the Jarocin festival.

Jaruzelski's Poland: Hardcore and New Wave

On a steamy night in late August 1982, SS-20 stepped onto a stage in front of several thousand Polish youth who had come for—as the sign onstage read in English—a "Punk Rock Concert." In the fall of 1981, SS-20 had played at Warsaw's Mokotow festival. Despite its hardcore sound (not to mention its provocative name, referring to the Soviet ballistic missiles that caused angst in the East and West alike), the young punk band received an award for its performance. No one was more surprised than the band members, who expected their aggressive brand of punk to shock audience and judges alike.[35] When SS-20 went to pick up the award in December, it was in for another surprise: the door was locked and the office was closed. Martial law had begun.

Just as Solidarity had affected Poland far beyond what might be expected of a labor movement, its suppression carried significance far beyond the union itself. New rules under martial law contained a ban on nonreligious gatherings, including entertainment and public art works, without prior local government approval. It mandated identity cards and reaffirmed the requirement that citizens serve in the military. The hours of 10:00 p.m. to 6:00 a.m. were declared "military hours," during which people could not appear in public. Freedom of speech and freedom of the press were limited, with a ban on the publication of books, works of art, written or recorded texts, and periodicals other than the Central Committee's *Trybuna Ludu* and a few other official publications. Breaking these rules would result in prison sentences.

Yet, a few months later, SS-20 was back for the annual punk festival in Jarocin playing in front of its biggest crowd ever. Hair disheveled, in a sleeveless shirt, guitarist Robert "Worm" Matera unleashed a riff of crunchy, staccato chords. Feedback screeched through the microphone clenched in the leather-studded fist of singer Dariusz "Scandal" Hajn as a band member called out the title "Aborted Generation" ("Poroniona Generacja"). "Worm" and "Scandal" shouted along with the guitar in semi-unison: "Scarce satisfaction, too much frustration / That's a sketch of my generation. / No goal, no future / No hope, no freedom."

In fact, before the festival, censors had struck the line "No hope, no joy" from an earlier version of the song; the band gleefully responded by replacing it with the still more provocative "No hope, no freedom." As Jarocin festival's organizer (and MMG impresario) Walter Chełstowski routinely told participating bands, "Officially I must inform you that you are not allowed to sing these texts, but sing what you want, because no one will pull you off stage."[36] SS-20 took the energy level up another notch on the subsequent songs, "Ask a Policeman" ("Spytaj Milicjanta") and "Bordello" ("Burdel"), both with the classic frenetic snare-cymbal-snare-cymbal drumbeat of hardcore punk. By the end of the set, audience members—hesitant and uncertain how to react at first—were thrashing in a small "mosh" pit in a combination of excitement, freedom, and fury.[37]

SS-20 gave martial law a sound, and that sound was punk. Seeing tanks roll down the streets with the declaration of martial law made a lasting impact on the psyche of all citizens, including punks. SS-20's members were notified after Jarocin that they would have to change the band's name in order to appear again in public. They chose Dezerter instead—which they considered to be at least as provocative, especially as punk bands were broken up by use of the military draft (the "Elvis method" of suppression pioneered in the United States). While some, especially members of professional rock bands, complied with service requirements, Dezerter's members had no intention of serving in the military, as the band's name clearly indicated. In fact, Tomasz Budzyński from brethren hardcore punk band Siekiera (and several others) instead went into hiding.

For young Poles who had not lived through the Stalin era, obvious signs of the state's violence had been limited to a few moments of localized suppression of striking workers, in Radom in 1976 and perhaps Gdańsk in 1970—not entirely different from the varied levels of awareness punks had of striking workers in the United Kingdom. Martial law revealed the exceptional repressive force of the state in Eastern Europe. Most concerts and festivals were canceled, but the curfew also made it much harder to organize informal gatherings to perform or listen to music. Even professional performers like Maanam had trouble practicing due to the curfew, which kept people closed inside during the evening.[38] Yet, as we will see, other factors were at work that made it possible not only for punk to survive in post–martial law Poland, but for it to reach its peak level of popularity.

Popular discourse about punk in the East (and often scholarly approaches as well) has tended to view it through a lens of whether it served as a political "safety vent" for youth rebellion against the communist regime or a political "accumulator" of resistance. In fact, neither side of this Manichaean framework adequately explains either the proliferation of punk or the sociopolitical role it played in the early 1980s—including in martial law Poland. Rather than a sinister master plan or heroic opposition, the punk explosion of early 1980s Poland emerged from the global economic and sociocultural transformations of the late Cold War world, filtered through the specific local circumstances of the People's Republic of Poland. While martial law was initiated to restore order and party authority, it was also an attempt to adjust prices, curb consumption, and increase production and exports in order to adapt to the global capitalist economy with which the Eastern bloc was increasingly becoming intertwined. After the initial show of force, the regime quickly sought to "normalize" conditions, resuscitate the economy, and win back at least a small measure of authority from the population through a range of initiatives to appeal to youth, develop culture, and introduce market reforms into the economy.

The particular local form that tensions took, as progressive reformers, party hardliners, and nationalist traditionalists clashed, was intertwined with broader global developments. As in the West, the 1980s in Poland brought together culturally neoconservative and economically neoliberal impulses in a volatile but potent formula. Despite the language of morality, national rebirth, order, and strength that flourished across the transforming political spectrum, the combined effect of market reforms and the normalization of the national culture and entertainment scene was to propel punk—and media-friendly new wave bands in particular—into the national spotlight. As in the United States and the United Kingdom, these transformations divided punk scenes in Poland, setting up spectacular clashes between hardcore and new wave bands within the punk scene, and also between punk bands and culturally conservative elites. Nowhere were these tensions more apparent than in the debate in early 1982 over whether to hold the punk-friendly annual Jarocin festival.

In February 1982, just two months after the declaration of martial law, the local Executive Committee of the Communist Party in the town of Jarocin debated whether to hold its annual alternative music festival. The local police commander emphatically rejected the possibility, stating, "The Review of Music of the Young Generation, which by the way attracts various types of scum, is a threat to the safety of the city." The question was tabled until the next week when the mayor and the local house of culture director would be present—yet, two other committee members couldn't help voicing their thoughts on such a provocative topic. One committee member called the festival "a bad example for youth"; the leader of the local socialist youth union begged to differ, cautiously offering his support.[39] It was an early indication that the conversation would be an intense one.

The next week, the Executive Committee discussed the festival under the topic of "developing culture in the city and community," explicitly framing it in the context of the ongoing national discussions about culture described in chapters three and four. Responses again were sharply divided. Speakers who supported the festival often argued for its continuation on cultural grounds. One noted the empty space left in the cultural arena after martial law: "The unions [i.e., Solidarity] were concerned with culture, and what now?" The local house of culture did a poor job catering to youth interests, another argued. But the socialist youth union leader voiced the most potent argument for the festival, cautioning against the party "playing the role of the grand inquisitor" and warning that canceling the festival meant that the party would be "resigning from the role of developing culture."[40]

The words echoed statements by the party in the IX Extraordinary Congress, held the previous year, before martial law, to formulate a response to Solidarity's challenge to party authority. But the youth union representative also had practical reasons to defend the festival. In the late 1970s, socialist youth unions were often seen by young Poles as the domain of careerists and sycophants. In 1980, the unions had asserted themselves, seeking to restore some of their reputation by supporting Solidarity. Martial law crushed that ambition, leaving unions hemorrhaging members just as the state was trying to attract the support of youth—youth who often were interested in punk and rock. In addition, many youth union members had open, reformist views of socialism that acknowledged forms of culture that would have been repugnant to hardliners.

Rather than challenging the premise of the youth union representative's argument, the festival's opponents disputed the character of the festival itself, taking up the classic Arnoldian position of identifying the festival as chaos, the very opposite of culture. One decried that it was "not a matter of music, but of the demoralization of society"; another suggested that they convert the alternative music festival into an "oldies festival." Needless to say, the police commander reaffirmed his suggestion that the festival not be organized that year—"or ever," he added. At the conclusion of the intense debate, the city's mayor voiced his support for the festival and Jarocin's party leader called the discussion to an end. The committee had reached a stalemate, leaving it to await confirmation from above.

The conversation about Jarocin was a microcosm for the cultural politics of punk in Jaruzelski's Poland. On one hand, the festival seemed like a perfect example of the chaos martial law was intended to stop, as the local police commander insisted. On the other, unless it was willing to rule by force alone, the party couldn't risk alienating youth or falling flat in its mission to promote Polish culture; nor could it miss an opportunity to take advantage of popular youth music as one of the few parts of the economy that could reliably be expected to turn a profit—particularly as the economy underwent market reforms.

After martial law, launching any successful cultural initiative was a major challenge. As theaters and concert venues reopened in the months that followed, the recording industry, the myriad concert agencies, radio, and television were expected to return to operation. However, many of the performers they relied on were part of Solidarity, and they refused to perform in order to protest the ban placed on the labor union. This was a significant political challenge to the party, since one of Solidarity's accusations was that the party was failing to adequately serve as the steward of Polish culture. Empty spaces where Solidarity cultural initiatives had once existed constantly threatened to confirm critiques of the party, granting the union a victory from the grave. Over the first half of 1982, party officials responsible for culture received reports from around the country of boycotts among Solidarity sympathizers in the cultural sphere—especially among musicians, one report noted.[41] In addition to the political challenge, boycotts presented an economic dilemma for the music industry: financial reforms drawn up at the IX Extraordinary Congress went into effect in 1982, making the industry economically self-supporting and making financial viability more important than ever.

In short, the conditions of martial law put festival organizers and music industry managers in the position of bargaining with politicians for leniency to produce the kind of records or concerts that would sell—and gave politicians good reason to acquiesce. Further, the same thing that made punk attractive to untrained young people made it a convenient substitute to fill in the silence left by martial law: punks could put together bands with minimal resources and training, and few of them were particularly loyal to Solidarity. Under better conditions, the conservative cultural gatekeepers of the music industry limited the access of punks to its resources, but when the choice was between filling a slot in a program with a punk band or leaving it empty, the former often seemed like a wiser option than the latter for an industry manager or an official familiar with the party's latest pronouncements on spreading culture and appealing to youth.

In fact, high-ranking cultural authorities had already been discussing the Jarocin festival at an organizational meeting for the Opole festival (Poland's most prestigious song festival and the site of Maanam's television debut in 1980), chaired by the vice minister of culture and art. The committee lamented that the sad state of the national budget and the boycott by many performers would make the Opole festival impossible for 1982. Astonishingly, though, the committee suggested that the Jarocin festival could serve as a substitute venue for celebrating Polish musical culture.[42]

Even with this powerful backing, Jarocin's mayor remained pessimistic until June, just weeks before the festival was scheduled to start. When the local youth union representative again proposed to organize the festival, even if in a different form from previous years, the mayor responded with resignation. "There is not a climate for organizing the Rhythms festival this year," he said, noting that it would depend on the judgment of the regional police commander.[43] His pessimism was understandable; if the local police commander was any indication of the sentiment of his superiors, there was little chance for holding the event. Then, two weeks before the festival was scheduled to take place, the mayor received a mysterious note from central authorities. Its contents were two words: "Do it."[44]

Amid the discussions about youth and culture under martial law and the weight of practical necessity, authorities decided that the need for the Jarocin festival outweighed the risks, and they gave the go-ahead to the town committee. As if confirming the soundness of the decision, a few weeks later, in October 1982, the minister of culture and art appeared on television and announced, "We have been, and always will be, a country of cultural openness." He promised that the state would not "organize boycotts of art or bands" and insisted that developing culture was "only possible with a great deal of social participation" representing "different worldviews."[45] This is precisely what would happen over the next two years as market pressures, a dearth of performers and plethora of amateur musicians, and flexible political slogans made more room for punk in the music scene than ever before, even as a vociferous opposition developed both inside the party and outside it.

The Jarocin festival not only took place in 1982 but also expanded dramatically. From fifteen bands and a modest audience in 1980, the 1982 festival developed into a three-day affair with between five and seven thousand audience members.[46] To accommodate this expansion, the festival was moved from the Jarocin Cultural Center to the city's amphitheater. One hundred sixty-one bands applied to perform, of which twenty-seven were accepted. Jarocin flourished even as the prestigious Opole festival was canceled; if Poles were going to attend a music festival in 1982, they would have to experience punk.

Many did: Jarocin was such a resounding success with youth that other events and festivals sprang up around Poland, capitalizing on the explosion of punk bands in the period following martial law, often sponsored by local state-sanctioned houses of culture and youth unions. For instance, in late 1982 and early 1983, a house of culture in Łódź sponsored a monthly concert under the title "Punk-rock-Estrada." The location offered an accepting environment, a hall, and decent amplification equipment—as well as a small-scale impresario in the form of a house of culture employee who "inspired and organized" the concert.[47] This was perhaps not typical of a house of culture, but it was not rare either; more than half of the punk bands at a typical festival in Poland were sponsored by their local house of culture.

Some local party officials weren't ashamed of sponsoring punk either. In 1983, the secretary of the PZPR in the county of Świebodzin wrote a letter to the regional division of culture requesting a bus for the local house of culture. His justification for this special allocation boasted about the region's bands winning sixth and eighth place at the Jarocin festival and two television performances by the group the System. It was a classic Orwellian Polish punk name, but in this case, its countercultural significance was outweighed by local pride and the need to promote culture and reach out to youth.[48] At a time of intense focus on youth and culture, the local party secretary believed (or at least feigned) that participation in the Jarocin festival and other punk-dominated events was not just acceptable, but grounds for special consideration by party authorities.

Support for punk was not limited to local authorities with creative interpretations of policy, however, especially as new market opportunities for punk opened up with the simultaneous globalization of the music industry and economic reform taking place in Poland. Under new economic policies, several music companies began operating in Poland in 1982, including international corporations and firms owned by Poles living in the West. These new businesses operated by permission from the Ministry of Culture and Art and were dependent on larger state firms for some materials and distribution, but they had more latitude in repertoire and production decisions as well as pricing. In these respects, they fulfilled a role analogous to independent labels in the West, but with a more explicitly capitalist business ethos.[49] Meanwhile, state firms had new cause for embracing punk, since market reforms left the industry desperate to find ways to support itself. No one had much money, but youth had consistently demonstrated they would find ways to spend it on music—provided it was the right kind.

However, these new potential opportunities did not apply equally to all punk bands. While the Polish festival scene attracted punk bands of all sorts, the recording and broadcast industry favored punk's marketable subgenre, new wave, dominated by bands like Maanam, Republika, and Lady Pank. From 1982 to 1984, the availability of new wave on television, radio, and records and cassettes expanded dramatically. Record companies—state and private alike—rushed to switch their classical and folk recordings over to the popular new wave bands and did whatever they could to package and sell new wave to youth without running afoul of politics. Both state firms and private firms produced albums by new punk bands—some classic and hardcore punk, but mostly new wave. The number of LPs by new wave bands pressed increased fivefold between 1981 and 1982, and then more than tripled again the next year to peak at over one million.

To capitalize on new wave, the music industry sought to justify the music in the context of ongoing national debates about culture, education, and youth. In 1983, the United Entertainment Industry devised a flashy new trade journal *Entertainment Forum* (*Forum Rozrywki*). It began with a section specially written in bureaucratese for officials, declaring its purpose to be "the development of entertainment art [*sztuka rozrywkowa*]" by "securing proper proportions and conditions for the development of entertainment culture" and "stimulating the further development and proper rating of phenomena currently existing."[50] But afterward, it included color images (a highly coveted commodity in 1980s Poland) and even a fold-out poster including Polish and international performers from mainstream rock and roll to new wave and punk—perhaps something for cultural authorities to present to a grateful young family member.

Blending quasi-socialist and quasi-capitalist elements, the publication presented punk and new wave as music that the entertainment industry was perfectly justified in producing. One article praised Maanam, noting the band's favorable reviews in the West (read: foreign currency opportunity) and its "provocative but humorous, surreal lyrics." Another offered an analysis of punk by sociologist Jerzy Wertenstein-Żuławski (whose essay had been critiqued by the Central Committee), based on scholarship on punk by Greil Marcus and Dick Hebdige—which he recommended to readers interested in understanding punk.[51] Besides hinting at its commercial potential, the periodical suggested that punk could be critiqued, studied, and understood like any art form (and, as Marek Wiernik argued, that its artistic value was ever increasing).

Meanwhile, the broadcast media were undergoing changes as significant as those in the recording industry. Party authorities viewed the broadcast media as an essential tool for reaching out to potentially alienated citizens. Following martial law, many young Poles regarded the national media with contempt, viewing it as complicit with an oppressive, untrustworthy system. Even before martial law, less than 2 percent of youth surveyed said they trusted the media's information about domestic affairs, for instance.[52] To combat this widespread distrust, the three-month break during which radio programming was cut off at the beginning of martial law was used to rework the radio's Third Program (Trójka) to cater to listeners aged sixteen and seventeen.[53] The most adventuresome program would appear on Saturdays at 8:00 p.m., when a "Hits List" (List Przebojów) would be presented live, "directed with the cooperation of listeners." To run the program, directors at Polish Radio chose the young DJ Marek Niedźwiecki.[54]

The Hits List brought audience choice to the radio. Each week, listeners could send postcards to the station or call in, voting for their favorite song. The fact that a station existed that allowed listeners themselves to select what was played was an unprecedented democratic opportunity in the entertainment industry. It was also tremendously popular among young listeners: the radio finally had a mechanism to keep up with changing listener tastes, or at least those of the majority of fans. Like John Peel's show in the United Kingdom, the Hits List brought bands to listeners who otherwise wouldn't have known they existed. For the first list, only a couple hundred votes went to the first-place song, but over the next few weeks, the number of letters and calls increased dramatically, and thanks to support from fans, new wave bands quickly took over the list.[55] Maanam rocketed to first place in week two and would dominate the list along with its new wave brethren for several years.

The Hits List allowed young Poles to bring new wave to the state media and hold it there unassailable. When authorities tried to intervene, it proved messy. In 1984, for instance, Niedźwiecki's boss came in and told him Maanam couldn't be played, since the band had refused to perform at an official function in Warsaw. Like the music industry in the United Kingdom after the Sex Pistols offended national pride, the Polish music industry responded by attempting to displace the band from its position on the charts. Niedźwiecki responded, "Are you ill?" There were three songs that week on the list by Maanam; he wondered, "I'm supposed to remove them, and say what to listeners?"[56] In fact, he devised a creative solution: he played a loop of the drum intro from Maanam's "To tylko tango" in the space where the banned "Simple Story" was supposed to appear. He later reflected, "Everyone amazingly knew it represented the intervention of censors. The ban was short, only three weeks. The radio was literally buried in letters."[57] In a gutsy maneuver, Niedźwiecki revealed the state's clumsy interference. Listeners played their part as well: they continued to vote for the song on the Hits List for nearly four months in 1984.

A number of new wave bands gained massive popularity during martial law, reaching wide audiences through the state media. Maanam, the group with the deepest roots in the Polish new wave scene, made its appearance first and was followed by two other hugely popular groups. In the list's seventh week, new wave band Republika showed up for the first time with "Kombinat"—a syncopated, new wave–style song set to dystopian lyrics that describe a pulsating, breathing factory, comparing it to a tissue in which the protagonist is a cell—a living cog in a cybernetic machine. This song reached the top position by week eleven. It was in week fifteen, however, that the quintessential new wave band of the post–martial law era made its Hits List debut, with Lady Pank's first single, "Little Lady Punk" ("Mała Lady Pank").

While hardcore bands like SS-20 ruled punk circles from 1982 through 1984, Poles who encountered punk through the media typically equated punk with the band Lady Pank. Lady Pank formed in late 1981 when Andrzej Mogielnicki, long a fixture of the Polish music scene as a lyricist, decided to put together a new wave band around his lyrics and the guitar of experienced rocker Jan Borysewicz.[58] Thirty-five years old in 1983, Mogielnicki was roughly the same age as punk impresarios McLaren and Gajewski. Unlike either, he was more interested in a successful business venture than in aesthetics or provocation. His skill at finding the right sound (in this case, strongly reminiscent of the Police in the United Kingdom), the right image, and the right words and negotiating the intricacies of the Polish music scene sent the group rocketing to the peak of popularity. Lady Pank thrived—and eventually died—by using the increasingly freewheeling music market of post–martial law Poland to funnel punk's subcultural capital into actual capital.

Five years after punk first appeared in the Eastern bloc, Lady Pank popularized the idea and image of punk and marketed it as a colorful, stylish rebellion to a younger audience. Stylistically distinct from both the simple attire of early punks and the studded leather of hardcore, the members of Lady Pank boasted a colorful and varied wardrobe, including flashy red boots, brightly colored ties, stripes and animal print patterns, and vivid face makeup. Their sound and performances were upbeat and playful—as were their lyrics. The band's first eponymous album was wildly popular, with the first three tracks (along with others) all becoming hit singles. Yet, Lady Pank often offered subtle critiques for careful listeners, providing a small amount of substance to buttress the aura of rebellion from listening to punk. "Crisis Fiancé" ("Kryzysową narzeczoną") told the story of martial law from the point of view of a man ironically lamenting his wife's absence, traveling abroad and missing the "good times" to be had in communist Poland getting high. He receives a postcard from abroad reading "Merry Christmas"—a tongue-in-cheek reference to martial law, declared just twelve days before the holiday.

Mogielnicki's skills (lyrical and managerial alike) not only got Lady Pank by censors; they also got the band plenty of deals with the music industry— including a music video. Television was a hugely popular medium, but most bands didn't have the wherewithal to utilize it due to the high cost of filming. Further, among punks, television had an even lower reputation than radio—much like *Top of the Pops* in the United Kingdom. Yet, the allure of television was too much for Mogielnicki to turn down. While Maanam also made videos, Lady Pank took the form to a new peak of musical spectacle. For instance, "Monkey Factory" ("Fabryka Małp") provided a farcical play on the violence of post–martial law Poland, as the band paraded around the "jungle" of socialist block-style housing, facing enemies with a slingshot while singing about the "state of total war" (*stan totalnej wojny*), linguistically proximate to the state of martial law (*stan wojenny*).

Bands like Lady Pank attracted a different audience with different tastes and behaviors than the first wave of punk. In particular, they appealed to younger teens who used punk's subcultural capital to provide a sense of independence as they approached adulthood. In 1983 and 1984, fan clubs for the most popular bands among younger listeners—especially Republika and Lady Pank—sprang up across Poland. These organizations, often run by the local youth club, mailed members pictures and articles about the featured band in exchange for a small fee. Some clubs' memberships reached the thousands, while other clubs were small and intimate. Like the Beatlemania of the previous generation, fans' feelings for these performers were often powerful and deeply personal. Fan groups often engaged in debates about new wave in the mainstream press, writing in editorials to defend their favorite band and organizing voting blocs for their band on the Hits List. They wrote to and about the bands and their members as though they were their friends, or even lovers. One fan wrote in a letter (one of many) to a music magazine, "I am pouring tears of emotion. I probably never loved anyone, or ever will, as I love [Lady Pank's] Janusz Panasewicz."[59] Another wrote, "When I listen to you, I want to cry and scream; I don't know what to do."[60] A third described her plans to leave home and move to Warsaw, simply to be closer to Lady Pank.[61] Fans were willing to exchange their own money to invest in the band's subcultural capital: one fan reportedly saved up the impressive sum of 17,000 zloty to buy boots like those worn by vocalist Janusz Panasewicz. New industries sprang up dealing in Lady Pank paraphernalia—with Lady Pank perfume reportedly going for 80 zloty a bottle at news kiosks. Fans used bands' posters and pictures to decorate their walls, sought out music magazines for precisely this purpose, and wrote in droves begging for more large-format, color images (even the archival copy of *Razem* is missing two pages where its Lady Pank poster was torn out).

Anyone with the slightest entrepreneurial acumen would have salivated at the business opportunity—including in the Eastern bloc. In fact, by 1983, Poland began exporting new wave, producing albums in English for international distribution and sending bands to tour in the West. Maanam and Republika both released English-language albums, combined with international tours (Maanam in continental Western Europe, and Republika in Britain). Republika also had the opportunity to tour Poland with UK Subs, a pioneering, ferocious UK punk band. Rather than being shepherded through huge auditoriums with Republika, the UK Subs would have surely been more at home underground with the Polish hardcore scene. Ironically, they got their closest brush with the bright lights and glamour of stardom not in the capitalist West but in the rapidly changing communist East, courtesy of the Polish Artistic Agency.[62]

The greatest marketing endeavor came in 1985, though, when the US music company MCA (whose president had canceled Black Flag's "anti-parent" EP in 1981) extended Lady Pank a five-year contract and brought the band over to the United States for a three-week visit to promote its English-language release, *Drop Everything*. The visit to the United States gave the band members a taste of the capitalist publicity machine. They had a chance to ride in a limo, performed on *American Bandstand*, and recorded a music video in Manhattan. The video for "Minus Zero" (an English language version of the hit "Mniej niż zero") assembled an absurd collection communist Polish tropes, including actors dressed as secret agents gorging on kielbasa performing with the band around the central prop, a pink replica military tank replete with swiveling canon – all with the New York City skyline in the background.

In Poland, new wave presented a rare opportunity for punk diplomacy, like the US jazz diplomacy of the previous decades in the Cold War, while also bringing badly needed foreign currency and positive press to the economically and culturally ailing People's Republic of Poland. The press took the opportunity to express national pride at the success of a Polish band in the United States: one article in the national weekly *Polityka* brandished *Newsweek*'s claim that Lady Pank was the "greatest Polish musical phenomenon since Chopin." For its part, the band was characteristically cool, describing the biggest revelation of the tour as learning that Americans "use a lot of ice in their drinks."[63] The renewed international contacts that new wave bands achieved after martial law were a great opportunity for just about everyone. From the perspective of the bands, they were a chance to gain international recognition. From the perspective of the industry and the state, they were rare opportunities to obtain foreign currency—while also enhancing the international prestige of Polish culture and recovering from the stigma of having declared martial law.

Exchanging punk's allure of rebellion—its subcultural capital—for international success provided Lady Pank with a massive, devoted fan base (albeit mainly in Poland, despite the best efforts of MCA). However, SS-20 percussionist Krzysztof Grabowski—and many hardcore punks—saw Lady Pank's success differently. From his perspective, Lady Pank and other bands that "sold themselves" to the music industry were "bootlickers that were getting profits from government concessions."[64] Lady Pank's success, and that of other new wave bands, proved that they were willing to compromise their principles and work with the system. As John Savage observed with respect to the United Kingdom, punk's popularization was a two-edged sword. In the view of punks who emphasized their uncompromising nature, prized their lack of widespread exposure, and preferred a faster, harder sound and a small but dedicated audience, new wave bands had traded in all of their subcultural capital and sacrificed their status as punks. They had become "official" bands, complicit with the system, and worthy only of contempt. This charge intertwined with an increasingly gendered discourse about punk credibility: the increasingly masculinized identity of punks (particularly in hardcore-dominated scenes) identified bands like Lady Pank as feminine, willing to "sell themselves" for money.

By the mid-1980s, Lady Pank and other bands that dominated the Hits List (and its DJ, Marek Niedźwiecki himself) became targets of these punks' rage. As with any hits list, listeners tended to vote for songs they already knew and liked, and, in turn, got to know songs that were voted for. This system lent itself to promoting the familiar rather than the new and different—much like the conditions of the industry as a whole. It provided access for a few of the more accessible new wave bands while excluding many others. Contributing to this tendency, unlike that of John Peel in the United Kingdom, Niedźwiecki's taste extended from progressive rock to new wave, stopping short of rougher-edged punk and hardcore. He and the organizers of the Jarocin festival alike developed many enemies among punks who resented cultural gatekeepers—even if the gates were wider than most in communist Poland. In fact, by 1985, a second hits list developed to compete with Niedźwiecki's, trumpeting its reputation for independence (as its name "Polish Independent" stated)—despite falling under the aegis of the official scouting organization, ZHP. As the bizarre scenario of the "independent" hits list operating under an official youth organization suggests, the barrier between "official" and "independent"—between dominant and subculture—was permeable, shifting, and ambiguous in post–martial law Poland.

While Lady Pank took new wave's capacity for mainstream appeal to its limit, even punk bands that touted their hardcore credentials like Dezerter faced difficult choices about working with the music industry in the post–martial law environment. Ironically, the growing subcultural capital that Dezerter generated made the band so popular among punk fans that it earned an invitation in 1983 to record a single with state record label Tonpress (whose new studio Brygada Kryzys had tested the previous year—and used to surreptitiously record its first album). Dezerter also had some help from open-minded industry insiders, including Tonpress director Marek Proniewicz and Marek Wiernik, a music journalist who was among the first to write about the band in mainstream media (one of the strategies was writing the band's name as De-zerter, disingenuously translated as "the zerter").[65]

Dezerter might have thought twice about accepting the deal, but its members had recently been reading about the Sex Pistols' manager, Malcolm McLaren, who had helped the band rise to notoriety on the back of the record industry.[66] Inspired, drummer Krzysztof Grabowski decided "it was necessary to seize the opportunity and create a provocation." And it was provocative. The band presented twelve texts to the censor, of which four were accepted. Somehow, among these was one of its hits from Jarocin, "Ask a Policeman" ("Spytaj Milicjanta"): "Ask a policeman, he will tell you the truth!"[67] Lest the audience mistake it for a genuine endorsement of the police, it starts out with a police whistle, the assertion of the policeman's repressive authority rather than his comradely assistance—a twist on the siren opening to the Ruts' "War ina Babylon," released the previous year in the United Kingdom. The hardcore sound was totally different from that of the Ruts, however, from the shocking opening to the barrage of hardcore guitars and drums, careening to the abrupt end just over a minute later.

Permeable as the boundary between "official" and "independent"—between subcultural and regular capital—may have been, it was nonetheless critically important to uphold for bands and their followers alike. Even with Dezerter's undeniably hardcore sound, some fans were upset by the band's appearance on a state label, reading it as a symbol of cooperation with authorities (much as when the Clash signed with CBS). Dezerter had traded in some of its subcultural capital, and the line between "official" and "independent" was incredibly thin. Signs of compromise could be found everywhere: in a record deal with the state industry, in a polished, well-rehearsed song, in lyrics written by a professional, or a particular hairstyle. Dezerter recovered its subcultural capital relatively quickly: it moved from the Sex Pistols' strategy to that of hardcore punks in the West, using the money generated from its single to purchase a tape recorder in order to self-release its next two albums under its own underground independent label, Tank Records.[68] However, from the perspective of Polish and international music industry officials alike, the contacts most worth cultivating were not those in the DIY punk scene, but the major new wave superstars. As a result, in just a couple of years, Poland's punk scenes began to divide into warring factions, seeking to cordon themselves off from the taint of collaboration with the music industry. As punks and new wave bands and fans devised increasingly dramatic methods for asserting and defending their subcultural capital, the resulting spectacles played into the hands of an emerging conservative coalition much like the ones developing in the United States and the United Kingdom, as the chapters that follow will show.

By the mid-1980s, Poland, the United States, and the United Kingdom (like many other countries) were undergoing momentous shifts under the transformative regimes of Jaruzelski, Reagan, and Thatcher. Economically, they corresponded to the third wave of globalization, as the Second and Third Worlds gradually integrated into global markets. Politically, they entailed a shift of emphasis from class-based politics to a class-blind politics based on identity and culture. The third wave of globalization expanded punk's reach—most dramatically in the Eastern bloc. Yet, simultaneous political developments invested punk with an increasingly clear symbolic meaning as the antithesis of the themes of order, stability, morality, and tradition trumpeted by the rising conservative right.

The unprecedented access to the global market favored some subgenres over others. As punks found their subcultural capital challenged by the surge of popular new wave bands in the media, some sought to restore it by seeking out ever more uncompromising hardcore identities. Others, however, sought a source of subcultural capital in the same reliable source that punks had drawn on for years: the Third World. Yet, the Third World was undergoing a transition of its own, analogous to and intertwined with those taking place in the First and Second Worlds. The result would be a transnational resonance between punk and its fellow travelers—a return of the spirit of the previous generation's *tiermondisme*, played out in the world's interconnected punk scenes. Other punks, however, were less eager to embrace these transnational connections turning to a fiercely local, communitarian identity that resonated with the language of the new right.

6

Punk *Tiermondisme*, Punk Tribalism, and the Late Cold War Roots of Antiglobalization

In the summer of 1983, Anglo-Jamaican reggae band Misty in Roots stood onstage and unleashed its trademark reggae barrage. Halfway through the set, amid cheers and applause, the drums thundered into a lead-in, with the keyboard and guitar hitting four deliberate, emphatic downbeats as the singer shouted, "No more life in Babylon." Over a profoundly bass-heavy reggae rhythm, the vocalist proclaimed the downfall of the corrupt civilization of Babylon: "No more life in Sodom and Gomorrah . . . Woe, woe unto you . . . Brimstone, fire . . . It must be total destruction." It was the same apocalyptic message the band had been delivering since the first days of Rock Against Racism years earlier. This time, though, the audience was a crowd of young Poles in the city of Wrocław in the communist East. The message of retribution and justice resonated powerfully in a country that had been under martial law until just the previous month. The average Pole in attendance may not have understood every word Misty in Roots sang in Jamaican-accented English, but at least one word translated perfectly: Babylon. Polish reggae fans knew that they too were standing in the heart of a corrupt civilization, and that reggae promised to destroy it in a storm of flames.

If the summer of 1982 belonged to hardcore punk and its new wave competitors, the summer of 1983 was Poland's summer of reggae. In July, Warsaw's foremost jazz club, Akwarium, introduced the Polish audience to the sounds of Jamaica with videos featuring celebrated reggae performers Bob Marley and Peter Tosh. The next month, following an extended visit to Africa, Misty in Roots arrived in Poland. As the band toured, it was followed by an entourage of young Poles wearing the red-yellow-green colors of Pan-African nationalism (their less cosmopolitan compatriots reportedly mistook them for fans of Warsaw's football squad, which wore red-white-green). Some of these inspired Poles declared themselves Rastafarians, adopting the belief in the inevitable collapse of corrupt modern civilization (be it capitalist or communist). Dick Hebdige suggested that the radical blackness of roots reggae alienated young white youth in the United Kingdom, who instead turned to punk.[1] The converse was true in the Eastern bloc: in the near absence of black people in Poland, reggae served as pure, distilled rebellion.

Misty in Roots was a particularly apt vehicle for the reggae invasion. It had a knack for appealing to punks, having regularly played alongside punk bands like the Clash and the Ruts in the United Kingdom. It also had experience handling an interventionist state: the band's practice space had been raided and the band manager brutalized by the United Kingdom's Special Patrol Group. Misty in Roots had also played in the Counter-Eurovision festival in Brussels, sponsored by Belgian socialists (Eurovision was Western Europe's music industry–sponsored festival). Certainly, the members of Misty in Roots were no fans of Thatcher's England or the imperialist West. From the perspective of the officials in the Polish Artistic Agency who invited the band, Misty in Roots presented a chance to make some money and demonstrate Poland's solidarity with those oppressed by racism, state violence, and imperialism in the First and Third Worlds.

When it came to its performances, however, Misty in Roots made less of an impression among the state and party apparatus than among young punks in communist Poland, who related strongly to the band's experience and ethos. At a press conference at the Akwarium jazz club in Warsaw, Misty in Roots manager Clarence Baker explained, "Reggae is combative. It can't adapt like other genres. . . . [Reggae] records don't show up in stores because stores are controlled by big firms, and if you don't work with them, they are able to block your record from normal circulation."[2] Baker's experience had been in the capitalist West, but it resonated deeply with Polish punks in 1983, just after martial law and amid the massive commercial success of new wave music. So did reggae music. Songs for the oppressed peoples of the world such as "Persecution" ("so long we've been exploited / they even take us for granted / no justice or equality / they persecute us day to day") were eerily appropriate to post–martial law Poland (the song was released by the state record label Tonpress in 1985). East and West alike, the oppressive, corrupt civilization of Babylon that roots reggae described sounded a lot like home.

Amid the third wave of globalization and the neoconservative/neoliberal restoration that punk helped provoke, a subset of punks (and their fellow travelers in reggae and, later, hip-hop) achieved the pinnacle of transnational consciousness in the mid-1980s, reaching out to each other across the borders of the Cold War world. Like the champions of *tiermondisme* ("third-worldism") of previous generations, these punks saw themselves as trapped in a corrupt system, and they recognized in the Third World a radical potential that could cure the ills of the modern world. Unlike traditional *tiermondisme*, this new punk variant rejected political solutions like socialism, instead focusing on culture—including a radical critique of European civilization and the notion of progress that extended beyond that of traditional *tiermondisme*.[3] Moreover, punk's new *tiermondisme* arose precisely as the political projects of the Third World (and Second World) crumbled in capitulation to the global capitalist order in the late 1970s.

Punk has been interpreted both as a global phenomenon and as a series of fiercely local attempts to resist globalization.[4] Both perspectives have merit. Scholars of globalization such as George Lipsitz, Homi Bhabha, and Rupa Huq have shown how transnational alliances and hybrid cultures have enabled people to find spaces, identities, and alliances that empower them to adapt to and engage with the globalizing world.[5] While each punk scene maintained local specificities, many punks became intertwined with a globally conscious cultural and stylistic critique of the emerging international economic order, portending the complex, spectrum-defying politics of globalization.

These macro-level struggles with globalization in the 1970s and 1980s intersected with a related struggle taking place at the micro level in punk scenes around the First and Second Worlds. As new wave bands brought punk music to the market with increasing success, punks sought ever more vehement expressions of rebellion to maintain their subcultural capital and to reject "the system." What "the system" was, and the best way to reject it, however, were hotly contested. For some, like those who joined Rock Against Reagan and even the formerly apolitical Crass, the rise of neoconservative identity and neoliberal economics as the political currency of the new right gave punks a clear enemy. Others, however, were skeptical of this political voice and global vision. For them, politicized punks affiliated with *Maximum Rocknroll* and their ilk represented the new dogma, a set of rules—something punk ought to assault, not embrace.

Punks everywhere were suspicious of international capital and the moralizing states that supported it. However, rejuvenating *tiermondisme* was only one side of punks' reaction. While some punks responded to globalization by forming transnational multicultural alliances, others withdrew to fiercely communitarian insularity and xenophobia. Despite their common roots, these different cultural responses to the developments of the late Cold War era and the onset of the third wave of globalization placed multicultural punk *tiermondisme* and punk tribalism on opposite sides of the emerging political spectrum, contributing to the struggles over multiculturalism that would define the cultural politics of the 1980s and 1990s.

Despite efforts to avoid politics, by the mid-1980s, punk scenes around the world found themselves dividing along the lines of an emergent culturally based political spectrum, split into warring factions of xenophobic reactionary skinheads and globally minded progressive punks. This divide was intensified by the overlying tension between bands that found market success and those that vehemently rejected any sign of it. Over time, the struggle to define the appropriate range of punk culture and to reassert punk's subcultural capital set the stage for a supreme clash with political forces that drew their power from the rhetoric of order, tradition, and authority.

Punk *Tiermondisme*

As new wave redefined punk as a highly attractive business proposition from the perspective of music industry entrepreneurs in the East and West alike, a similar change was underway with reggae. Reggae's fate was intertwined with that of the Third World project, and by the end of the 1970s, both had lost much of their political cachet, including in the Third World itself.[6] As Thatcher, Reagan, and Jaruzelski embraced a combination of free markets, moral revival, and social order, a number of Third World leaders began to accept similar values.[7] In Jamaica, in the early 1970s, Michael Manley's People's National Party (PNP) had joined the orbit of the Third World nonalignment movement and had risen in popularity alongside Bob Marley as a result of popular enthusiasm for radical Afrocentric culture and politics. However, with the global economic crisis, the PNP government pursued assistance from the US-dominated International Monetary Fund. Among the conditions of IMF loans were structural adjustments—austerity measures that were intended to streamline the government and encourage private industry, but that resulted in mass unemployment and a withering social safety net.[8] The crisis provided an opening for the Jamaican Labour Party (JLP), the main opposition to the PNP, spurring an extended violent conflict between warring groups backing each party at the end of the decade. In 1980, JLP leader (and former music industry entrepreneur) Edward Seaga was elected president due to a variety of specific local factors—but also on promises to restore order, provide stability, implement responsible economic policy, and defend the national interest, reminiscent of his neoliberal/neoconservative northern counterparts in England and Poland.[9] Seaga rose to power as hope in a radical Third World alternative faded, and the global South joined the global capitalist economy from a position of weakness. The very meaning of the term "Third World" shifted, redefined as the impoverished ("underdeveloped") lower echelon within the global capitalist system—the meaning of the term that dominates today.

As Jamaica accommodated itself to the neoliberal capitalist world order, roots reggae transformed from a subcultural phenomenon into a marketable commodity. Jamaica's tourist industry, once anxious to dissociate itself from Rastafarian militancy, began to use reggae (and particularly Bob Marley) to promote island tourism.[10] Some bands reportedly got turned down from record deals for *refusing* to wear dreadlocks, which became associated with laid-back Jamaican beach culture rather than a radical Rastafarian identity.[11] Roots reggae increasingly became an export good—one of the few besides bauxite with an international demand.

Like the Jamaican tourist industry, the international music industry began marketing reggae as beach party music rather than militantly anticommercial, anti-imperialist Rastafarian music. The international reggae smash hit of 1982, "Pass the Dutchie," put reggae in the mouths of Jamaican preteens, and changed the "pot" (marijuana, the truth-revealing herb of Rastafarianism passed around in a *kouchie*) into a "pot" (a cooking basin, or "dutchie") to avoid upsetting mainstream Western sensibilities.[12] Among the biggest hits in continental Europe (West and East) in the early 1980s was the West German Goombay Dance Band's "Sun of Jamaica," which used black actors onstage to conjure an image of island life, including fire-eaters and children playing with a beach ball. In a similar spirit, the (all-white) Polish vocal group Vox performed "Bananowy Song," a catchy smash hit about relaxing island life.

There was still one place left where roots reggae's alternative potential remained unimpeachable, however: among punks in the communist Second World. Misty in Roots had once helped rejuvenate punk through Rock Against Racism—and it also had experience enduring the truncheons of an oppressive state. The band was a source of inspiration in the West, but it was nothing short of a revelation for punks in the East when it crossed the Iron Curtain. As in the West, reggae bolstered punk by offering it ties to the culture of Third World rebellion, while Second World punks like Robert Brylewski and his new band, Izrael, recaptured the radicalism of reggae in solidarity with the Third World.

"Reggae is life," Robert Brylewski told a journalist for the popular youth magazine *Non Stop* in the summer of 1983—the summer of the Misty in Roots tour of Poland. Izrael played reggae—or, to be precise, "punkreggae," he explained—in order to break free from corrupt, degenerate modern European civilization, a civilization with which the band had "nothing in common." Brylewski then handed the interviewer a pamphlet about Pan-African nationalist pioneer Marcus Mosiah Garvey, quoting, "We stand face to face with a highly developed civilization that cannot last—it must fall because it has no spiritual foundation. It is a civilization that is vicious, greedy, dishonest, immoral, a-religious, and corrupt." From Izrael's perspective, Jamaican immigrants in the United Kingdom, people in the Third World, and Polish punks were all in the same situation, and "punkreggae" was their best hope.[13]

Warsaw punk-Rastafarians were not the first to make the argument about the parallel conditions of the Second and Third Worlds. The Eastern bloc had long trumpeted its support for the Third World against the common enemy, capitalist imperialism. In 1955, Poland hosted the Days of Solidarity with

Colonial Youth in Warsaw. Six years later, Poland received a brotherly visit from Ghana's president, Pan-African nationalist and Third World revolutionary Kwame Nkrumah. Despite the decline of Third World radicalism, residual connections between the Second World and Third World continued into the 1980s. Exchange students from the Third World continued to visit the Eastern bloc—among them, a young woman named Vivien Quarcoo from Ghana (where, as in Poland, reggae continued to thrive even as its popularity waned in Jamaica). In the mid-1980s, Quarcoo met (and eventually married) Robert Brylewski, the former guitarist of Brygada Kryzys, solidifying the Third World inspiration that the band proclaimed.

For its part, Brygada Kryzys had been ready to move on to something new after months of wrangling with authorities under martial law. Just weeks after martial law was declared, Brygada Kryzys's members returned to Poland from a trip to Yugoslavia to see that they had been invited to perform at a Warsaw concert series. Or, rather, "Brygada K" had been invited; the band's name had been shortened by programmers. No doubt, the full word "Kryzys" ("Crisis") struck too close to home just weeks into martial law. Yet, from the band's perspective, changing the word "crisis" to the inert letter "k" would have meant giving in to the system, a major forfeit of subcultural capital. Brygada Kryzys chose not to play under the shortened name, and organizers responded that the band would not perform at all—ever again. They meant it: the band was no longer invited to perform in Warsaw—effectively banned from performing publicly in their own city.

Brygada Kryzys established a reputation as an uncompromising, unassailably alternative band. It also got in one last laugh: among the great ironies of martial law is that one of the first bands to be silenced was also one of the first to record an album. Roughly a month after the ban, the state record firm Tonpress opened a new studio that needed to be tested.[14] The members of Brygada Kryzys knew someone who worked there, got hired as equipment testers, and used their time in the studio to record their first, eponymous album—a classic of Polish punk. Shouting out from the silence of the ban on performing, on "There is Nothing" ("Nie ma nic") they systematically rejected the regime's worldview, declaring in nasal monotone, "If there is a new world, . . . Certainly it's not this one . . . There is nothing left here to lose."[15] While some copies made it to retailers, rumors circulated that many copies of the album were intentionally destroyed—just as A&M had done in the United Kingdom with the Sex Pistols' "God Save the Queen."

While Brygada Kryzys had managed to achieve the rare feat of slipping an album through the net of the state music industry, the ban on live performance following martial law had made life difficult. After a year of being unable to perform—and watching new wave bands like Republika and Lady Pank rule the state media (and sell off punk's subcultural capital)—Brygada Kryzys picked up reggae, changed its name to Izrael, joined Misty in Roots on the tour, and took up many of the components of Rastafarian philosophy. Brylewski's bands had been influenced by reggae since the late 1970s, but Izrael took its Third World inspiration particularly seriously. The band chose the name Izrael for local reasons—because it "had the fog of the enemy" in communist Poland due to Cold War geopolitics and because it was irritating to Polish anti-Semites.[16] But it also was meaningful metaphorically according to the beliefs of Rastafarianism, which identified Zion as the promised land, and Babylon as the oppressor. By playing reggae, reading texts by Marcus Garvey, and using marijuana, the band found a "new awareness." Izrael explained, "You smoke herb and your third eye opens. . . . the world is set in place, you know, you see the light, and you must rise and fight for your rights."[17]

Izrael was just one part of a growing reggae scene in Poland. In 1983, the first annual Robrege festival took place in Warsaw, sponsored by the University of Warsaw's official student club and frequent punk venue, Hybrydy. The club's manager, Sławomir "Gąsior" Rogowski, was not a party member, but he used his connections with the leadership of the student organization ZSP and the PZPR's student committee to gain authorization and protection for the festival.[18] As a result, bands and huge audiences gathered in the middle of Warsaw amid the ubiquitous smell of marijuana—and a surprisingly low presence of censorship and the secret police.[19] Robrege transformed Warsaw into a reggae paradise. Jacek Słowiński, a writer for the youth magazine *Razem*, marveled, "Marcus Garvey, the deceased prophet of Rastafarianism, would be shocked if he found himself in Warsaw today." Słowiński evidently shared Garvey's surprise, remarking on people "walking around the streets dressed in red-yellow-green colors—the national colors of Ethiopia," as well as hairstyles "in the rasta fashion," including dreadlocks.[20] By the next summer, the festival was attracting some of the edgiest alternative punk and reggae acts from across the Eastern bloc.

Izrael and its brethren recognized reggae's racial politics and sincerely identified with the Third World. Like Misty in Roots, Donovan Letts, and many others, they saw reggae and punk as fighting the same struggle. Both cultures rejected and attacked the corrupt, decaying modern world: punk did it through irreverence and realism, while reggae worked through allegory and revelation. Thanks to its catchy, bass-heavy rhythm, reggae gained popularity in the Eastern bloc that rivaled that of punk—and even exceeded it in some places. If punk was a rebellion against indulgent progressive rock, the music industry, and Western modernity, it made little sense in parts of the Second and Third Worlds without commercial rock scenes—or Western modernity, for that matter. However, reggae's sound instead built on classic R & B, allowing it to thrive where punk was slow to make inroads, in the Third World and the interior of Soviet Russia.

Among those interested in reggae in the USSR was one of the country's most revered alternative rock bands, Akvarium. Akvarium had spent the early 1980s performing underground after losing its professional status in the wake of a scandal at the Tbilisi rock festival. The band spent its time away from the spotlight seeking out a diverse palette of sounds from around the world. Alongside new wave influences, its next album, *Radio Africa*, offered an eclectic mix of rock, jazz, funk, new wave, and—in the case of the title track—Afrobeat, including an introductory sax solo reminiscent of Nigeria's anti-imperialist musical superstar, Fela Kuti. In 1983, as progressively minded elites in the USSR sought to integrate young people back into the system much as they did in Poland, Akvarium performed at the first festival of the Leningrad Rock Club.[21] Along with "Radio Africa," it performed "Babylon," bluntly singing, "We live in Babylon / This town is Babylon"—a blatant rejection of modern Soviet life in the language of reggae.

New wave followed close behind reggae in the Soviet Union, traveling along the same combination of personal and systemic networks as punk elsewhere. It arrived first in Leningrad, Russia's historic "window to the West." Among its carriers was little-known punk singer Joanna Stingray, who traveled from Los Angeles to Leningrad in 1984, where she met members of Akvarium and Leningrad's first full-fledged superstar new wave band, Kino, led by Korean Russian singer Viktor Tsoi. Stingray was so enthralled with the scene developing around the new wave club that she stayed and married Kino's guitarist, helping bridge the scenes by transporting music and videos between the East and the West in both directions. Stingray was just one link in the cultural exchange between the First, Second, and Third Worlds: in 1985, Misty in Roots toured the Soviet Union before stopping back in Poland to play at the annual Robrege festival.

By then, the collaboration between Poland, West Indian immigrants in the United Kingdom, and Jamaica had matured to full fruition. In 1986, Warsaw radio presenter Włodzimierz Kleszcz brought Norman Grant of the Twinkle Brothers, a Jamaican reggae band active since the 1960s, to Poland. Roots reggae may have been on the decline in Jamaica and London, but Grant found a lasting cultural kinship in Eastern Europe among the mountain folk culture of southeastern Poland. Forming a union of the world's oppressed people—Jamaicans and marginalized East Europeans—the Twinkle Brothers collaborated with a Tatra mountain folk band, Trebunie-Tutki, in a partnership that maintained its relevance through the transition from the Cold War era to the subsequent era of neoliberal globalization. Their message and their sound appealed in the West as much as the East and South: when they released their first single, it made West European charts.[22]

As Second World punks rekindled the fires of reggae and directed them against what they saw as widespread corruption extending from the global order down to local politics, a coalition of *tiermondisme*-inspired punks in the First World underwent a similar globally engaged politicization, explicitly targeting Western imperialism and the expansion of global capital. While the vehemence of the antiglobalization movement of the early 1990s took many observers by surprise, its origins are readily discernible in the punk scenes of the 1980s. Punk's Cold War roots gave it a transnational scope that lent itself to global critique in the changing environment of the late Cold War world.

In the West, punks' links to Third World ideology via reggae provided a ready-made critique of imperialism, Westernization, and Eurocentrism. The Clash is an obvious example: in December 1980, it released *Sandinista!*, which included "Washington Bullets," a sharp critique of US foreign policy set to a bouncy Caribbean rhythm. One by one, the song called out First World Cold War interventions of the previous decades as acts of violence against the people perpetrated by dictators armed with "Washington bullets." Nor was the Second World safe from the Clash's rebuke: the song also shouted out against the "Moscow bullets" in Afghanistan and those of Chinese communists in Tibet. With the song, the Clash placed itself solidly on the side of the Sandinista rebels in Nicaragua, who by 1980 had managed to successfully fight back against the US-backed dictator Somoza. Reminiscent of his first gig with the 101ers at a benefit for Chileans after the US intervention against the Allende government, Strummer invited a spokesman for the Committee in Solidarity with the People of El Salvador to rap in "Washington Bullets." The Clash's vision and worldview had been global from the beginning, but after more than a year of traveling constantly between New York, London, and Kingston (home to *Sandinista!*'s producer Mikey Dread), the band had developed an increasingly acute sense of the brutal consequences of First and Second World Cold War policies in the global South.

A second potent strand of global critique among punks in the West and East alike was an intensifying engagement with the proliferation of nuclear weapons. Concern (and fascination) about nuclear weapons was present in punk from the beginning. The Weirdos, a pioneering punk band in LA sang "We Got the Neutron Bomb" in 1977, and the Minutemen's "Paranoid Chant" (1980) wryly remarked on the extent to which daily life had been infiltrated by thoughts of the coming apocalypse. Concern about nuclear warfare grew increasingly dire over the first few years of the 1980s, however, as Reagan sought to expand American military supremacy, flanked by Thatcher stationing missiles in the United Kingdom. In 1980, Crass released "Nagasaki Nightmare / Big A Little A"—the B-side riffing on a Dr. Seuss children's book for a critique of nuclear armaments. Pacifists repulsed by the militant rhetoric of the Thatcher and Reagan administrations, Crass began to donate the proceeds from its music sales to the Campaign for Nuclear Disarmament.[23] In the early 1980s, nuclear tensions rose to a level that was greater than at any time since the Cuban Missile Crisis. The Doomsday Clock maintained by the editorial board of the *Bulletin of the Atomic Scientists* was moved three minutes closer to midnight (which represented nuclear apocalypse). This was its highest threat level since the 1950s—and it would get worse before it got better.[24] Even the typically playful Circle Jerks released "Stars and Stripes" in 1982, warning, "Everybody's building bombs / ... Modern technology digs your grave / Care of Moscow and DC / Votes you never gave."[25]

As neoliberal/neoconservative globalization expanded in the 1980s, these strands of punk's incipient global critique interwove into a ferocious activism across punk scenes in the United Kingdom and United States. In the United Kingdom, a key catalyst was the Falklands War in 1982, which brought a new urgency to the critique of bands like Crass. When Argentina invaded the Falkland Islands off its eastern coast in April 1982, the impact on the wounded post-imperial British psyche outweighed any strategic or economic impact on England. The Falklands crisis presented the opportunity to embrace and harness repressed British colonial nostalgia and nationalism, however, and the United Kingdom sent its military to recapture the islands. The Falklands changed the tenor of the Thatcher regime, which transcended its association with social unrest and economy hardship and replaced it with a claim to be restoring the glory of the British Empire.[26]

While Crass once reveled in political ambiguity and contempt across the spectrum, it refocused its assault as the United Kingdom prepared for war. Since Crass was already attracting attention from authorities ("Reality Asylum" provoked a visit from Scotland Yard's vice squad, which threatened charges of criminal blasphemy), it adopted a guerrilla strategy for its next action.[27] The band produced an anti-Falklands and anti-Thatcher album like a bootleg, pressed in France to avoid interference. Then, Crass had sympathizers in the music industry slip it in with popular albums by respectable pop stars like Sheena Easton and Robert Palmer, using pop as a Trojan Horse for its punk assault. It registered as a potent threat: the military worried that copies had made it to sailors fighting in the war and warned soldiers not to listen.[28]

When the inevitable victory of UK forces came, Crass did everything it could to interrupt the celebration, and in the process, broke into public awareness as punk had not done since the Sex Pistols showed up for the queen's Silver Jubilee five years earlier. When everyone else prepared for the parade, Crass released "How Does It Feel" ("to be the mother of a thousand dead?", the lyrics continued). Once again, punk attracted attention not just from local law enforcement and cultural authorities but also from Members of Parliament. Conservative MP Tim Eggar was enraged and wrote to the attorney general requesting that Crass be prosecuted under the Obscene Publications Act. Crass's newfound activism also found sympathetic collaborators in the punk scene, especially 2 Tone, whose bands shared Crass's aversion to the rising violence and saber-rattling. The Specials reached back to the 1960s, remaking Dylan's "Maggie's Farm," which found new relevance in the Thatcher era as an antinuclear anthem at rallies—a movement that would peak in a 250,000-person march in London in 1983. Meanwhile, 2 Tone labelmates the Beat contributed "Stand Down Margaret," with all proceeds to benefit the Campaign for Nuclear Disarmament.[29]

Thatcher was not about to be drawn into a battle with punks. Shortly after Crass released "How Does it Feel," the prime minister declared she would not "give these people the dignity . . . of having a public platform." Crass and Penny Rimbaud were less and less interested in speaking anyway. Rimbaud reflected, "As young men died in their hundreds, Crass' songs, protest and marches, leaflets, words and ideas seemed suddenly worthless."[30] Rimbaud took up a new motto, borrowed from his nemesis, the military, as an explanation for civilian casualties in the Vietnam War: "It was necessary to destroy the town to save it." In Rimbaud's case, the town was London. Over the next nine months, Crass supported three "stop the city" actions organized by London Greenpeace in 1983 and 1984. Seeking to disrupt the "business as usual" mentality and bring the war back home, the actions blockaded London's financial district. Amid the smoke bombs, broken glass, and arrests, Crass's figurative guerrilla war strategy had gone from metaphor to reality.

Like any good insurgency, Crass launched its own information campaign. As the battle raged on, a tape purporting to contain conversation between Reagan and Thatcher surfaced in 1983 with the UK press, suggesting the latter had sacrificed soldiers to keep Prince Andrew out of the line of fire. The accusation was serious, and the recording was convincing—so much so that the scandal was dubbed "Thatchergate" and blamed on the KGB.[31] When it was linked to Crass nearly a year later, the band got everyone's attention, attracting surveillance by the British security and receiving contacts from groups hostile to the capitalist United Kingdom, including the KGB, the IRA, and Baader-Meinhof. Through its newly found militancy, Crass had placed itself solidly in the camp of opposition to Thatcher. It was a very uncomfortable place for a band that eschewed partisan politics, but it nonetheless deeply inspired Crass's punk comrades in arms across the Atlantic as they too delved into explicitly global political concerns.

In the fall of 1983, the Reagan administration faced an analogous situation to that of the United Kingdom in the Falklands. In another former colony of the United Kingdom, the tiny island of Grenada in the Caribbean, a left-wing coup threatened the Cold War calculus of the capitalist world.[32] The United States invaded and quickly defeated the insurgency, bringing cries from the international community of a violation of Grenadan sovereignty. Meanwhile, the punk scene of San Francisco had already been radicalizing at the urging of *Maximum Rocknroll*, abandoning all scruples about politicizing punk. By the mid-1980s, *Maximum Rocknroll*'s radio show had expanded to over thirty stations around the United States, and the 'zine itself was distributed globally, including scene reports on all of the inhabited continents of the earth by the late 1980s. In one issue alone in 1984, for instance, the 'zine reported on violence in Nicaragua, an anti-imperialist anti-American Japanese punk band called Stalin, Polish punk, and a raid on the music of Crass and the Dead Kennedys in a UK record store. *Maximum Rocknroll* refocused on its hometown scene as well, opening a new punk venue on Gilman Street founded with rigorous standards of nonviolence and inclusivity. If that meant "rules" from the perspective of some punks, then so be it. Some San Francisco punks were even willing to take cues from the hippies that punks so often viewed with contempt, spawning a new subset of punks who came to be known as "peace punks." They became so ubiquitous, in fact, that by 1984, *Maximum Rocknroll* presented a comical sketch of peace punks as a "punk type," identified by their obligatory Crass apparel.

Peace punk was more than just a fashion statement, however. Peace punks and other politically active punks in San Francisco looked to Crass and London's "Stop the City" actions for inspiration. After organizing a punk subset of the Livermore Action Group that protested the Lawrence Livermore nuclear defense laboratory, they joined the group's "Hall of Shame Tour" through San Francisco's financial district. The next spring, the punks themselves led the charge, organizing another tour on Tax Day, invading the lobbies of military-connected corporations, staging "die-ins," interrupting business, and finally protesting a speech by former secretary of state Henry Kissinger, stirring up the crowd enough to provoke mass arrests from the mounted police.[33]

Punk activism in the United States found its most dramatic expression, however, against the backdrop of the Democratic War Chest Tours, which coincided with the Democratic National Convention in the summer of 1984. While most punks vehemently opposed Reagan, many saw the Democratic Party as merely a lesser evil—and the Democratic Party establishment returned their skepticism. Punk had a long tradition of hostility toward organized politics in general, and San Francisco was atypical in that its political spectrum extended mainly from the moderate left to the far left. However, punks' involvement in the Democratic National Convention also presaged the complex, seemingly political spectrum-defying politics of globalization, bringing together punks concerned with globalization on both *tiermondiste* and tribalist grounds. Between the two sides, they caused a commotion and response befitting an uprising in communist Eastern Europe. While the San Francisco police managed the protests through frequent arrests, on the final day of the convention, when the protests coincided with an all-punk Rock Against Reagan concert, punk protesters had an audience of five thousand to back them up. More than one thousand joined in a march to the city jail, as the crowd chanted "Let them go!" The result was 282 additional arrests.[34]

San Francisco and *Maximum Rocknroll* were the hub of *tiermondiste* punk activism, but scenes elsewhere in the United States politicized as well, sometimes finding themselves fighting alongside traditional political parties in the shifting political landscape. By 1984, with the prospect of four more years of Reagan, the editor of LA 'zine *Flipside* reconsidered the strategy of equal contempt for both sides—even for the 40 percent of readers who described themselves as anarchists: "You can say fuck the system, whoever you vote for government wins, but it's like one government will kill you and [with] the other you may have a fighting chance." He added, "If Ronnie Ray Gun does get the security of another 4 years he will probably get his war. And we're talking life and death, perhaps of the whole planet, so I can see where, hmmm, that involves anarchists too."[35]

The pinnacle of global punk activism and *tiermondisme*, however, emerged on both sides of the Atlantic in response to apartheid in South Africa, the official division of society into hierarchical categories based on race. Many punks around the world identified with the plight of black South Africans. In the United Kingdom, Jerry Dammers of the Specials—founder of 2 Tone—had dedicated his life to breaking down racial boundaries. In 1983, Dammers attended a concert in London by radical black South African trumpeter Hugh Masekela. After hearing the crowd chanting, "Free Nelson Mandela," Dammers wrote a ska song by that title, to be performed by a new incarnation of the Specials, "The Special AKA."[36] The result not only reached the Top 10 on UK charts by March 1984 but also garnered letters of praise from the African National Congress. He continued the fight by helping found the organization Artists Against Apartheid in the United States. It fit perfectly with what was already in the works in Washington, DC, where punks had declared 1985 to be "Revolution Summer." One of their projects would be to work with the nonprofit organization Transafrica to protest apartheid in South Africa in a "punk percussion protest" outside the embassy in June 1985.[37]

Even DC's Ian MacKaye, master of the politics of the personal, began to turn his attention in a global direction by the mid-1980s. Like Crass when the Falklands War broke out, he found that revolutionizing the self and forsaking politics was insufficient when confronted with brute force from those who wished to co-opt punk for hatred and mindless violence. In early 1985, he had traveled to the United Kingdom and met with Crass. He had been familiar with the band's music and ethos previously, but now he was undergoing a similar evolution to the band's, from apolitical anarchism to engagement. It was becoming increasingly clear to McKaye as to other punks in DC, that oppression in other parts of the world wasn't just a distant, unrelated issue. Again, apartheid served as an obvious example. At a concert, Guy Picciotto, who would join MacKaye in the unabashedly political Fugazi, picked up the set list, written on the back of an anti-apartheid poster and commented, "It's not really that far away."[38] From the perspective of punks, the regimes of the First, Second, and Third Worlds were all versions of the same oppressive system, and increasingly, they sought to join forces against it.

Punk *tiermondisme* was also significant in one other respect: it provided an important interface with hip-hop culture, the new cultural phenomenon arising among the black population of New York. This new culture shared features like a heavy bass line and DJ "toasting" with Jamaican dub, but its combination of rapid-fire vocal "rapping" and acrobatic breakdancing distinguished it as a culture of its own. During a week-long residency at Bond's International Casino, the Clash shared the stage with hip-hop pioneers Grandmaster Flash and the Furious 5, whose first hit was as attuned to social justice as the Clash, but from the perspective of black New York rather than working-class London.[39] According to Rick Rubin of Def Jams records, the Clash was "the first band to really embrace that cross-cultural revolution" of hip-hop.[40] Like Paul Simonon with reggae, Mick Jones in particular was inspired, recording "Radio Clash," a breakdance track. The connection went both ways: the Clash's "Magnificent Dance" was a hit on black station WBLS. The band became regular visitors to Club Negril, along with luminaries of the early New York hip-hop scene. As Don Letts observed, much as with reggae years before, "There was a punky hip-hop party going on and the Clash were at the centre of it."

Among others, the band met hip-hop pioneer Afrika Bambaataa, who Letts noted "was really intrigued by all these punks getting into hip-hop." In fact, he got a chance to check it out for himself. In 1984, Bambaataa joined John Lydon (who was already connected to reggae and dub through his new band, Public Image Ltd) to create the band Time Zone. The single "World Destruction" picked up in 1984 where the Clash's *Sandinista!* left off, unleashing a furious shout of rage against the global North, asserting solidarity against the likes of the CIA and KGB. Not to be outdone, as the Clash was starting to disintegrate, Mick Jones and Letts formed a new punk/reggae/hip-hop fusion band, Big Audio Dynamite. Malcolm McLaren joined the new hip hop-trend as well, releasing a hip-hop-tinged album, *Duck Rock*, in 1983. Meanwhile, back in the United Kingdom, hip-hop artist the Phantom picked up on a familiar punk theme, releasing his "Thatcher Rap" at the peak of Crass's assault in 1983.[41]

By the middle of the 1980s, punks were sharing their space on the alternative music stage with reggae and hip-hop—and, in many cases, happily so. For punks seeking to rejuvenate their scenes, these opportunities to draw inspiration across national, regional, and racial boundaries were transformative. However, punks who chose to respond to the changing landscape of the late Cold War world by seeking out multicultural alliances were just one subset of punk's diverse and multifaceted scenes.

Punk Tribalism

As a new wave of globalization spread across the Cold War world and a neoliberal/neoconservative alliance in the West ramped up rhetoric of strength and order, many punks radicalized and refashioned themselves as world citizens in a new *tiermondisme* suited to the transition from the late Cold War world to the era of neoliberal globalization. However, another option was available for punks who were skeptical of what seemed like an emerging progressive, internationalist punk movement. Rather than embracing punk *tiermondisme*, they turned inward, fiercely defending their subcultural community, its subcultural capital, and its boundaries from encroachment, retreating into what might be called "punk tribalism."[42] While they were seldom interested with politics as such, in some cases, these punk communities' symbols and language resonated with those of the emergent right, focusing on order, hierarchy, and self-defense. In this context, a split emerged in punk scenes around the world in the mid-1980s—one that remains present in punk scenes today.

In part, this inward turn was a reaction against new wave and its commercial success: bands rejected commercialization by cordoning themselves off from the market and finding ever more extreme ways to amass subcultural capital. It also was a reaction against the perceived leftist politicization and cosmopolitanism of punk. However, there were long-term systemic forces at work as well. Over the 1970s, elements of 1960s radical discourse had gradually become integrated into mainstream European and American politics. While globalization demanded order to maintain trade, it also relied on a degree of willingness to engage with potential partners and customers across borders to facilitate the international exchange of goods and capital. Slogans about tolerance, equality, and diversity were mouthed by elites across the political spectrum, even as obvious inequality endured. In this manner, the legacy of 1960s radicalism transformed in some quarters into "political correctness" in the 1980s. Rather than identifying and addressing racism and sexism as ubiquitous systemic problems, political correctness focused on merely censuring the expression of sexist or racist sentiment.

For many punks, political correctness was precisely the kind of obfuscation and doublespeak that made politics repugnant, whether it came from the Left or the Right. Rejection of political correctness could easily shade into bigotry, however. When faced by the disjuncture between slogans of equality and an unequal reality, one option for punks was to point out the lies and hypocrisy behind the empty words ("God save the queen, the fascist regime"). The other option, however, was to reject equality itself as a value. If mainstream society could agree on mouthing support for tolerance and peace, then shouting about bigotry and violence could serve as a conspicuously nonconformist alternative. Over the first half of the 1980s, the violent, masculine, destructive side of punk, and particularly hardcore, intersected with these developments and coalesced into a distinct skinhead subculture.

Music journalist Greil Marcus had first noticed a change starting to take place in the LA punk scene in 1981 while he was reviewing an Adolescents album filled with rage directed against the black, Jewish, Latino, and homosexual populations. Rather than aiming its fury at power as punk had initially done, he noted that "L.A. punk directs its rage against the other, the powerless—and that is a stance no less American than a happy barbarianism."[43] As in hardcore scenes everywhere, the atmosphere at shows in Los Angeles was growing increasingly tense. Chuck Dukowski (another First World punk who took a Polish surname in solidarity with his maligned East European comrades) from hardcore punk band Black Flag noticed that slam-dancing started as just good fun but began to turn into something far more sinister when "assholes" started coming to shows beat up punks. "Then factions formed, and it was like war. . . . It definitely was not our intention."[44]

Yet, Black Flag and its hardcore brethren walked a fine line. When violence erupted at shows, vocalist Henry Rollins fought back, much like Oi! bands in the United Kingdom. Rollins was no Nazi, but his sculpted masculine physique and tough guy persona appealed to some skinheads. While San Francisco "peace punks" and Crass were protesting against war, by the mid-1980s, Rollins, like many hardcore punks in the East and West, had given up on peace. Rollins embraced the apocalypse with nihilistic vitriol and black humor: "Personally, I am pro–nuclear war. I want to destroy the earth, 'cause it will get rid of everyone. All the mafia, all the club-owners, all the neurotic cocaine-sniffing wenches, all the fucking scumbags. I want to start clean and after the bomb drops, there will be nothing left but big old roaches, mutants, and stuff like that."[45] While Rollins's punk paradise of mutants and roaches differed substantially from an idealized Aryan society, the theme of purification through violence resonated disturbingly with the discourse of the far right. Meanwhile, the Black Flag song "White Minority" addressed white people becoming the minority in Los Angeles. As the band saw it, the controversy around the song meant that it succeeded, since it unsettled people's existing views, forcing them to reflect and consider.[46] In late 1981, the band finally explained in an interview that the song was intended to be ironic—a claim that carried some weight considering the original vocalist who performed it was Puerto Rican Ron Reyes.[47] However, like Oi! in the United States, Black Flag had gotten caught up in the fracas as its fans struggled over competing visions of punk – globalist versus tribalist – that were sweeping not just the United States but much of the world.

In fact, Black Flag had noticed the first signs of change taking place when they were touring Europe, where Rollins found himself fighting off skinheads identifying themselves as fascists. Paradoxically, punk tribalism also spread along punk's global networks, creating a global community of fiercely insular punk scenes. In Western Europe, right-wing punk groups in France joined the Rebelles Européens label and looked to the far right in reaction against the multiculturalism of the socialist Mitterrand government.[48] In West Germany, right-wing punks gathered around the Rock-O-Rama record label. Both connected with right-wing punks in the United Kingdom—most notably, the white supremacist band Skrewdriver. Skrewdriver had existed briefly in the late 1970s, only to fold in the face of indifference and outright opposition. In the new environment of the 1980s, though, Skrewdriver came back to life and found itself at the center of a racist skinhead culture by 1984.[49]

Punks who were inclined toward *tiermondisme* fought this emerging trend. In 1981, as the Dead Kennedys blasted the religious right in "Moral Majority," they simultaneously took on bigotry within the punk scene with the B-side, "Nazi Punks Fuck Off." Jello Biafra reminded punks that while they might "think swastikas look cool," the "real Nazis" were the school principals, coaches, businessmen, and cops—and that punks would be among the first to be eliminated in the event of a "fourth Reich." In a collaborative effort to help get US punk scenes back in order, the Dead Kennedys' Biafra traveled from San Francisco and led DC crowds singing "Nazi Punks Fuck Off." For any who remained unconvinced, the Dead Kennedys got help from Bad Brains when the latter came to visit San Francisco: Who better to take on white supremacists than an impeccably hardcore black punk band? Biafra credited Bad Brains with neutralizing the disturbing trend he saw of increasing fascist influence in the punk scene. However, it was impossible to deny that a change was taking place. The boundaries between punks and skins had initially been unclear, but by the middle of the decade, skinheads increasingly staked a claim to a racist, violent machismo as their identity.[50]

Some of the same ideas and images that were popular among tribalist punk scenes in Western Europe also appealed to their Eastern European counterparts. Working-class politics in Eastern Europe had been realigning since the dramatic failure of reform on the Left with the suppression of the Prague Spring in 1968. With the Left monopolized by the communists and the moderate right occupied by dissident elites, some punks found a potential wellspring of subcultural capital in the symbols, ideas, and identities usually associated with the far right. For some groups, there was an ironic distance or blatant absurdity in the right-wing references, as had been the case with the New York Dolls or the Sex Pistols appropriating swastikas, or the Jam claiming to support the Conservative Party. In a similar spirit, some alternative thinkers in Czechoslovakia embraced monarchism as a political philosophy that was safely untainted by association with the Communist Party.[51] For other bands, though, it was far more difficult to tell where ironic appropriation ended and actual right-wing politics began.

That was certainly the case in northwest Yugoslavia, where the Slovenian band Laibach thrived on the ambiguous boundary between appropriating fascist imagery and embracing it. Like its closest Western counterpart, the UK band Throbbing Gristle, Laibach was as much a visual art group as a band, with connections to the Neue Slowenische Kunst (New Slovenian Art) movement. Its intent was to provoke: the name "Laibach" hinted at fascism, as the German title for the capital city Ljubljana, used during the Nazi occupation. The dark imagery in the name complemented Laibach's heavy, ominous atmospheric music and its combat attire and symbolism taken from the regimes of dictators from across the political spectrum, including Mussolini, Tito, and Poland's Jaruzelski.

There were elements of irony in Laibach's use of authoritarian imagery. For instance, Neue Slowenische Kunst cleverly brought out the Yugoslav regime's uncomfortable similarities with fascism by submitting a (successful) proposal for a socialist youth festival poster based on a design from the 1936 Olympics in Berlin. Laibach also employed anti-Nazi appropriation of fascist imagery, using German anti-Nazi John Heartfield's pastiche of fascism on a record sleeve. One of the band members described the music as waging "psychological terror" on listeners—a concept that certainly jelled with punk and the tactic of bricolage, combining wildly incompatible symbols for shock value. The band's close associate, punk manager Igor Vidmar, was certainly no fascist—although his proud display of lapel badges for the Campaign for Nuclear Disarmament and the Dead Kennedys' "Nazi Punks Fuck Off", which depicted a crossed-out swastika, got him arrested by confused authorities.

Despite these hints that Laibach was toying with fascist imagery rather than embracing it, the typical punk irony of seeing swastikas used by bands like the Sex Pistols evaporated under the intensity of Laibach's deathly serious, dark music. A swastika combined with a waifish teenager with torn pants and spiky hair singing in a bratty, nasal voice to a simplistic punk song about being a degenerate may indeed be bricolage; a swastika combined with military uniforms and video projections of fascist rallies is a different matter. Laibach convinced people that it was serious about the right-wing symbols it used—including authorities in the Yugoslav state, which banned Laibach in 1983. While its performances were clearly theatrical, as Sabrina Petra Ramet has noted, Laibach never stepped out of character.[52] In this respect, Laibach exemplified a postmodern approach to punk: the line between fictitious personas created for shock value and real identities became so thin that it sometimes disappeared entirely. Laibach circulated its imagery and sound to both consternation and acclaim in Eastern and Western Europe alike. In 1983, despite being banned in Yugoslavia, the band launched its "Occupied Europe" tour—which tellingly included both Eastern and Western Europe. When it stopped in Poland to play at Gajewski's former club Riviera-Remont, however, even the punk-conditioned audience had trouble making sense of Laibach. Its song "Jaruzelsky" might have gone over fine if it had been accompanied by punk sounds and ironic lyrics, but the overlaid recordings of military bands and official news reports left the audience uncertain how to react.[53]

Polish punks would have no such trouble, though, when hardcore punk band Siekiera played at the Jarocin festival the following summer. In Poland, too, the combination of a growing global punk trend of experimenting with xenophobic and misogynist symbolism and a powerful reaction against new wave's mainstream success began to transform and divide the punk scene. Siekiera's performance of "There Were Only Four of Us" ("Było tylko czterech nas") at Jarocin in 1984 made even SS-20's performance from two years earlier seem like a calm, orderly affair. Siekiera took every tool Dezerter had used to stake its claim to hardcore punk status and intensified it, including the frenetic tempo, rapid bass-snare-bass-snare pattern, and the shredding distorted electric guitar. In particular, Budzyński's gruff, vocal cord–shredding bellow stood out from his hardcore punk peers. Sounding like a furious, deranged Louis Armstrong, he bellowed, "There were only 4 of us / Her alone, a dark forest / Without rescue and without chance / ... Four skins [skóry], free time." The repeated final yell, "All is well with us," contrasted menacingly with the threat of sexual violence in the first three. Siekiera's audience at Jarocin enacted the confrontational atmosphere that the lyrics suggested. A mosh pit formed in front of the band, where fans feeling the intensity of the music demonstrated their commitment by thrashing and slamming into each other, leaving a pit of dust and mud.[54]

Suggestions of violence in songs and performances were not new to punk, dating back at least to Sex Pistols performances in the mid-1970s. In this case, though, much like the trend Greil Marcus noticed in LA, punk's typical self-effacement and rebellion against the mainstream were replaced by empowerment through violence against an outsider—the woman in the woods with no identity other than as a victim. Siekiera took the hardcore ethos to its maximum extent, seeking to differentiate itself from punk bands deemed to have become too conformist. The band unflinchingly proclaimed that it endorsed "conflict at every level"—right down to between its own members.[55] In place of punk irony, Siekiera found "freedom in destruction."[56]

Vocalist Tomasz Budzyński recalled being asked constantly if the members of Siekiera were "punks" or "skins." Not surprisingly, they refused to categorize themselves. However, many of the characteristics of skinheads' new turn to the Right were there. To distinguish himself from punks, Siekiera's guitarist Tomasz Adamski shaved his head and grew a beard. Budzyński recalled that it "drove audiences crazy because punks didn't do that. Punk was like a uniform, but we wanted to be more."[57]

Above all, Siekiera relied on hardcore toughness and masculinity to distinguish itself from mainstream society and effete punks and new wavers alike. As new wave bands got airplay, music videos, and record contracts, bands like Siekiera redoubled their efforts to assert their subcultural capital by distancing themselves from new wave bands that had gone "soft" to appeal to popular audiences. In Poland, this charge was directed especially at Lady Pank, particularly after its performance at the prestigious Opole song festival in 1984. With their brightly colored dress, young fans, professional manager ("pimp"), and popularity ("selling themselves"), the members of Lady Pank found their masculinity and authenticity simultaneously challenged. As a reader of the music periodical *Non Stop* accused, "They paint themselves like girls . . . does no one know that they are puppets that only play as Mister Mogielnicki tells them to?"[58] He characterized Lady Pank as feminine and submissive—implying that subcultural capital came from being dominant and masculine. Lady Pank dressed in bright colors; Siekiera wore leather. Lady Pank's Jan Panasewicz had stylish curly hair; the members of Siekiera shaved theirs off. Panasewicz playfully half-sang; Budzyński growled and yelled. Lady Pank blended pop into its music to appeal to audiences; Siekiera banished any hint of pop and directed its music *against* its audience. Lady Pank acted like girls; Siekiera dominated them.

By 1984, Lady Pank and other bands that existed on the boundaries between mainstream and alternative came under attack from within Poland's punk scene. In place of the fan clubs that had proliferated around popular new wave bands like Republika, Maanam, and Lady Pank two years earlier, a new phenomenon took place: anti-fan clubs. Their members dedicated themselves to mocking new wave bands and their fans and would go en masse to concerts of groups they disliked in order to jeer at the bands and antagonize their fans.

As in the West, punk scenes in Poland were dividing into warring camps, and the popular press took notice. In April 1985, a survey of fans appearing in *Razem* magazine announced an odd pair of awardees for the "Noose" award for the greatest harm to new wave and Polish rock: Lady Pank came in second place, beaten out only by the state Ministry of Culture and Art.[59] In this context, a press panel of punk enthusiasts asked whether the new wave revolution had finally come to an end. Curiously, Lady Pank guitarist Jan Borysewicz—whose band was number two on the Hits List at that very moment—responded, "It lives on in our hearts." Three months earlier, Borysewicz had told an interviewer that his favorite band was Siekiera.[60]

For all their ambiguity, Black Flag, Laibach, and Siekiera were not neo-Nazis or white nationalists. In fact, in 1985, Siekiera appeared side by side with Robert Brylewski's globally minded Izrael on the first above-ground compilation of hardcore punk and reggae, released under the title *Fala* by the semiprivate label Polton—an important reminder that bands with seemingly different cultural politics often moved in similar circles. In other cases, though, the inspiration from the far right was more explicit. Over the 1980s, as in the West, skinheads in the East became increasingly associated with radical right-wing ideas and symbols—including those of neo-Nazism and white nationalism.[61] In Hungary, a lively Oi! scene developed in the wake of UK Oi!, with the band Mos-oi staking claim to the international skinhead movement's blue-collar, masculine, militaristic white identity with its "Skinhead Marching Song." The band faced some of the same question about its relationship with the radical right and violent nationalism as UK Oi!—and answered unmistakably with songs like the xenophobic "Immigrants' Share" and "Freezone," calling for exterminating gypsies with a flamethrower.[62] Meanwhile, in Estonia, punk band Propeller launched a nationalist assault on ethnic outsiders like Russians and Jews (promising to "finish what the Germans began").[63] In East Germany, nationalist elements of the punk scene leapt into the spotlight in 1987 when a performance by the new wave band Element of Crime—performing in a church where East German punk bands sometimes found refuge—precipitated violence from skinheads in the audience.[64]

The same networks between East and West that inspired punk also fueled a transnational skinhead movement across the boundaries of the Cold War world. In 1982, a new band appeared on the DC scene on Ian MacKaye's Dischord label under the name Iron Cross. Vocalist Sab Grey had returned from the United Kingdom inspired by Oi! and brought its tortured racial attitudes into the DC scene. For those who missed the obvious right-wing resonance in the band name, reminiscent of interwar Eastern European fascist parties like Arrow Cross (Hungary) and Iron Guard (Romania), Grey made the connection obvious by claiming in an interview that everyone was a Nazi.[65] Meanwhile, a new group calling itself the "Rat Patrol"—which started up like the punk self-defense squads in LA that formed against hostile outsiders—began to redefine its mission as beating up homosexuals in the gay-populated Dupont Circle area. Prominent among them was a most unlikely person to wear a swastika, a young black woman who, evidently grasping the irony of her situation, went by the nickname "Lefty." As skinheads entered the orbit of the far right, even Iron Cross's Grey was alarmed, recanting his words about Nazism as "numb-skulled provocation." True skins (like him) were different from the fascists, he now argued.[66] Yet, if there was indeed a difference, he was one of the few who could still tell. It was an increasingly subtle distinction that he himself had helped efface.

This time, not even black DC hardcore pioneer Bad Brains could help. In fact, they had also fallen victim to the growing tensions within the world's punk scenes. Vocalist HR had grown increasingly interested in reggae and Rastafarianism over the early 1980s—so much so that his bandmates started having trouble getting him to play punk.[67] HR even adopted a Jamaican accent when the band performed—and is often credited for coining the term "mosh" (a Jamaican-inflected pronunciation of "mash") for the intense slam-dancing that accompanied hardcore punk. More troubling than his growing indifference to hardcore punk, though, was his increasingly vocal condemnation of homosexuality in the punk scene—a trend that grew to a near feud when the band traveled to Austin, whose gay-friendly punk scene had once been home to MDC.

Animosity toward homosexuality was typical in many sectors of American society; it was certainly not an invention of punk. However, HR's position placed the band in the uncomfortable company of the emergent cultural right. HR consistently explained his objection to homosexuality in the language of Rastafarianism, but the fact that bigotry arose out of a philosophy ostensibly about empowering the weak and downtrodden was small comfort. *Maximum Rocknroll* predictably responded with a full spread denouncing Bad Brains, including the image of a cross folding into the shape of a swastika. *Maximum Rocknroll* wasn't alone this time, though: the *Flipside* 1982 reader poll awarded

Bad Brains third place for "Asshole of the Year"—only two slots behind Ronald Reagan. Like Lady Pank competing with the Ministry of Culture and Art for the "Noose" award, Bad Brains found itself in awkward company.

By 1984, as punk scenes around the United States were marred by internecine strife, venue after venue closed their doors—or closed their doors to punk, as was the case with the popular Wilson Center in Washington, DC. In San Francisco, the largest punk venue, On Broadway, closed in 1984.[68] A disturbing trend started where instead of uniting against the police, punks had to call the police in for protection. On the cover of its spring 1984 issue, *Maximum Rocknroll* asked, "Does punk suck?" For many, the answer seemed to be yes.

In fact, some of the most influential hardcore punk bands were moving away from punk and gravitating toward a new variety of heavy metal—including Black Flag. Heavy metal was not new, but as hardcore punk arose at the cusp of the 1980s, it inspired and intertwined with a new wave of heavy metal that was faster, darker, and fiercer than ever before.[69] Whereas punk mocked power, metal embraced it, as bands like Iron Maiden took the thick, orchestrated sound, elaborate costumes, theatricality, powerful amps, lighting, sound effects, and virtuoso performances of progressive rock and intensified them. The new brand of metal spread to the East as well, with Iron Maiden's World Slavery Tour spanning both sides of Europe's Iron Curtain. In fact, Polish metal fans voted the tour the number one musical event of 1984 in *Non Stop*.[70] In the East, too, metal abandoned social critique and gender-bending, instead converting spectacle into a symbol of masculine virility. The leader of pioneering Polish metal band TSA rationalized his choice of heavy metal as his musical style explicitly in terms of gender: "It is music for men. . . . The rebellion of punk rock quickly was reborn in commercial opportunism. This will never happen with our music."[71] Compared with punk, which had been commercialized (even within socialist Eastern Europe), metal was saved by its masculinity.

Most punks avoided formal politics from the beginning, loathing conservatives, contemptuous of the Labour establishment, disgusted by Democrats, and skeptical toward the political far right and far left. However, over the 1980s, politics, culture, and identity increasingly intertwined across the late Cold War World, framing everyday life (and phenomena like punk) as struggles between order and chaos, righteousness and dissolution (from the perspective of the Right) and between progressives and reactionaries (from the perspective of the Left). While many punks remained skeptical of formal politics, the forces of globalization (particularly the effects on the music industry) combined with the emerging political spectrum to exacerbate a divide in punk scenes around the world.

As the world moved from the ideologically based categories of the Cold War toward the identity- and culture-based framework of the era of global neoliberalism, many punks were deeply skeptical of the emerging global order. However, their differing reactions nonetheless placed them on opposite sides of the emerging political spectrum. Some punks embraced a new *tiermondisme*, forming connections across national boundaries with punks, Rastafarians, emerging hip-hop scenes, and other fellow travelers. Others, however, turned to tribalism, joining a network of fiercely local, xenophobic communities that meshed with the symbolism of the emergent political right. As punk scenes divided, their internal struggles intertwined with cultural-political clashes taking place around the world. In this manner, punk scenes were drawn into a series of struggles between political traditionalists and progressives that, by the late 1980s, became an all-out global culture war.

7

Culture Wars

Between 1982 and 1984, as new wave popularized and punk scenes broke down into warring factions, a flurry of controversy over punk arose in the media across the Eastern bloc. In 1982, an article in the East German periodical *Junge Welt* entitled "Between Rage and Conformity" attacked punk as threatening yet also conformist. In 1983, a similar jeremiad appeared in Czechoslovakia under the mysterious authorship of "Jan Kryzl" and the title "A 'New' Wave with Old Contents," denouncing new wave for its decadent behavior, flamboyant dress, and drug use—ultimately alleging it was a capitalist conspiracy (evidently one that the capitalist world had already unleashed on itself). In Soviet Ukraine, authorities deemed punk to be an offshoot of right-wing Ukrainian nationalism and sought to ban it, to the consternation of those who had counted on leniency from officials for years. In the USSR, the reaction went all the way up to the new general secretary, Iurii Andropov, who took a stand against new wave as part of his campaign to reverse the consumerism and corruption of the Brezhnev years. In July 1983, at a plenum of the Central Committee of the Communist Party, Andropov declared, "It is intolerable to see the occasional emergence of a wave of popularity of musical bands with repertoires of a dubious nature."[1] It was not an idle threat: the Ministry of Higher and Specialized Education followed up with Order 67, "Measures for the regulation of activities of vocal/instrumental groups in higher and intermediate specialized educational establishments ..."

Without a doubt, this new attention from the state was bad news for punks in the East. Yet, anyone perusing the news in the West would have been surprised by the similarity between the situations on each side of the Iron Curtain. At precisely the same moment, US international radio broadcasting took a conservative turn: in 1983, Voice of America programmer Frank Scott issued a directive to not play music that might offend any portion of the audience.[2] Voices of cultural conservatism in the United States also intensified in the months that followed. In June 1984, the national convention of the Parent Teacher Association (PTA) in Las Vegas decided to take up the matter of objectionable content in popular music. With the well-being of the nation's youth involved, the issue quickly developed from a topic of concern for a group of citizens to a barrage of hyperbolic editorials in the press and on television, several high-profile trials of punk bands, and a hearing in the US Senate.

To punk scene insiders, it was the strangest things that provoked the international panic and reaction in the East and West. It was not hardcore punk, not the War Chest actions and mass arrests in San Francisco, not skinheads or Siekiera's all-out war against everything. Rather, it was the mass-market spin-offs of punk most likely to reach young people—the new wave and new metal bands showing up in the mass media in the East and West. In the United Kingdom, no one would have been surprised that Crass finally faced legal charges after years of provocations, but it was the band's "obscene" feminist lyrics, not Thatchergate or alleged collaboration with the KGB, that got its members sentenced. In short, it was not politics—at least in the classic, ideological sense—that was at issue; rather, the basis of the uproar was moral, cultural, and aesthetic. The same basic list of characteristics aroused concern on both sides of the Iron Curtain: allegations of low musical quality, mindless consumption, sex, drugs, violence, profanity, and the occult. By the mid-1980s, even as punk ceded the spotlight to heavy metal and hip-hop, it nonetheless found itself at the center of a struggle over decency, values, order, and youth. It was not so much that punk had politicized (although some punks had); rather, it was that social and political discourse had "culturalized." Punk and its offshoots helped provoke a reaction that defied conventional political categories, fracturing society and politics along new lines.

Andrew Hartman has demonstrated how the dramatic cultural changes in the 1960s United States spurred intellectual fermentation in the 1970s and eventually a political realignment as cultural values overtook socioeconomics as the determining factor in politics.[3] This chapter shows that punk and related subcultures were crucial aspects of this "war for the soul of America," making culture an increasingly visible and polarizing force. Punk had evoked strong opinions from the beginning, but by the mid-1980s, it became entangled in an all-out culture war. Over time, the effect was a far-ranging political realignment. In what James Hunter once described as a "new ecumenism," new coalitions and alliances formed across old boundaries, and new divisions sprang up within existing institutions.[4] In place of the Cold War divisions between labor and capital, working class and bourgeoisie, the new political fracture lines were determined primarily by identity and culture.

In fact, there was a war taking place not just for the soul of America but for the souls of states around the world as they realigned politically amid the global transition from the late Cold War era to that of neoliberal globalization. A similar process of cultural warfare and realignment to that which Hartman and Hunter describe in the United States was also at work in the communist Second World in the middle to late 1980s. Social divisions with respect to Marxism-Leninism and the Communist Party in the East became less substantial as elites and citizens alike coalesced into emerging constellations organized along different lines. On one side were those who looked inward, seeking to defend tradition, order, culture, and the nation from the forces of chaos. On the opposite side were those who looked outward and were willing to tolerate or even defend subcultures like punk in the name of freedom of choice and pluralism. Punks, for the most part, were skeptical of the politics associated with either. Nonetheless, they were drawn into the repolarizing struggle that set in place the global framework that would survive the fall of communism in 1989 and define the subsequent era.

In contrast to the culture wars in the West, the culture wars that swept the Eastern bloc in the 1980s have typically been read in the context of Cold War politics—as a series of thaws and crackdowns by the Communist Party and the state, and struggles between "the people" and "the system." In fact, when viewed in global context, the process taking place closely resembles a political realignment arising out of a culture war, remarkably similar to what was taking place in the capitalist West. Of course, the People's Republics of the Eastern bloc lacked access to directly changing the political landscape through voting. There were, however, vociferous debates both inside and outside the party and state apparatus, and a wide range of views and coalitions both within and beyond conventional politics. Eventually, they would coalesce into opposing sides that had little to do with communism or the Cold War.

The panics and subsequent bans in the communist world were not usually planned and coordinated attacks. There typically was no coherent strategy, and frequently there were powerful voices that argued back. After Kryzl's attack on punk in Czechoslovakia, the Jazz Section of the Musicians' Union published a passionate editorial lambasting Kryzl for having "nurtured hate and mistrust in thousands of young people"—precisely the language that would evoke scruples in a progressive communist, for whom disaffected youth at home were a more immediate concern than capitalist infiltration. In fact, the Jazz Section argued, punk had solid left-wing credentials—so suppressing it was misguided.[5] Similarly, in Ukraine, managers of discos, youth clubs, and youth unions argued back against the strange new line, quoting lyrics by the Clash to police to convince them of the band's anticapitalist credibility. They had good cause to be confused: the Ukrainian socialist youth periodicals sent in from Moscow continued to print lyrics to songs by the Clash—including "Guns of Brixton" and, remarkably, "Know Your Rights"—even at the peak of the anti-punk campaign.[6] The press was more than just a one-way conveyor belt of party ideals, and there was considerable debate over what those ideals were within the communist parties of Eastern Europe.

In Poland, too, behind the hyperbolic language, there was a serious debate both inside and outside the Communist Party—and it was not always party hardliners in the driver's seat. Progressives defended punk as a flourishing amateur movement, consistent with the party's vision of socialism, the nation, and culture. However, its opponents could turn the argument around and assert that new wave was harming "true culture," socialism, and the nation by monopolizing airwaves and other resources. As often as not, the divide between these positions had nothing to do with allegiance or opposition to communism. Rather, it indicated an emerging fracture between globally minded progressives and inward-looking traditionalists. As the voices of moral outrage grew louder, they created a great chasm that ran straight through key institutions in the state, the party, the opposition, and the rest of society.

Conservative Crackdown in the East

The panic in Poland began in the summer of 1983, when cultural critic Daniel Passent decided punk had gone too far. In the national weekly magazine *Polityka*, he published an article under the poetic title "Electrification Plus Epilepsy"—sensationally redirecting Lenin's slogan that socialism is "power to the soviets plus electrification" at new wave music.[7] Passent blamed the forces of the "market . . . ruled by rock, rock, and more rock" for replacing the "old guard" of Polish songcraft with new wave, which he characterized as musicians "connected to electricity . . . moving violently to the beats of music." The result, he lamented, was nothing short of the extinction of the heart of national musical culture, now "relegated to the museum." It wasn't hardcore punk's violent nihilism, the dark, fantastical, masculine mysticism of heavy metal, or even reggae's call for solidarity of the oppressed against evil Babylon that brought out Passent's vitriol. Rather, it was the appearance of some of the most popular new wave bands like Lombard, Republika, and Lady Pank at the prestigious Opole national song festival that year—and, to add insult to injury, Lombard receiving second place in the jury competition for premier acts.

Passent's critique was not orchestrated by the party. In fact, the official newspaper of the Central Committee, *Trybuna Ludu*, explicitly rebutted Passent's claim that the Polish song tradition was dying out—tantamount, after all, to claiming that the party was failing as steward of Polish culture. At its heart, Passent's invective was a culturally conservative attack that might as easily have come from Thatcher's England or Reagan's United States. In fact, in the United States, traditional-leftist-turned-cultural-conservative Allan Bloom would famously make similar arguments about the latest trend in rock music a few years later in *The Closing of the American Mind*.[8] Passent's critique of popular music was similarly politically ambiguous in Poland, appealing to cultural conservatives of all stripes.

A steady stream of criticism of new wave followed Passent's in the press over the next year and a half—and it quickly expanded from a critique of musical culture to a sweeping social diagnosis, identifying punk with malaise in Polish society from gangs to drug abuse. As the Reagan administration stepped up the war on drugs in the early 1980s in the United States, the Polish media had its own panic over the alarming growth of "narkomania," described in sensational reports of wars between drug- and music-related subcultures. In April 1984, *Polityka* published an article discussing violent gangs of punks and other youth subcultures roaming the streets of the Stalinist-era industrial city Nowa Huta—a phenomenon that was combated by distributing pamphlets to schools to aid in identifying members of youth subcultures.[9]

The panic over punk peaked just in time for the Opole festival in Poland the next summer, when Lady Pank performed its smash hit "Monkey Factory" ("Fabryka Małp") in the heart of the official song competition. The jovial humor in the song, reveling in the chaos of the urban jungle of Warsaw, was evidently lost on culturally conservative critics. Urszula Biełous reported that the festival "shocked audiences" and was "no longer a festival of song."[10] Adam Ciesielski confirmed this sentiment in *Życie Warszawy*, deeming the festival's focus on new wave groups "monotonous," dictated by the tastes of fans of the radio's Hits List.[11] These conservative critiques also sprinkled in a measure of traditional leftist criticism reminiscent of the Frankfurt School. For instance, Biełous charged new wavers with being cogs in the music industry machine: Lombard was "professional," and Lady Pank's hair, makeup, and outfit were "part of the scenography." Ciesielski likewise critiqued the "manufactured sounds" of bands like Lady Pank, which he suggested led even their fans to abandon them for other acts. A coalition began to emerge defining itself against new wave, combining cultural conservatives across the ideological spectrum, including Stalinists, nationalists, and culturally traditionalist ex-leftists and workers, whose long-standing political differences faded as punk came under the spotlight.

As the coalition of citizens concerned about punk grew, the moral panic over new wave that started in the press reached the government. In mid-1984 Poland, a delegate at a party conference rose to voice his objections to "anti-educational" (*antywychowawczy*) contents in "youth vocal compositions"—a euphemism for the new wave of rock sweeping the nation—demanding their suppression by state censorship organs.[12] Another delegate agreed, suggesting that the state limit the presence of "youth music" of "dubious quality" on airwaves.[13]

At first, many elites responsible for culture were reluctant to respond—much as they had been when they first confronted punk years earlier. The Main Office of Control of the Press, Publication, and Entertainment released a dry reminder that "organs of control are licensed mainly to eliminate contents propagating alcoholism, drug use, violence, and pornography"; artistic quality was outside their purview.[14] The radio noted defensively that it had to "respond to the tastes of all types of listeners." When the barrage of criticism of new wave in the press peaked after the Opole festival in 1984, though, the party Central Committee's Division of Culture finally considered taking action. While the Division of Culture argued that the festival had succeeded at providing "another example of openness in cultural politics of the party and government" and at "relaxing the social mood," it was tainted by "the ruthless domination of "rock" (with "rock" cordoned off by quotation marks, indicating the inability or unwillingness of the authors to name the new musical trend they were describing). This new, unspeakable genre of music was particularly problematic because it demonstrated "a low musical level, little cultured performance," and texts "devoid of literary values." Instead, the Division of Culture observed, bands expressed "moods of apathy, doubt in the sense of action, and rebellion"—and, ominously, "a few of them even contained unambiguous allusions of a political nature."[15]

For conservative elites concerned about youth, culture, the nation, and the party, the opportunity was ripe. Referencing Ciesielski's *Życie Warszawy* article that described punks' "cold reception" of "Lady Punk [sic]," the Division of Culture issued a list of directives for the future. Declaring, "It's not just a matter of profit, it's a matter of defense of our culture," it insisted on more "ideologically and artistically valuable" music, greater oversight by artistic councils, and "consequences" for those who violated restrictions.[16] In clear, forceful language, the division voiced the growing concern that punk and new wave were not culture but in fact the antithesis of it—and even their popularity and economic allure were insufficient to compensate.

The next month, the consolidating forces of conservatism directed their attention at the annual Jarocin festival, dialing up their scrutiny precisely as punk and new wave bands were engaged in spectacular efforts to assert their subcultural capital in the face of new wave's unexpected popular success. Quoting a western Associated Press article celebrating punk as resistance to communism, now repurposed as a supplement to the Polish security service, the Division of Culture reviewed what was taking place at Jarocin, blue pencil at the ready. Particularly disturbing were one band's name (Moskwa—i.e., "Moscow"), an example of a song title ("Everything Rots"), the number of youth exposed to it (nineteen thousand), and a quotation from Siekiera bass guitarist and lyricist Tomasz Adamski.[17] In fact, the quotation was taken from Polish journalist Urszula Biełous's investigative report on Jarocin, translated from Polish to English by the Associated Press, and then back to Polish again for the Division of Culture. But its meaning was as potent as ever: "Destruction means freedom." Adamski had been trying to cause a stir, but he would no doubt have been surprised to know his words would be circulated globally and then carefully considered by the Central Committee of the Communist Party.

The note was accompanied by a comprehensive security report about subcultures of disaffected youth prepared for the Division of Culture and the Group on Youth Matters. Under the title "Information on Phenomena of Social Pathology among Youth," it outlined the major pathologies affecting youth at the time, placing "the growing problem of cultural contestation" alongside drugs, alcohol, prostitution, crime, and suicide as the greatest threats to youth.[18] Using the classic Eastern bloc expression of disdain, it observed that "so-called Youth Subcultures" were guilty of disturbing public opinion in their manner of dress, their music, and their attitudes. Foremost among them was "the PUNK movement," identifiable by its unfashionable dress, colored hair, mohawks, and safety pins in clothes and bodies. Punks favored anarchism, arrogance, aggressive and shocking behavior, mocking of "normal citizens," social nihilism, and extreme egocentrism. Its slogans (written in English, with Polish translation) were "No future" and "Hate and war." And, of course, punks were "fanatics of rock music and its singers." While the report contained a few nods to progressives and reformers (such as acknowledging the need for more good jobs), the dominant message was a call for "preventing and eliminating" punk, giving a mandate to conservatives who had been calling for its suppression.

Indeed, the new year started with a clear indication that the state would use its power to promote bands with safer sounds and reputations, while suppressing others. In January 1985, the ZSMP youth union planned to have new wave bands Lombard, Republika, and Banda i Wanda represent Poland at the Festival of Political Song in Berlin. In the face of the backlash from punk fans for their commercial success (and loss of subcultural capital), however, these bands refused to participate in the festival—although they were willing to play in the postfestival concert. Such a politically charged posture had always attracted a strong response from authorities, but this time the matter went all the way up to the party's Central Committee, where the Division of Culture announced it would cut back radio and television presentations of those bands, forbid their tours abroad for half a year, and "conduct conversations with the bands."[19] At the request of the ZSMP, progressive rock bands Budka Suflera and Kombi were invited to perform instead.[20]

Objections to new wave grew in spheres responsible for the media as well. The party Group on Matters of Disseminating Culture complained that under new market conditions, Poland was "surrendering to the commercial model of pop music of Anglo-Saxon countries" despite the negative consequences for Polish culture.[21] The Division of Culture echoed these concerns, criticizing Polish television for blindly buying popular music and failing to eliminate bands that "promote trash"—singling out the "punk lifestyle" and its "hopeless artistic quality, . . . eccentricity, and . . . stupidity." A month later, a committee responsible for the radio announced that it was taking up a firmer policy. Besides "reducing the presence of western commercial music," it called for eliminating all recordings from non-state-controlled record firms from the airwaves—effectively excising a sizable portion of punk from the media.[22] Even live performance came under fire: cultural authorities unveiled a new, more stringent policy for "verification" of musicians for their pay categories.

The year 1985 was a tough one for new wave bands, squeezed from one side by culturally conservative critics and from the other by punks who accused bands of trading in subcultural capital for popular success. After its reprimand from the state at the beginning of the year, Republika was nearly booed offstage by "anti-fans" at Jarocin that summer. Popular new wave bands Maanam and Lombard faced similar pressure, with serious consequences: all three bands broke up within a few months of one another in 1985, and Lady Pank followed soon after. While the breakups of new wave bands were not directly orchestrated by the state or party, conservatives relished their demise nonetheless: in early 1986, the Division of Culture noted with smug satisfaction that its "stimulation" efforts had led to a "gradual decline in rock music." Despite the appearance of new punk and heavy metal bands, the "leaders of the movement" like Lombard and Maanam had broken up, while others were professionalizing.[23] The conservative crackdown, in combination with the impulse in punk circles to assert their subcultural capital, took its toll—much as it would in the capitalist West.

Conservative Crackdown in the West

As Poland's panic over new wave peaked in 1984, the United States plunged into a moral panic of its own. It started early that year, when an Ohio parent listened to her child's recording of "Let's Pretend We're Married" by Prince and found its reference to casual sex offensive. The presence of sexual innuendo in a pop song was certainly nothing new. However, a growing coalition had been emerging over the previous decade, spanning the conventional right and left, fueled by fears that the cultural permissiveness of the 1960s had led to the deterioration of morality and standards.[24] After years of punk provoking society while simultaneously making ever greater inroads into the mass media, concern over offensive music caught the attention of the Cincinnati PTA in 1984 and then became a focus of the national convention in Las Vegas. The national PTA drafted a letter to the Recording Industry Association of America (RIAA) calling for it to take greater responsibility over its records and help parents protect youth. The RIAA initially ignored the recommendations from the PTA; as in Poland, the financial incentives to produce and market music on the edge of social acceptability were significant enough to risk some backlash. However, the movement quickly picked up momentum when it was endorsed by powerful women with political connections on both sides of the aisle: Tipper Gore (married to Democratic senator Al Gore) joined forces with Susan Baker (married to James Baker, President Reagan's Chief of Staff), and together they sought to address objectionable content in music.

In the context of the revival of politicized morality with the Moral Majority in the Reagan years, there was a growing group of activists ready to join them. The early 1980s saw a resurgence in record burnings and lectures against the hazards of "rock" (as in Poland, US conservative critics recycled the terminology of the 1960s to address the new musical phenomena of the late 1970s and 1980s).[25] Gore and Baker were soon joined by Jeff Ling, an evangelical youth minister and anti-rock activist who spoke to a mass meeting of concerned parents at a DC church, and, later, Dr. Thomas Radecki of the National Coalition on Television Violence, which was growing increasingly preoccupied with music. In early 1985, Gore, Baker, and others formed the Parents Music Resource Center (PMRC) with the goal of giving parents the tools to discern which music was harmful and prevent it from falling into the hands of youth. However, the combination of the charged cultural politics of the 1980s and the Washington connections of Gore and Baker propelled the question of objectionable content in music to the forefront of national conversation.

The PMRC identified several objectionable themes in youth music: free love and sex, sadomasochism, rebellion, the occult, drug use, violence, and obscenity—many of the same themes that concerned citizens and elites in Eastern Europe fretted about.[26] Most of these themes were not difficult to find in punk, new wave, and heavy metal (or the blues or opera, for that matter). Soon after, the PMRC announced its "Filthy Fifteen"—a list of songs from across the musical spectrum tainted by one or more of the objectionable characteristics it had identified. Initially, the focus was not on hardcore or avant-garde punk bands but, rather, on those that came into regular contact with masses of white suburban youth—above all, the new wave and heavy metal bands that turned up in living rooms around the country on MTV. Once the PMRC started looking, though, its attention quickly fell on the far more contentious music that even MTV refused to air—including the Dead Kennedys' "Nazi Punks Fuck Off," outrageously misinterpreted as endorsing Nazism by the PMRC, just as it had been by Yugoslav authorities three years earlier when the same slogan got punk band manager Igor Vidmar in trouble.[27]

Undoubtedly, the most provocative of the objectionable themes was sex. An article appeared in *Newsweek* entitled "Stop Pornographic Rock," coining the label "porn rock" that immediately stuck with both PMRC activists and the media. *U.S. News & World Report* asked, "Why do we allow this filth?" in its examination of "X Rated Records." Gradually, federal authorities joined in the panic, much like their counterparts in Poland. In May 1984, Surgeon General C. Everett Koop claimed that MTV fans were "raised with rock music that uses both pornography and violence."[28] The designation "porn rock" was more than just empty media sensationalism. Pornography was regulated and kept out of the hands of children; perhaps music should be as well, the PMRC suggested in an editorial to the *Washington Post*. Soon after, the National Association of Broadcasters sought to protect its business and image by asking recording companies to send lyrics to radio stations in order for them to decide whether the music was appropriate to play.[29]

No doubt concerned parties on both sides of the Iron Curtain would have been surprised to learn that analogous reactions to youth musical culture were building in the capitalist West and communist East. Like opposition to the Sex Pistols nearly a decade earlier, concern over youth music didn't neatly fit Cold War ideologically based political categories. For a concerned parent like Gore, it was not an ideological issue but rather a moral and cultural issue any citizen should take interest in. As Andrew Hartman has shown, cultural conservatives from the traditional left had been alienated by the progressive cultural views dominating the new left, and they were increasingly willing to form alliances with culturally conservative Republicans.[30] Gore's alliance with Baker, the wife of a prominent member of the Reagan administration, emerged thanks to expanding common ground on cultural and moral issues between elites across the aisle. Other cultural conservatives on the Left included fellow southern Democrats like former president Carter and Jesse Jackson—the latter of whom had spoken out against punk and "sex rock" on behalf of the National Federation for Decency a few years earlier.

If scrambled cultural-political categories and identities were the hallmark of the late 1970s and early 1980s, however, by the middle of the decade, politics and culture were settling into a new alignment. As Gore would discover, cultural issues like those that the PMRC dealt with were becoming the new political currency of the age, and discourse about tradition, decency, morals, and standards was increasingly owned by the Right. The PMRC's initiative resonated powerfully with the surging conservative social movements linked to President Reagan's Republican Party. In fact, Reagan himself would soon personally join the fray in the press as the debate escalated to the highest echelons of the US government in one of the most heavily attended and highly publicized Senate hearings of the decade.

In September 1985, the Commerce Committee of the US Senate invited the leadership of the PMRC and RIAA, as well as expert witnesses and musicians, to a hearing on offensive content in records. The polarizing forces that punk had helped provoke pushed those in attendance into irreconcilable positions, with one side defending the nation and youth from the predation and perversion of rock, and the other defending free expression from parochial lummoxes and religious zealots. Even in the Senate, usual rules of gentility gave way to culture war, with a script that could as easily have played out in a meeting of the Division of Culture of the Polish United Workers' Party.

Throughout the hearing, Al Gore and Tipper Gore both insisted that they were seeking not government regulation but voluntary self-regulation by record companies. Yet, the entrenched positions of the culture war that had been dug out over the previous few years left only an uninhabitable no man's land between the two sides, as conservative senators and progressive witnesses both pushed the conversation into a polarized debate about government censorship. Indeed, for some in the room, censorship was the best solution: Senator Hawkins clearly stated that there was no "absolute right" to free speech, while Senator Hollings cited the precedent of the Federal Communications Commission enforcing decency on the airwaves. Predictably, the musicians selected to testify – Frank Zappa, John Denver, and Dee Snider of Twisted Sister – argued passionately against government censorship on the grounds of free speech.

Regardless of how its organizers tried to cast it, the Senate hearing posed the threat of government involvement, as most of the people in the debate were eventually willing to concede. There was a tension between the position that the hearing sought only "private action" and the fact that it was taking place in the Senate—as Zappa incredulously observed, gesturing around the chamber, "This is private action?" The debate was still more vitriolic outside the Senate, as impassioned editorials appeared in the media railing alternately about tyranny and about the corruption of youth. Even President Reagan joined the fray, declaring in October, "I don't believe that our Founding Fathers ever intended to create a nation where the rights of pornographers would take precedence over the rights of parents, and the violent and malevolent would be given free rein to prey upon our children."[31]

The PMRC had an even greater asset than Reagan, though. As the hearing took place, the RIAA was simultaneously lobbying for a tax on blank cassettes—a tremendous potential boon to address losses from personal recording that bypassed the music industry. By acquiescing to suggestions of senators in the hearing that businesses in the recording industry "clean up their act," the RIAA could win some support for their Home Audio Recording Act. More likely than government censorship, and just as damaging from the perspective of the musicians present, there was a strong possibility that the RIAA, PMRC, and US government would unofficially collude and leave musicians stranded.

In fact, that is what happened. Two days before the RIAA's Home Audio Act came up for debate, Stanley Gortikov, head of the RIAA, announced that the association had established a policy for labeling objectionable content in music. The line between censorship and voluntary self-regulation—encouraged in this case by threats of impending government intervention—was thinner in effect than in theory. Once objectionable records were labeled, gatekeepers ranging from legislatures and media executives all the way down to local store managers had the power and incentive to take further action. Sears and JC Penney announced that they would not carry labeled records; Walmart followed soon after. Malls and department stores unwilling to risk boycotts found it safer to exclude music with the parental advisory label than to risk a protest. MTV relied on self-censorship by its Standards Department to ensure that objectionable content was excluded.[32]

Whether blacklisting took the form of censorship by legislatures or censuring by major corporations and institutions in the face of combined public and legislative pressure, the result was much the same. In fact, several state legislatures did introduce bills to restrict the sales of labeled music. Local government and law enforcement had more leeway than the Senate: free speech may have been protected, but precedent also existed for prosecuting obscenity as a breach of community standards.[33] In fact, a member of Congress anonymously commissioned a study to explore the constitutionality of federal legislation to prosecute retailers that carried albums with advisory labels using the Child Protection and Obscenity Enforcement Act.[34]

The one reprieve for musicians who found themselves labeled objectionable was that advisory labels took a long time to produce. In the meantime, the tone of the debate in the public gradually shifted as a progressive counteroffensive coalesced—much as it soon would in the Eastern bloc. The PMRC had initially benefited from favorable or at least receptive attention in the media. News of the Senate hearing, however, inspired a wave of editorials and letters in support of musical subgenres and subcultures. Likening the PMRC to the former generation's crusaders against the Beatles, Elvis, and jazz, a nascent coalition of cultural progressives portrayed the organization as stodgy, reactionary, self-righteous, and silly. The PMRC wasn't waiting idly, though. Its activists kept a lookout for objectionable music, and eventually, they set their sights on punk.

At six o'clock one morning in April 1986, responding to a PMRC complaint, the police raided the home of Jello Biafra of the Dead Kennedys, searched it thoroughly, and confiscated several copies of his most recent album—and a copy of punk 'zine *Maximum Rocknroll*. Ironically, the album included a parental advisory label (on the wrapper, not on the album itself, the PMRC would emphasize).[35] A trial was set not just for Biafra but also for several employees of his independent record label. For the first time in the United States, a criminal trial was held for the contents of a music album.[36] Having just dealt with state intervention himself, Frank Zappa gave Biafra a call and advised him to remember that he was the victim—and not to allow himself to be portrayed as an outlaw because of his music.[37]

For those keeping tabs on the international punk scene, the signs were not good. Biafra's compatriots across the Atlantic, Crass, had recently been found guilty of obscenity in UK courts. After nearly a decade of affronting just about every possible value—and even sharing the spotlight with the KGB as a perceived threat to UK security—Crass fell victim to the restoration of tradition and values under the Thatcher administration. As with Biafra and the Dead Kennedys, it was the charge of obscenity that provided the legal grounds for the verdict, in this case under the United Kingdom's Obscene Publications Act. Evidence was taken from a song the band considered to be feminist, "Bata Motel"—deemed offensive to public morals for its disturbing first-person account of a prostitute allowing herself to be abused by men. The verdict against Crass upheld Victorian morality, lamenting the "creeping lowering of standards in society"—language that would have been equally at home in Andropov's campaign for renewal, the Polish Communist

Party's Division of Culture, or the PMRC hearings in the United States. The judge found that Crass's records had "a tendency to deprave and corrupt people likely to come into contact with them." By that time, the band had grown tired of constant surveillance and intimidation and had run out of money due to court fees. Crass was not alone: over the next two years, authorities cracked down on the annual Stonehenge festival, and issued the Public Order Act in 1986.

Biafra's position was similarly precarious. The latest Dead Kennedys album, *Frankenchrist*, would have been sufficient to attract the ire of cultural conservatives by itself. However, it was once again sex that provoked the severest reaction. The album included a poster by artist H. R. Giger, an Escher-like representation of sex in which everyone is fucking and getting fucked—exactly how Biafra interpreted modern capitalist America. However, conservatives (and the prosecution) emphasized the shocking images and lyrics as problems themselves rather than as critiques of underlying social issues. Prosecutors in California sought to prove that the Dead Kennedys' album appealed to prurient interests, that the average California adult would deem it offensive to minors, and that it was without redeeming value.[38] In a scene that recalled the debate over the term "bullocks" in the Sex Pistols trial eight years earlier, the defense called an expert witness who upheld the value of the poster as a work of art. Despite a hung jury, a judge skeptical of the prosecution's case declined to entertain a new trial. However, even with a favorable outcome, the legal charges exhausted the independent record label's resources: it was forced to close down despite the help of donations from hundreds of punks.

Between mid-1984 and mid-1985, the media amplified the vitriolic struggle to define the standards by which culture should be judged, with decency, tradition, and morals on one side, and free expression, open-mindedness, and choice on the other. Even as punk became more familiar and established, some of the controversy remained: in 1983, the organizer for concerts in New York's Central Park specifically cited the Clash as a band that wouldn't be allowed to perform due to its tendency to attract "hoodlums."[39] As the moral crusade against music picked up over the 1980s, though, the question of whether the public performance of punk should be regulated showed that not even the highest court in the United States was immune to the culture war.

When the New York Police Department demanded that Rock Against Racism turn down the volume at performances in 1987, it set off a series of trials that made it all the way to the Supreme Court by 1989. While the Supreme Court strived to maintain its distance from the partisan political bickering below, in fact, the justices also divided into camps of cultural conservatives and progressives. One opinion argued that the interest of the government in controlling the volume level on behalf of its citizens outweighed the right of bands to amplified free speech, while the other argued that only preexisting statutes would have the authority to trump the right to expression.[40] In this case, the former prevailed.

But even more significant than the outcome was the hardening division in politics and society along lines of culture. Even the arcane legal terms scarcely obscured the court's division into conservatives and progressives around the question of punk.[41]

Progressive Counteroffensive

As traditionalist and progressive blocs coalesced and faced off around the question of youth musical culture in the United States and United Kingdom, the struggle between the traditionalist forces of order and progressive forces of openness took a new turn in the East. After decades of continuity and stagnation in the one-party state, one after another aging party leader passed on the torch in the USSR in the first half of the 1980s. Iurii Andropov remained general secretary for just over a year—thankfully, from the point of view of Soviet new wave fans. Konstantin Chernenko lasted not even as long as Andropov. The ravages of old age, in combination with the ravaged economic system designed to flourish in era of mass production rather than the globalizing economy of the late twentieth century, convinced the Politburo to look outside its inner circle of aging party elites for someone with the strength to lead (or at least survive) the reforms that appeared to be necessary. It found someone with fresh ideas (and relatively few years of age) in Mikhail Gorbachev, who promised to restore the dynamism of Soviet communism. To the surprise and consternation of those who selected him, he exceeded even those expectations a year after taking office with an ambitious restructuring program known as perestroika. However, Gorbachev faced an enormous barricade of bureaucratic inertia seeking to preserve the familiar system of the Brezhnev years. The only way to move it was to mobilize a force of his own—a powerful coalition of progressive, reform-minded communists and, more boldly, reformers and critics outside the party. To support perestroika, he advocated glasnost—a policy of openness. If he could mobilize the latent forces for reform within society and use them against conservatives, his reforms might have powerful enough backing to have a chance.[42]

As with previous leaders, culture and popular music were important components of Gorbachev's reforms. Whereas Andropov lashed out against rock as part of his effort to cleanse the Soviet Union of corruption, Gorbachev harnessed the power of new wave rock bands to buttress his new approach of openness and reform. By 1986, the rock club concept that Leningrad experimented with expanded across the union, including a "rock lab" in Moscow backed by the Komsomol first secretary.[43] Meanwhile, in Leningrad under glasnost, Akvarium saw its opportunities to perform expand dramatically in live concerts and even a recording with the state firm Melodiya. For good reason, Leningrad critic Alexander Kan deemed Akvarium to be "the banner of perestroika."[44] In the face of conservative opposition to Gorbachev's reforms, new wave was becoming a rallying symbol for progressives both inside and outside the party.

Gorbachev's changes made an impression on the leaders and citizens of the satellite states on the USSR's western periphery. Each regime took its own lesson from the reforms: leaders in East Germany and Czechoslovakia hunkered down, much as they had in the era of de-Stalinization. In Poland, however, the reforms merely heightened the struggle already raging between progressives and conservatives inside and outside the party. Even before Gorbachev announced his reforms, the consensus in Poland was tipping in favor of cultural progressives by early 1985 as some members of the party's cultural wing worried that the reaction against new wave was going too far. That year, the director of the Division of Culture wrote to the director of the Committee on Matters of Radio and Television expressing concern about having "gotten signals" from musicians and journalists that the media was considering cutting music produced by nonstate record companies from the airwaves. While the impulse was understandable, he cautioned that they avoid restricting records and cassettes containing "valuable compositions and performers" approved by the Ministry of Culture and Art.[45]

As the Division of Culture reviewed the matter, it also grappled with the possibility of taking an alternative approach to popular culture. A document circulated within the division warned against a programmatic line of music on radio and television set by "specialists" and "bureaucrats" lest the party create an impression that it was trying to steer artistic production through "demands and prohibitions." Banned records became "forbidden fruit," which "always tastes the best"—and were regularly exploited by Catholic organizations and foreign radio stations, it wryly noted. Paraphrasing John Stuart Mill's classic liberal argument for allowing free speech, it suggested that even songs of low quality would serve to inspire "discussion about Polish recreational music." This standard applied even to hardcore punk: the document explicitly cited the most extreme record officially available in communist Poland, the hardcore punk and reggae compilation *Fala*. While the album was "interesting exclusively from a sociological point of view," it was also an important opportunity for "creative cultural discussion." This argument was convincing—enough so, in fact, that the director of the Division of Culture wrote a response to the radio director warning against an "embargo" on controversial broadcasts in order to avoid an "an atmosphere of sensation" and spreading "false myths about the state's cultural politics."[46] The response included a list of approved songs—among them, compositions by new wave bands Lombard and Lady Pank. The response to the radio from the Division of Culture marked a key turning point: it was the beginning of a progressive counteroffensive in the culture war that would realign Polish politics from top to bottom over the rest of the decade.

Precisely as the Division of Culture reconsidered its cultural policy, a related conversation about punk took place in the popular press. In 1985, *Na Przełaj*, the periodical of the official scouting organization, hosted a forum asking young people to write in about what punk meant to them. In the issues that followed, a struggle over culture played out that was emblematic of the coming age not just in Poland but in much of the post-punk world. In December 1985, the editors published two letters under the title "Punk according to Two Views." The first was from "Agrawa," a young Polish woman who wondered why people harassed her and fellow punks. The other was from "Beata," who wrote an exposé about a group of punks that turned against her when she did not want to devote herself completely to the punk agenda.[47] The magazine editors asked what punks had to say "in their defense"—and it turned out to be a lot.

Over the next months, letters from readers filled the pages of the official scouting union's magazine. Some defended punk as a legitimate choice of music, style, and identity, while others attacked it as a threat to culture, order, and decency. Aska M. sharply rebuked punks, calling them an "army of Satan"—and dirty to boot.[48] Another reader called attention to what she perceived as a contradiction between punk's ideals and actions, while a third objected to punks' irresponsibility, writing, "What will Agrawa do when she is old enough to have to earn money and take care of herself?"[49] In response, punks like "Agatha Insane" (Agatka Wariatka) mounted a counteroffensive. It was not punks who needed to defend themselves but, rather, "normals," who smelled bad, were always drunk, and behaved much worse at soccer games than punks did at their concerts.[50] Several other letters defended punk with classic liberal arguments, based on freedom of conviction, freedom of choice, and the right to an individual identity. Another confirmed that "in punk, philosophy is the most important," blaming the media for misrepresenting punks as "hooligans" and "bandits"—adding that "all are free to their own style, even if it is fantastic."[51]

As the upper echelons of the state and party divided into conservatives and progressives over the question of punk, the young readers of *Na Przełaj* did the same. Young conservative readers rejected punk in the name of order, tradition, and decency, while progressives defended it in the name of freedom of choice and the right to alternative identity and social critique. Most readers implicitly accepted the identity-based fracture line of the debate, which divided anti-punk traditionalists from tolerant progressives. Only a few letters, mostly sent in by self-identified punks, rejected the debate and its categories altogether. Self-proclaimed punks accused the periodical of arranging a sensationalist account so its readers could "sneer" at punks.[52] They doubted whether the original letters were even about "real punks"; more likely, their source was some other pseudo-punk subculture like hooligans, fascists, "poser-punks," or perhaps "panks" (the

Polonized version of the word from which Lady Pank took its name).[53] The idea that punk was a coherent "movement" (*ruch*) that could be defined by editorials in a youth periodical was ridiculous, one suggested.[54] The whole enterprise was a sham, since "no real punk would answer your question."

Yet, *Na Przełaj* continued to promote the conversation—eventually taking up the progressive banner itself by embracing punk. The magazine started including a regular column entitled "Koalang," presenting punk lyrics as avant-garde art. Taking a proactive defense that might assuage conservatives, the editor suggested that punks could be the next vanguard of Polish national literature, the 1980s version of the revered nineteenth-century Skamander poets. Apparently among the new founders of the nation was hardcore punk band Siekiera, whose fierce, misogynistic "There Were Only Four of Us" was included among the artistic texts.[55]

The revolution taking place in the Polish scouting organization's publication mirrored similar developments in other official youth organizations, also claiming a progressive identity through their discourse on punk. Two months after the debate in *Na Przełaj*, the national directors of the other three socialist youth organizations, the ZMW, SZSP, and ZSMP, staked their claim to punks and other marginal youth in the youth magazine *Razem*. An article boldly proclaimed a natural sympathy between punk and socialism, claiming that socialist youth organizations "exist for punks, skins, and hooligans."[56] If socialist organizations were losing out to punk, it was "not because they style their hair less effectively, but because they lack passion"—something punks had in abundance. The ZSMP director added that they sought out those who "long for change" and "people who doubt, complain, have reservations"—precisely the qualities of punks.[57] With the support of rhetorical prowess, the leaders of youth unions were able to link punks and other marginal youth groups to progressive reform efforts (and to their need to attract more members).

Some punks had resented having their identities negotiated on the pages of the scouting organization periodical; serving as part of a membership drive for youth unions was still worse. However, ownership of punk had long since transferred from the small like-minded avant-garde in Warsaw. It had entered the mainstream via new wave, where it provoked a culture war and became a litmus test for political-cultural identities. None of these identities had the least bit to do with communism (or capitalism, for that matter). Rather, those who wanted to present themselves as open-minded, outward-looking, and progressive (and who had flexible cultural ideals) could draw on punk as a resource. For those who wished to take a stand for tradition, nation, culture, and order, however, punk was equally useful, as a source of chaos to rally against. The culture war between these camps would peak the next year, in 1986, when a battle over the annual Jarocin festival pulled together conservatives across Polish society and institutions of the state and party—and, eventually, an equally powerful group of progressives opposing them.

The Battle over Jarocin

Jarocin had been a battleground in the struggle over Polish culture and youth since its reconstitution as a new wave festival in 1980. Increasingly, however, this struggle was not between communists and anticommunists; rather, it delineated the two new camps of progressives and conservatives. Progressives of all stripes sought to use the festival to demonstrate their open-mindedness and attract youth. The local ZSMP union served as a sponsor of the festival: the union's local leader identified Jarocin as an ideal location to establish a dialogue with youth. While the union stopped short of presenting punk to potential recruits, it offered another lure—an on-site ZSMP beauty contest, including a swimsuit competition.[58] The state and party weren't the only ones staking their claim to the festival, though. The most progressive among Catholic priests began making regular appearances at the Jarocin festival, carrying posters, handing out flyers, and sometimes even wielding guitars and leading folksy hymns. One local church even held a mass for deceased musicians during the festival to attract young rock fans.[59]

Meanwhile, conservatives coalesced in opposition to the festival, seeing it as an opportunity to defend the nation and order from unruly punks and heavy metal fans. Hardliners in the party and state stepped up the presence of security services at the 1986 festival, and for the first time, in addition to surveillance and reporting, they made some arrests. Music journalist and DJ Paweł Sito wrote boldly that the festival's black and red symbol had been reversed that year—now, there was a black dot in the middle, surrounded by the "red" circle of communist authorities.[60] Beyond the state security service, though, most ardent conservatives had no interest in attending the festival. Instead, they preferred to register a protest from a distance—which is precisely what they would do once news of the festival's outrages broke out.

As punks, reggae fans, and metalheads got caught up in the struggle between conservatives and progressives hammering out their identities and agendas through the Jarocin festival, they lashed out, just as they had on the pages of *Na Przełaj*. Kazik Staszewski from the punk band Kult angrily announced on the microphone that he would not be returning to Jarocin, since the excessive intervention of censors had left his band with almost nothing to play. The reggae band Immanuel interjected its Rastafarian message with a declaration of its independence, singing, "We don't need the CIA / We don't need the PZPR / I sing the praise Jah / I sing so the people will be free."

Perhaps the most extreme backlash, though, was directed not against communist authorities but against the growing Catholic presence at the festival. Roman Dostrzewski of heavy metal band Kat certainly had no interest in being "rescued" by Catholic clergy, as he made clear by confronting a pair of priests at the festival and explaining that the inverted cross around his neck symbolized his disagreement with the church.[61] That night, his band Kat performed "Oracle," a thunderous black metal tour de force that featured Dostrzewski in leather, dark makeup, frizzed long blond hair, and an inverted cross as he screamed about hell, locusts, "witches bathed in blood," and "necklaces of bone." Kat recreated the apocalyptic world of dark, evil forces characteristic of the new wave of metal that was provoking outrage around the world, from the Eastern bloc to the PMRC's "Filthy Fifteen." Kat wasn't even the most controversial: another metal band, Test Fobii Kreon, destroyed a cross onstage. Meanwhile, reports of black masses and exhumed graves near Jarocin reverberated through the media.[62]

The outrage that followed solidified an awkward incipient alliance between conservatives in the church and party. Test Fobii Kreon was brought to trial for "attacking the Christian faith," prosecutable as a crime of religious intolerance—an interesting charge in an ostensibly atheist socialist state.[63] The reggae band Immanuel was arrested and sentenced to three months in prison or an 80,000-zloty fine. Longtime director Walter Chełstowski also faced legal charges, accused by Poland's national court of discriminating against certain varieties of music, and resigned from his role as organizer.[64]

It would take a high-profile progressive defender to rescue the festival and its participants from conservatives. As it turned out, that was precisely what Jarocin would get. In 1987, the vice director of the Division of Culture forwarded the minister of youth, Aleksander Kwaśniewski, a letter from a Jarocin resident objecting to the annual festival. While agreeing that the "phenomena" described in the letter were "reprehensible and undesirable," Kwaśniewski nonetheless affirmed that the festival was necessary for the "interests and needs of youth."[65] As minister of youth (and occasional festival attendee), he threw his lot in with progressives and young people inside and outside the party.

Conservative opponents of the festival were not pleased. The Forum for Catholic Social Thought wrote an open letter to the mayor of Jarocin expressing great concern. Dredging up the term for rock music from two decades earlier, the letter conveyed horror that the festival was sanctioned even though "most known hard beat bands officially propagate Satanism." As Poles and citizens, the group demanded that the state begin "propagating and promoting healthy and decent forms of entertainment . . . to the benefit of Polish youth, and also to the nation"—precisely the kind of language that both conservative communists and conservative anticommunists could get behind.[66] The letter was sent to the highest officials of the state and the church, including the marshal of the Polish parliament, the president of the national council, and the Polish primate.

The letter also landed on the desk of the first secretary of the Communist Party, who was faced with the choice of siding with hardliners and social conservatives or with reformers and progressives. Like the rest of Polish society, both the Ministry of Internal Affairs and the Ministry of Culture and Art were divided.[67] The former likened the festival to a war between youth subcultures but also noted that it served to concentrate an "uncontrolled movement" in one place.[68] The latter lamented punk's "protest against established norms and the social-political establishment" but admitted that punk and heavy metal were "accepted by a decided portion of the young generation," that reggae was a music of "peace or even optimism," and that the Jarocin festival had "become an enduring element of youth culture with a nationwide reach."[69] If Jaruzelski had held a plebiscite on whether to allow the Jarocin festival to continue, the results would have driven a wedge down the middle of the presumed groupings of 1980s Poland—the Communist Party, the opposition, the Catholic Church, and Polish society in general.

Of course, in 1988, decisions were not made by plebiscite. Instead, behind closed doors, senior representatives from the party's Division of Culture and the state's Ministry of Culture and Art met and passed a resolution that would have surprised conservatives and progressives alike: they resolved to make the Jarocin festival "the main site for the presence of state patronage in the milieu of youth subcultures."[70] No doubt it helped that the proposal for that year's festival included representatives from the Ministry of Culture and Art, the Ministry of Youth Affairs, and the Committee on Radio and TV. Also noted was the fact that a Catholic bishop had recently issued an appeal for believers to "care" for the festival—placing progressives in the party in a bidding war with progressive Catholics for the support of Polish youth who were interested in punk. There were also some key concessions to conservatives, such as an "ideological-education program," the promotion of "cultural and aesthetic awareness," anti-drug sessions, and events designed to promote solidarity between generations.

Punks and other fans of alternative music were not impressed. The next year, Jarocin festival crowds responded by chanting for the death of the new festival organizer. Rock elder statesman Zbigniew Hołdys declared the festival dead in an obituary in *Non Stop*.[71] In his view, the festival had been co-opted by the system, losing its subcultural capital. However, it was less a strategy on the part of the state than a byproduct of the struggle between conservatives and progressives—groupings that would grow in relevance when the Communist Party began its fall from power a few months later.

The culture wars of the 1980s have frequently been identified as constituting a watershed in US politics. In fact, they were significant on a much broader level. As the ideological and sociopolitical categories that structured the Cold War world crumbled over the late 1970s and 1980s, their significance was overtaken by new categories based on culture and identity. In both the East and the West, the culture wars that began in the mid-1980s vaulted considerations of culture and identity to the peak of political significance, fueling a realignment along cultural grounds, with the opposition between progressives and conservatives, rather than ideology or socioeconomics, serving as the most significant fracture line.

Punk and related subcultures were crucial to this transition. In the West and East alike, new wave and heavy metal brought together a coalition of conservatives who opposed them—and, eventually, a group of progressives who arose in their defense. Self-identified punks and bands remained marginalized in this struggle; their focus was not on politics but on striking the delicate balance to maintain their subcultural capital and avoiding unwelcome interference from both governmental and grass-roots attacks. Nonetheless, by the late 1980s, they found themselves dragged into the realigned political spectrum—which, in many cases, seemed just as restrictive and corrupt as the political categories of late Cold War world that they had helped bring to an end.

1989: Conclusion and Epilogue

In September 1987, as conservative Polish Catholics and communists came together against the Jarocin festival, nearly six thousand miles away in San Francisco, Dave Dictor and MDC prepared for the arrival of Pope John Paul II— formerly Cardinal Karol Wojtyla of Poland. With the local punk stalwart the Dead Kennedys sapped by the protracted legal battle over the album *Frankenchrist*, MDC took the offensive, grabbing its instruments, donning papal miters, and playing "This Blood's for You," and "Multi-Death Corporation" from Dictor's rooftop as the pope departed the nearby chapel. When the police arrived, they asked if MDC wanted to "learn to fly," searched the band members for weapons, and turned them over to the local precinct. There, Dictor explained that he was raised a Catholic and that they were "peace punks."[1] He wasn't advocating violence; he simply disapproved of the coalition of oppressive forces that had gathered in the church and state.

Just three weeks earlier, John Paul II had concluded a visit to Poland—the third since he first returned to his homeland as pope in 1979. Papal appearances were momentous occasions that brought out huge crowds of Poles. Western observers declared the pope's presence to be a powerful blow to the Communist Party, presenting Poles with an alternative source of authority.[2] For most Polish punks, though (as for MDC), organized religion was hardly an alternative. Or, as Robert Brylewski succinctly put it, the church in Poland was "a bitch," kowtowing to those in power.[3] After all, the state had allowed the papal appearance to take place, so how much of a challenge could it really be? Of course, the same could be said of punk.

By the time the pope returned to the East for another appearance in 1991, Eastern European communism, the Second World, and the three worlds framework itself had collapsed. The political transformation began in Poland, where members of Solidarity, the church, and the Communist Party sat down together in early 1989 and negotiated the Round Table agreements. The Communist Party no longer had the authority to rule by consent and no longer had the collective will (or backing from Moscow) to rule by force alone. At the Round Table, party members pursued a last-ditch effort to preserve some authority by bringing in their opponents, now eligible for a percentage of seats in the Polish parliament. By the time elections came around, however, the party was trounced. It became clear that the Round Table's power-sharing agreement was the beginning of the end of communism in Poland, and over the next few months, all of Eastern Europe followed.

The political truce between the opposition and the Communist Party had been prepared by the social and cultural changes of the previous decade—including those surrounding punk. With each passing year of the 1980s, the cultural differences within the party and Solidarity had grown, making the divide between the two groups less substantial. Contrary to partisan rhetoric, progressives in the opposition and the party had as much (if not more) in common with one another as with the conservatives in their own organizations. The same could be said of cultural conservatives inside and outside the party. Communism fell less through opposition than entropy—there was little holding it together anymore beyond empty symbols and rhetoric. This confirms Stephen Kotkin's characterization of 1989 not so much as the triumph of dissent as the mass resignation of the communist parties of the East, which had lost confidence in their ability to lead in the emerging new era.[4] While Kotkin describes Poland as an exception due to the remarkable strength of Solidarity, there too 1989 can be read as the effect of the party acknowledging its own obsolescence rather than a struggle between a united party and a united opposition, as the preceding account has demonstrated.

The united front of the Communist Party had also been fracturing in the Soviet Union, provoked in part by glasnost—Gorbachev's efforts to mobilize progressives inside and outside the party behind his reforms. Glasnost also gave rise to a countervailing conservative alliance, however.[5] After the brief opening for punk and other music subcultures in 1986 and 1987, a conservative power bloc with an eye to suppressing subcultures re-emerged in the late 1980s. Increasingly vocal Russian nationalist groups began to voice critiques of punk, rock, and metal, speaking out in defense of the nation and accusing rock of destroying culture, stupefying youth, and damaging their brains.[6] The accusations resonated with those of both cultural conservatives in the West and the culturally conservative hardliners in the Communist Party who had been challenged by Gorbachev. Whatever their disagreement about politics, the rabidly anticommunist Pamyat and party hardliners agreed that heavy metal and punk were threats to the nation and to youth.[7] Gorbachev and the progressives eventually won, but not without a coup d'état led by hardliners protesting his reforms—less for the sake of communist ideals than a desire for order in the face of chaos. As Lilia Shevtsova has argued, the coalition that formed in opposition to postcommunist president Boris Yeltsin brought together a seemingly odd combination of ex-communists, nationalists, and authoritarians—in fact, just the sort of coalition that had been emerging in states across the Eastern bloc over the previous decade and a half.[8]

The Round Table agreement and the subsequent revolutions that ended communist rule around Eastern Europe were undoubtedly momentous events in the history of the world. The year 1989 brought a decisive end to the late Cold War era and marked the beginning of a new world order, an era of reinvigorated globalization and ascendant neoliberalism. While 1989 was most visible in the arenas of politics and economics—the fall of communist regimes and their replacement by liberal democracies—the concomitant underlying cultural shift has been at least as significant. In an ambitious and enigmatic account, Jonathan Clover has sought to identify the spirit of 1989, from the viewpoint of the West, through the popular musical culture of the United States and United Kingdom.[9] That year, Clover argues, marked a turn inward in culture, the end of the era of "the social. This turn is embodied by the shift from punk's slogan—"This is a chord, this is another, this is a third. Now form a band"—to Kurt Cobain's "Learn not to play your instrument." The difference is subtle but significant—a loss of faith in collectivity and a turn inward, from society to the individual.

In fact, Clover's account of 1989 could be amended and adapted to the Second World, the epicenter of that year's transformation. In Poland, a song by reformed punk veterans Tilt, "The Last Wall Has Fallen" ("Runał Już Ostatni Mur"), rose to popularity in the late 1980s, capturing the fall of communism magnificently. Despite its promise of communal redemption, however, the refrain "Nothing divides us" ("Nie dzieli nas nic") rang hollow after 1989 in the face of fault lines that emerged rapidly once the country no longer could unite around widespread disdain for the Communist Party. Much more befitting the new era was punk band Big Cyc's 1993 "Song about 'Solidarity,' or Everything Rots," ("Piosenka o 'Solidarności' czyli wszystko gnije"), bitterly contrasting the heroic solidarity of the 1980s with the atomized, self-interested society that followed. In the East and West alike, punks too became wrapped up in this transition, paradoxically combining aspects of a social movement with fierce individualism and wide-eyed idealism with crushing cynicism. More than a moment, 1989 was the climax of an ongoing global transition from the late Cold War world to the era of neoliberal globalization, spurred on by the spectacular sociocultural clashes that punk helped fuel in the First and Second Worlds alike, in close connection with the Third.

Who could possibly have envisioned the end of the Cold War, the collapse of the framework that had structured the world for half a century? Punks, of course. They had felt the weaknesses of the systems on both sides of the Iron Curtain and cheered on the demise of the late Cold War world order for years with the slogan "No future." Punk arose, East and West, amid crisis, making a name for itself by spectacularly mocking the values and symbols on which the societies of the East and West were based. Instead, punks chose to create something fun and vital, overcoming the high barriers to creativity from the music industry and the world of high art. Drawing inspiration from the urban ethnoscapes of Berlin,

New York, Warsaw, Kingston, and London, interconnected across the borders of the Cold War world, punks like Joe Strummer, Walek Dzedzej, and Donovan Letts devised identities that embodied their rejection of the current world order through fashion, art, and music.

They only reached full force in collaboration with an older generation of experienced radicals and artists like Henryk Gajewski and Malcolm McLaren, however. They brought punk into contact with a wider current of postmodern art, drawing on movements like Dadaism, Situationism, and especially Fluxus and Pop Art to perfect the art of blurring the boundaries between high and low culture, and between aesthetics and everyday life. Postmodernism's tendency to reject metanarratives also resonated with punks' skepticism of the value systems of the modern Western world—communist or capitalist. These punk-friendly artistic gurus' transnational networks helped make punk a "third culture"—connected to each of the local scenes, but intelligible among punks spanning the boundaries of the Cold War world.

Punks' artistic connections overlapped, however, with equally significant—and far more visible—connections to the globalizing music industry, which propelled punk to notoriety in the First and Second Worlds alike. The forces of globalization in combination with with punk's postmodern characteristics—its skepticism toward metanarratives and blurring boundaries between aesthetics and everyday—made for an exceptionally complex relationship between punk's subcultural capital and actual capital. Balancing between these two forms of capital was highly volatile, leading to a wide variety of strategies in the punk scenes around the world, from Malcolm McLaren's efforts to maximize the clash between alternative and mass to Henryk Gajewski's constant effort to cordon punk off safely from penetration by the music industry. Everywhere that punk encountered the media, punks had to restore their subcultural capital by flaunting norms. The result was a chain reaction, provoking mass outcries from the public and, eventually, political and cultural elites.

Making sense of punk proved difficult, however. It fit neither the Left's narrative of class struggle nor the Right's narrative of tradition and nation. A few politicians, particularly those on the margins—in the National Front and the Socialist Workers Party in the West, and in socialist youth unions and the anti-communist opposition in the East—sought footholds in punk for their own ideals and objectives. For the most part, though, punk fit poorly with partisan politics anywhere, leaving elites on both sides of the Iron Curtain falling back on an Arnoldian framework of chaos versus order. When amplified by the media, punk's open skepticism toward the metanarratives and central values of the East and West provoked moral panics, prompting responses from political and cultural elites who tried to make sense of punk. Punk thereby accelerated emerging fault lines within the political formations of the East and West, dividing cultural progressives from conservatives within each group.

While punk defied the political spectrum of the 1970s, the panics it provoked helped consolidate a group of dedicated opponents seeking to end the chaos and restore national greatness. A new batch of leaders in the United Kingdom, United States, Poland, and elsewhere rose in the late 1970s and early 1980s; together they would redefine the global political order over the next decade. Each leader was a caricatured foil for punk—authoritarian, capitalist, orderly, nationalist, and conservative. There was Reagan, the revival preacher/Hollywood actor; Thatcher, the uncompromising matriarch; and Jaruzelski, the impassive aging general. The Iron Curtain between them and the stark difference in their basis of authority—popular support in the United States and United Kingdom, and authoritarian quasi-coup in Poland—obscure surprising similarities in their rhetoric and methods for handling the crises facing their countries. Where punk was chaos, they promised order. They embodied what punk mocked—strength, hierarchy, tradition, nation. Yet, they also embraced the market economics that propelled punk into the spotlight, including in Eastern European countries like Poland and Hungary.

Punk scenes around the world gradually reacted to the changes taking place around them, from the globalization of the music industry to the conservative counterrevolutions enveloping their societies. By the mid-1980s, punk scenes in the East and West began to fracture. One subset of punks organized in self-conscious opposition to the new conservative right, forming a globally minded transnational alliance that resembled the *tiermondisme* of the previous decade but trading faith in a race-blind global socialism for a progressive multiculturalism. However, another subset responded to the challenges of growing inequality and globalization with tribalism, turning inward, becoming xenophobic and sometimes racist, sexist, and authoritarian. Both subsets were skeptical of emerging global capitalism. However, the latter lashed out against the "global" (and against the punks who seemed to be co-opted into the progressive politics of the Left), while the former embraced the "global" and blamed capitalism. As this division split punk scenes around the world, it portended the grand political shift of the late Cold War era toward a political framework divided primarily between cultural conservatives and cultural progressives.

As punk scenes were at war with themselves, punk once again got caught up in a broader social and political debate about culture, reaching the highest authorities in the West and East—the upper echelons of the communist parties of Eastern Europe, the government and courts of the United Kingdom, and the US Senate and Supreme Court. Punk didn't fit the political categories of the 1970s, but by the mid-1980s, politics were adapting, taking shape around identity and culture rather than ideology. The periodic panics over punk metastasized into a war over culture that would consume the whole system, redefining it in the process. The change was perhaps most dramatic in Eastern Europe, where by the second half of the 1980s, punk helped divide the Communist Party and the opposition alike into progressive and conservative/traditionalist factions.

Most punks certainly had little interest in either progressive or conservative political identities. However, punk (like other new musical subcultures) was of interest to elites as an opportunity to bolster their credentials as either open-minded progressives or stalwart conservatives defending culture and tradition. A decade of punk had unwittingly contributed to a political paradigm shift from a Cold War world defined by capitalism versus communism and capital versus labor, to a globalized world defined by widespread acceptance of a market (and the order necessary to maintain it) and a political spectrum restricted to one's choice of cultural identity as a conservative or progressive within the new order.

Punk's Lessons

Punk's appropriation as a pawn in the culture wars of the 1980s has led many punks to resist the impulse to understand punk at all. For every politically informed and engaged punk, there were others for whom being an anarchist, communist, or Nazi meant roughly the same thing. As is true for most people, late Cold War era punks' worldviews were inchoate. Unlike most other people, however, punks had their momentary utterances recorded by journalists and scholars, frozen in print, published, and footnoted. Little wonder, then, that they did not fit into the political or socioeconomic categories of the time. Punks' refusal to fit neatly into Cold War era ideological categories should not be mistaken for a lack of meaning, however. Quite the contrary: punk's meaning derived from its deviation from the categories and framework itself. Punk meant a great deal to both its practitioners and its critics, it shaped the world around it, and it says much about where our world came from and what it has become.

Seen from the perspective of punk, the differences between the "first" and "second" late Cold War worlds were not profound. Both were corrupt, oppressive, dying systems. Both relied on a combination of acceptance, complacency, and brute force to maintain order. Both had institutions that operated with varying degrees of balance between market forces and political/cultural ideals that had little to offer for skeptical, creative young people. Of course, there were very real differences between the systems (for instance, the West had democratically elected governments). However, the experiences of punks remind us that the rhetoric about a free capitalist West and an enslaved communist East was a discourse of the Cold War, not an objective assessment of it. Punk not only challenged the late Cold War world order; it also helps us see past the ideological blinders that it put in place.

In many respects, governments and societies in the East and West reacted to punk similarly. Political and cultural elites were initially reluctant to deal with punk, preferring to ignore it. When punk intersected with the mass media, however, it provoked mass outcry, and elites responded. When they did, the worldview of Matthew Arnold, registering culture as a source of order and enlightenment against the forces of chaos and anarchy, resonated with elites in the West and East alike. Whether Arnold's predominance in Eastern Europe was a holdover from the nineteenth century that survived Leninism or a post-Stalinist emergence after the collapse of ideological communism, his model of culture has shown remarkable resilience.

East and West, suppression was one response to punk: media bans, censorship, censure, and collusion between music industry elites and politicians have been recurring themes for punk bands everywhere. There are countless stories of local officials, industry representatives, and social organizations seeking to guard the youth and culture of England or the United States or Poland or the USSR from punk. Often, though, elites took a more balanced approach, grasping at elements that could fit with their own needs and worldviews. Economic incentives were decisive in some cases, while political and moral imperatives were in others, resulting in a mishmash of repression and commodification in the East and West alike. However, the lens of the Cold War has obscured these similarities: the relatively diffuse political and economic systems in the West make the diverse, scattered responses to punk appear to be pluralistic and idiosyncratic, while in the East, the same scattered response registers as a strategy by a monolithic, scheming state strategically crushing or incorporating all independent activity.

A central feature of punk scenes everywhere was their preoccupation with identity and their indifference to ideology—a key reason punk skirted the defining categories of the Cold War. Punk's focus on identity was intertwined with a global sea change in the late 1970s and 1980s, as capitalist liberalism rose to global hegemony. The era of three worlds and its ideological disputes between capitalism, communism, and *tiermondisme* gave way to a new world order, divided between two interdependent halves, one wealthy and "developed," the other impoverished and "developing." In the absence of ideological alternatives, the main fracture line in the new world order became identity—cultural, religious, and ethnic. This transformation wasn't caused exclusively by punk. However, punk's currency was culture and identity, and when people responded to it, they also emphasized their own identities, invoking culture, religion, the nation, family, and youth. Over time, these conversations shaped the new major sociopolitical constellations of the West and East: globally minded progressives and inward-looking conservatives. Even the countries of the "developing world," each with its own local political idiosyncrasies, shifted from the Cold War struggles over which ideological model to follow to identity politics, often in the form of ethnicity.[10]

In all these ways, the myriad stories of punk are part of the wider story of globalization. This is not to say that punk was universal, or that it was diffused evenly around the world. Punk shows how globalization is not a process of disembodied "flows" or generic "cultural hybridity" but of specific ties that brought together distant places, individuals, and movements at key moments. Seen from the perspective of punk, globalization is less about diffusion and universality than about specific connections, less about erasing boundaries than about redefining them, and less about leveling out inequalities than about creating new kinds of hierarchies. Through it all, local specificities remained important. However, punks also moved across boundaries, drawing ideas from each other, and reacting locally with an eye to the global.

The emergence of identity as the primary fault line in society and politics by the late 1980s suggests why communism withered away so quietly in Poland and elsewhere in the East: the clash between communism and liberal democracy was no longer the key issue for societies around the world. If punk helped bring down communism in the East, it was not because it attacked the party but because it made the divide between communists and anticommunists seem secondary compared with the struggle between conservatives and progressives. Little wonder, then, that Eastern Europe emerged from the fall of communism in 1989—a moment of triumph and unity—to find itself immediately divided between a newly aligned set of antagonistic parties.

In the West, punk bolstered the formation of new constellations on the Right—especially a coalition of social/cultural conservatives across class lines. The efforts of Reagan and Thatcher to equate the interests of the working class with the nation, tradition, and order—and thus with conservatives—were reinforced from the opposite side by punk. By the late 1980s, though, a new left would also coalesce, emphasizing uncertainty, inclusiveness, heterogeneity, and open-mindedness—all of which were also defined and refined in part through conversations about punk.

As this account demonstrates, punk was profoundly significant in its effects on society, culture, and politics. However, identifying its political significance is far more complex than a matter of scouring songs or interviews for clues identifying punk as left-wing, right-wing, liberating, repressive, resistant, or co-opted—whether with respect to politics, class, race, or gender. As scholars of popular culture have long suspected, "resistance" is not a particularly helpful concept for understanding how punk (or popular culture in general) operates in the world. While punks sometimes spoke in terms of resistance and co-optation as part of their struggle to assert their subcultural capital, these terms were prescriptive assertions, not descriptions of actual groups of people or their actions. Punk did not bring "the people" together against "the system" in the West or the East. In fact, it often brought people together against punk, uniting Catholics and communist hardliners in Poland, right-wing nationalists and Stalinists in the USSR, socially conservative Democrats and Republicans in the United States, and workers and elites in the United Kingdom. Once we abandon the effort to make punk fit with the ideological categories of the Cold War world, punks' apparent mishmash of political and apolitical views is less enigmatic. Resistance is not something that exists in a cultural form, even one as spectacular as punk. Rather, punk was politically relevant as a phenomenon through which the post–Cold War world's identities and social constellations—progressives and conservatives—formed and oriented themselves. This transformation took place in a complex interplay of developments and interactions that spanned the boundaries of the Cold War world.

Epilogue

In 1991, MDC's Dave Dictor arrived in the collapsing USSR just a few months after the failed coup, playing in Minsk, Leningrad (returning to its identity as St. Petersburg), and Moscow. Staying with Russian squatters and a group of visiting Polish punks, he was surprised to learn that there had been a community of punks in the East who had long loved and followed MDC's music. After years of hearing about one another, they finally had a chance to discuss in person the deep connection they had shared across the Iron Curtain.[11]

Where did punks fit within the new global order and its cultural politics? Nowhere, as many punks saw it. In the new capitalist East, communism was briefly replaced (in theory, at least) by neoliberalism, whose global appeal peaked as faith in the Second and Third World alternatives dwindled. New governments in the East disassembled state institutions, replacing them with a market. In place of the party, a new oligarchy arose as privatization allowed a few well-connected citizens to buy up huge resources owned formerly by the state. Roles within the previous system—affiliation with the party or the opposition—continued to be politically relevant for a few years after communism, but increasingly as identities rather than political platforms. In Poland, former Solidarity members and party members alike became prominent politicians from the local level up to the presidency, including Solidarity's Lech Wałęsa and Aleksander Kwaśniewski, former minister of youth and defender of the Jarocin festival. In terms of their actual politics, however, post-Solidarity and postcommunist political identities came to mean very little. Instead, the primary fault line was based on cultural and social views, between nationalist and traditionalist Catholic parties and secular, globally oriented progressive parties. The split that began at least a decade earlier—broad versus narrow definitions of the nation and culture, and identity as conservatives or progressives—became the primary difference between the Right and Left in Poland, as in much of the rest of the world.

Many punks felt comfortable with neither. Nearly everyone involved in the punk scene greeted the fall of communism with relief, but they didn't necessarily embrace the new capitalist system. KSU's Eugeniusz "Siczka" Olejarczyk put it more succinctly: while he had followed Solidarity and admired its outspoken critique of the Communist Party, he reflected in 2003, "When I look at what the movement became today, I want to puke."[12] Krzysztof Grabowski, Dezerter's drummer, felt similarly: "I always thought the government was more or less violence against the people; I still do."[13]

Capitalism came with new opportunities, even for some punks. There are a few success stories, including that of Kazik Staszewski of punk band Kult, who has done well in the music market after communism. His 2000 crossover hit "Cztery pokoje" captures the disillusionment with the transition since 1989, portraying the main difference from the communist era as having four parties instead of one—but with only superficial, identity-based differences between them. In turn, Staszewski's success grates on punks who continue to see themselves as outsiders to the system. So, too, does the resurgent popularity of new wave acts like Lady Pank and Maanam, as the 1980s have become mythologized as the time of Poland's finest popular music.

Success is not entirely comforting even for the punks who manage to achieve it, however. With the fall of communism, Siekiera's Tomasz Budzyński noted, he became a "rock star." Before then, this had always been a pejorative term.[14] He and others have had to find new strategies for asserting their subcultural capital. Staszewski, for instance, emphasizes his association with a small record label rather than a major company. Even so, he observed that the media in communist Poland and under capitalism operated in much the same way, privileging the mainstream over the marginal.[15]

Tomasz Lipiński from Tilt also had a jarring experience with the new capitalist system. He got a job with the major international music firm BMG, hoping that "after communism there would be civilized, just rules for the music industry." He soon quit, though, when he realized this was not the case. He sang about Babylon during communism, but after communism, he believes that "globalization is today's Babylon"—a sentiment he shares with many other punks around the world. Now, he's calling for "another revolution, a change of the political establishment, not just another oligarchy beyond social control."

Robert Brylewski from Kryzys, Brygada Kryzys, and Izrael is equally unimpressed: while the communist system was oppressive, he notes, "Today we have another system. It operates more discretely, less oppressively, but it still imprisons and bans."[16] Instead of bureaucrats, now Brylewski sings about "VIP's, a new phenomenon, politicians, businessmen with special privileges." Although he admits he would not choose to go back to the communist era, he argues, "It was easier to live in the time at the end of the [People's Republic of Poland] . . . as a musician, it was possible to do more, because there was chaos. The reds had their own problems, so they stopped being interested in us. And more people wanted to listen to us."[17] Ironically, the loss of state-sponsored houses of culture and student clubs removed the most popular venues for amateur punk bands: it was actually easier to play under communism.[18]

Poland was not unique in this respect: punk bands around the Eastern bloc had trouble adapting to new capitalist conditions. This was certainly the case in Hungary, which had enough leeway for bands to form and play, but also protected them from the forces of the free market—until communism fell.[19] East German punks faced the added challenge of competing in the national scene with West German bands already adapted to the capitalist marketplace. While punk's ethos was as relevant as ever in the Eastern bloc from the satellites to the USSR, it faced new challenges from the market, and also from conservative and nationalist forces that soon proved they were still willing to use the power of the state to suppress dissent, as Big Cyc forcefully articulated in its 1993 "Song about Solidarity, or Everything Rots." Even those who had experienced the communist system firsthand wondered how much had been gained: in 1994, UK punk émigré Tom Robinson released "Living in the DDR," reflecting on the time he spent living in the Eastern bloc. For years Eastern Europeans had longed for the end of communism; yet, the song noted with irony, unemployed and left behind by liberal capitalism, they now found themselves secretly longing for it to come back.

As the East rushed to bury communism and privatize its labyrinth of institutions, the West briefly basked in its victory in the Cold War. Finally, the world seemed to be on its way to embracing liberal democracy. The political spectrum in the West had also been subtly changing over the previous decade, however. In response to the conservative revolution of 1980 that led to the rise of a new right behind Thatcher and Reagan, a rejuvenated left coalesced in the second half of the decade, exemplified by "Third Way" politicians like Bill Clinton and Al Gore in the United States and Tony Blair in the United Kingdom.[20] To the alarm of traditional leftists, who saw the Third Way as neoliberalism obfuscated by slogans about equality and social justice, Clinton embraced capitalism and global free trade no less than his opponents in the new right. However, he was miles away in terms of identity. Clinton leveraged his identity as cool, worldly, and progressive, playing the sax and reaching out through youth-friendly media like MTV. Not surprisingly, his running mate, Al Gore, now distanced himself from the PMRC, which no longer fit with the emerging progressive democratic identity. Increasingly, the Left accommodated itself to subcultural symbols, using them to bolster its progressive credentials. In the United Kingdom too, Tony Blair shifted Labor's identity in the direction of progressive cultural politics, taking a "cultural turn," as Rupa Huq has shown.[21]

Many punks weren't convinced. A decade after the triumph of the First World, punk scenes surged back into action with a critique directed at the West and its new undisputed place of leadership in the global neoliberal order. In 1999, when the World Trade Organization met for a conference in Seattle, Washington, tens of thousands of people showed up to protest. As in San Francisco a decade and a half earlier, punks were at the heart of it, protesting the coalition of business interests and state power that privileged some people and regions over others. The link was more than philosophical: among the key organizers was Dave Solnit, a West Coast punk who also participated in the War Chest actions in San Francisco in the 1980s.[22] As with the punk protests over wars in Grenada and the Falklands, punks were among the only voices of antiglobalization protest in the West, joined by a ragtag assortment of other marginal groups. Analysts on all sides of the political spectrum were dumbfounded: opposing the WTO didn't make sense in the new era, when both the mainstream Left and the Right agreed on supporting global capitalism. Once again, punk fit poorly with the new political order. Amid a political spectrum defined by different cultural identities within broad neoliberal consensus, many punks rejected that consensus.

In part for this reason, punk has found unprecedented appeal in the Third World since 1989. Punk's rebellion against the modern Western world attracted interest, sympathy, and camaraderie in the global South in the age of three worlds, but the music and culture itself remained culturally alien. Globalization has begun to change that. Punk rose in the 1990s everywhere touched by global capital, including Bali, Nepal, and sub-Saharan Africa.[23] Even so, hip-hop has arguably surpassed punk as the go-to music of the disenfranchised. Hip-hop appeals to those who relate to the experience of African Americans in the United States and draw inspiration from their rebellion against the system and self-empowerment through art, creativity, and solidarity (as well as misogyny and violence; hip-hop has plenty of internal struggles to negotiate, much like punk). Hip-hop avoids punk's tendency to collapse into the solipsism of individual identity, since it is inextricably tied to a social identity by the concept of race. It is an art form well suited to globalization's underdogs—be it Polish migrant laborers in the European Union, South Asians in the United Kingdom, or Mexicans and Pacific islanders in the United States.

However, punk retains its ability to provoke. In February 2012, the punk band Pussy Riot, part of a radical art collective, staged a performance of "Punk Prayer" at Moscow's Cathedral of Christ the Savior, much to the surprise of elderly church patrons. In the subsequent music video it released, Pussy Riot launched a furious critique of the alliance of church and state under Putin. Shortly after, the band members were arrested and then tried for "hooliganism motivated by religious hatred." Despite impassioned speeches defending their actions as political protest, they received two-year sentences in prison with hard labor.

In a concluding statement at their trial, their lawyer observed with disgust that nothing had changed since the times of communism.[24] Indeed, the verdict against Pussy Riot, bringing together conservative forces of the church and the state, was nearly identical to the charge of religious intolerance brought against the metal band Test Fobii Kreon when it destroyed a cross onstage in communist Poland twenty-five years earlier. From the perspective of punks, the similarity between the communist and postcommunist authoritarian state is obvious, with the new generation of politicians holding as little regard for the ideals of democracy as the previous generation of leaders had for communism.

In retrospect, none of the three worlds emerged from the Cold War victorious. The triumph of the First World's liberal democracy lasted just a moment before it was met by a new challenge: the "evil empire" of communism had been replaced by the "axis of evil" of terrorism, and by ascendant state capitalism in East Asia. Neoliberalism in Eastern Europe did the unthinkable—it made some people nostalgic for Stalinism. In the USSR, they ended up with something similar: Putin accepted the market but brought back a powerful regulatory state and sought a return to national greatness through strength and order. Once again, punks were there to give it the finger.

Notes

Introduction

1. John Lydon, Keith Zimmerman, and Kent Zimmerman, *Rotten: No Irish, No Blacks, No Dogs* (New York: Picador, 2008), 234.
2. Robert Brylewski and Rafał Księżyk, *Kryzys w Babilonie: Autobiografia* (Cracow: Wydawnictwo Literackie, 2012).
3. For comparative histories of the Cold War era, see Eric Hobsbawm, *The Age of Extremes: A History of the World, 1914–1991* (New York: Pantheon Books, 1994); Odd Arne Westad, *The Global Cold War: Third World Interventions and the Making of Our Times* (Cambridge: Cambridge University Press, 2005); and Mark Mazower, *Dark Continent: Europe's Twentieth Century* (New York: Knopf, 1999).
4. Sex Pistols, "God Save the Queen," A&M AMS 7284, 1977.
5. Brylewski and Księżyk, *Kryzys w Babilonie*.
6. Sex Pistols, "Anarchy in the UK," EMI 2566, 1976.
7. For the story of punk centered on the Sex Pistols, see Jon Savage, *England's Dreaming: Anarchy, Sex Pistols, Punk Rock, and Beyond* (London: Faber, 1991).
8. Stuart Hall and Tony Jefferson, eds., *Resistance through Rituals: Youth Subcultures in Postwar Britain* (London: Hutchinson, 1976).
9. See Timothy W. Ryback, *Rock around the Bloc: A History of Rock Music in Eastern Europe and the Soviet Union* (New York: Oxford University Press, 1990), or, for an opposing view, Jolanta Pekacz, "Did Rock Smash the Wall? The Role of Rock in Political Transition," *Popular Music* 13, no. 1 (1994): 41–49. Sabrina Petra Ramet, *Rocking the State: Rock Music and Politics in Eastern Europe and Russia* (Boulder, CO: Westview Press, 1994), seeks to navigate the state-society binary by interpreting rock as "contested terrain." Padraic Kenney, *A Carnival of Revolution: Central Europe, 1989* (Princeton, NJ: Princeton University Press, 2003), further complicates this model by emphasizing the difference between the culture of the opposition and counterculture like punk.
10. This debate dates at least to Dick Hebdige's *Subculture: The Meaning of Style* (London: Routledge, 1979). In response, Roger Sabin has called attention to punk's right-wing elements in "I Won't Let That Dago By," in *Punk Rock, So What? The Cultural Legacy of Punk* (New York: Routledge, 1999). Others emphasize punk's openness and heterogeneity, like Ashley Dawson, "Love Music, Hate Racism: The Cultural Politics of the Rock Against Racism Campaigns," *Postmodern Culture* 16, no. 1 (2005), https://muse.jhu.edu; and Ian Goodyer, *Crisis Music: The Cultural Politics of Rock Against Racism* (Manchester: Manchester University Press, 2009).
11. See Ryback, Ramet, and Pekacz in note 9 above. This trend continues: see Grzegorz Piotrowski, "Punk against Communism: The Jarocin Rock Festival and Revolting Youth in 1980s Poland," in *A European Youth Revolt*, ed. Knud Andresen and Bart van der Steen (Houndmills, Basingstoke: Palgrave Macmillan, 2016), 203–216.

12. Tricia Rose, *Black Noise: Rap Music and Black Culture in Contemporary America* (Hanover, NH: Wesleyan University Press of New England, 1994).
13. Paul Hodkinson and Wolfgang Deicke, eds., *Youth Cultures: Scenes, Subcultures and Tribes* (New York: Routledge, 2007); Remigiusz Kasprzycki, *Dekada Buntu: Punk w Polsce i Krajach Sasiednich w Latach 1977–1989* (Cracow: LIBRON, 2013).
14. Observe the transition from sweeping narrative and theoretical accounts by the likes of Hebdige's *Subculture*; Savage's *England's Dreaming*; and Greil Marcus's, *Lipstick Traces: A Secret History of the Twentieth Century* (Cambridge, MA: Harvard University Press, 1989), to disjointed, multivocal, scene- and band-specific interview collections like Legs McNeil and Gillian McCain, *Please Kill Me: The Uncensored Oral History of Punk* (New York: Grove Press, 1996); Marc Spitz, *We Got the Neutron Bomb: The Untold Story of L.A. Punk* (New York: Three Rivers Press, 2001); Lydon, Zimmerman, and Zimmerman, *Rotten*; and Jack Boulware and Silke Tudor, *Gimme Something Better: The Profound, Progressive, and Occasionally Pointless History of Bay Area Punk from Dead Kennedys to Green Day* (New York: Penguin, 2009).
15. Nan Enstad, "On Grief and Complicity: Notes toward a Visionary Cultural History," *The Cultural Turn in U.S. History: Past, Present, and Future*, ed. James Cook (Chicago: University of Chicago Press, 2008).
16. Jonathyne Briggs, "East of (Teenaged) Eden, or Is Eastern Youth Culture So Different from the West?," in *Youth and Rock in the Soviet Bloc: Youth Cultures, Music, and the State in Russia and Eastern Europe*, ed. William Jay Risch (Lanham, MD: Lexington Books, 2015), 267–284.
17. For accounts of Eastern European popular culture with respect to transnational connections, Westernization, and modernity, see Adriana Helbig, *Hip Hop Ukraine: Music, Race, and African Migration* (Bloomington: Indiana University Press, 2014); William Jay Risch, *The Ukrainian West: Culture and the Fate of Empire in Soviet Lviv* (Cambridge, MA: Harvard University Press, 2011); S. I. Zhuk, *Rock and Roll in the Rocket City: The West, Identity, and Ideology in Soviet Dniepropetrovsk, 1960–1985* (Baltimore: John Hopkins University Press, 2010); Timothy Scott Brown and Lorena Anton, eds., *Between the Avant-Garde and the Everyday: Subversive Politics in Europe from 1957 to the Present* (New York: Berghahn Books, 2011); and Marta Marciniak, *Transnational Punk Communities in Poland: From Nihilism to Nothing Outside Punk* (Lanham, MD: Lexington Books, 2015).
18. Kevin Dunn, *Global Punk: Resistance and Rebellion in Everyday Life* (London: Bloomsbury, 2016). See also Jim Donaghey, "Punk and Anarchism: UK, Poland, Indonesia" (PhD diss., Loughborough University, 2016).
19. Recent scholarship on punk that combines some of the best insights from CCCS with post-CCCS approaches can be found in Hilary Pilkington, *Russia's Skinheads: Exploring and Rethinking Subcultural Lives* (London: Routledge, 2010), and The Subcultures Network, ed., *Fight Back: Punk, Politics, and Resistance* (Manchester: Manchester University Press, 2015). Dunn's *Global Punk* likewise combines close attention to lived experience with an insistence on punk's broader social significance.
20. Stuart Hall, "Notes on Deconstructing the Popular," in *People's History and Socialist Theory*, ed. Raphael Samuel (London: Routledge, 1981), 227–249.
21. Michael Denning, *Culture in the Age of Three Worlds* (New York: Verso, 2004).
22. See Anoop Nayak, *Race, Place and Globalization: Youth Culture in a Changing World* (Oxford: Berg, 2003).
23. The initially innovative and subsequently maligned concept of cultural "flows" stems from Arjun Appadurai, *Modernity at Large: Cultural Dimensions of Globalization* (Minneapolis: University of Minnesota Press, 1996). For more on punk and globalization, see Alan O'Connor, "Local Scenes and Dangerous Crossroads: Punk and Theories of Cultural Hybridity," *Popular Music* 21, no. 2 (May 2002): 225–236.
24. Mike Featherstone, *Global Culture* (London: Sage, 1990); Featherstone, *Undoing Culture: Globalization, Postmodernism and Identity* (London: Sage, 1995). On postmodernism, see Perry Anderson, *The Origins of Postmodernity* (New York: Verso, 1998). On punk and postmodernism, see David Muggleton, *Inside Subculture: The Postmodern Meaning of*

Style (Oxford: Berg, 2000), and Ivan Gololubov, "Immigrant Punk," in The Subcultures Network, *Fight Back*, 77–98.
25. Sarah Thornton, *Club Cultures* (Hanover, NH: University Press of New England, 1996); Rupa Huq, *Beyond Subculture: Pop, Youth, and Identity in a Postcolonial World* (London: Routledge, 2006).
26. James Davison Hunter, *Culture Wars: The Struggle to Define America* (New York: Basic Books, 1991); Andrew Hartman, *A War for the Soul of America: A History of the Culture Wars* (Chicago: University of Chicago Press, 2015).
27. Jonathan Clover, *1989: Bob Dylan Didn't Have This to Sing About* (Berkeley: University of California Press, 2009).
28. Lauren Gail Berlant, *The Queen of America Goes to Washington City: Essays on Sex and Citizenship* (Durham, NC: Duke University Press, 1997).

Chapter 1

1. Nina Hagen, Marcel Feige, and Jim Rakete, *Nina Hagen: That's Why the Lady Is a Punk* (Berlin: Schwarzkopf & Schwarzkopf, 2003).
2. Arjun Appadurai, "The Ethnographic Imagination: Textual Constructions of Reality," *Theory, Culture and Society* 7 (1990): 295–310.
3. Hodkinson and Deicke, *Youth Cultures*, and The Subcultures Network, *Fight Back*, offer useful historiographical summaries of subcultural theory. For globalization and punk, see O'Connor, "Local Scenes and Dangerous Crossroads"; Dunn, *Global Punk*; and Sam Quinones, "Mexico's Globophobe Punks," *Foreign Policy*, no. 138 (September–October 2003): 78–79.
4. Nayak, *Race, Place and Globalization*.
5. Huq, *Beyond Subculture*.
6. See Gololubov, "Immigrant Punk." Stephen Duncombe and Maxwell Tremblay survey the full spectrum of punk's tortured relationship with race in *White Riot: Punk Rock and the Politics of Race* (New York: Verso, 2011).
7. Everett True, *Hey Ho Let's Go: The Story of the Ramones* (London: Omnibus, 2005).
8. McNeil and McCain, *Please Kill Me*.
9. Ralph Blumenthal, "Punk, and Jewish: Rockers Explore Identity," *New York Times*, June 12, 2009, http://www.nytimes.com/2009/06/13/nyregion/13punk.html?_r&_r=0.
10. Ben Brumfield, "Punk Rock Icon Tommy Ramone Dies," CNN, July 13, 2014, http://edition.cnn.com/2014/07/12/showbiz/tommy-ramone-dead/index.html?hpt=hp_c2.
11. "Ivan Král Biography," www.ivankral.net.
12. Pat Gilbert, *Passion Is a Fashion: The Real Story of the Clash* (Cambridge, MA: Da Capo Press, 2005).
13. Chris Salewicz, *Redemption Song: The Ballad of Joe Strummer* (New York: Faber and Faber, 2007).
14. Ibid.
15. Ibid.
16. Gilbert, *Passion Is a Fashion*.
17. Don Letts, *Culture Clash: Dread Meets Punk Rockers*, ed. David Nobakht (London: SAF, 2007).
18. Ibid.
19. Kevin O'Brien Chang and Wayne Chen, *Reggae Routes: The Story of Jamaican Music* (Philadelphia: Temple University Press, 1998).
20. Letts, *Culture Clash*.
21. Ibid.
22. Salewicz, *Redemption Song*; Gilbert, *Passion Is a Fashion*.
23. Letts, *Culture Clash*.
24. Hagen, Feige, and Rakete, *Nina Hagen*.
25. Quoted in Ryback, *Rock around the Bloc*.

26. Wiesław Królikowski, "Czas Jak Rzeka . . . ," *Magazyn Muzyczny*, August 1984. See Przemysław Zieliński, *Scena Rockowa w PRL: Historia, Organizacja, Znaczenie* (Warsaw: Wydawnictwo Trio, 2005) for a deeper treatment of the history of rock in Poland.
27. Ryback, *Rock around the Bloc*; Mark Fenemore, *Sex, Thugs and Rock 'n' Roll: Teenage Rebels in Cold-War East Germany* (New York: Berghahn Books, 2007).
28. G. Ann Stamp Miller, *The Cultural Politics of the German Democratic Republic: The Voices of Wolf Biermann, Christa Wolf, and Heiner Müller* (Boca Raton, FL: Brown Walker Press, 2004).
29. Hagen, Feige, and Rakete, *Nina Hagen*.
30. Ryback, *Rock around the Bloc*.
31. Ibid.
32. Hagen, Feige, and Rakete, *Nina Hagen*.
33. Ibid.
34. Ibid.
35. Lydon, Zimmerman, and Zimmerman, *Rotten*; Zöe Street Howe, *Typical Girls? The Story of the Slits* (London: Omnibus Press, 2009).
36. Hagen, Feige, and Rakete, *Nina Hagen*.
37. Howe, *Typical Girls?*
38. Ibid.
39. Ibid.
40. Hagen, Feige, and Rakete, *Nina Hagen*.
41. Cezary Łazarewicz, "Porter John: Nie Zgubiłem Się W Tralala," *Polityka*, no. 47, 2009.
42. Gilbert, *Passion Is a Fashion*.
43. Liner notes to *Victim of Safety Pin: Polski Punk Underground 1977–82*, Supreme Echo SE 01, 2003.
44. Piotr Milewski, "Walek Dzedzej—poeta Przeklęty 1953–2006," *Nowy Dziennik*, October 19, 2006.
45. Ibid.
46. Ibid.
47. Ryback, *Rock around the Bloc*; Kasprzycki, *Dekada Buntu*.
48. Igor Mirkovic, *Sretno Dijete* (Croatia: Gerila DV Film, 2003).
49. Risch, *The Ukrainian West*.
50. Gilbert, *Passion Is a Fashion*.
51. Dave Thompson, *Wheels Out of Gear: 2 Tone, the Specials and a World in Flame* (London: Helter Skelter, 2004).
52. Duncombe and Tremblay, *White Riot*.

Chapter 2

1. Katarzyna Urbańska, "Galeria Remont: Nieznana Awangarda Lat Siedemdziesiątych," *Sztuka i Dokumentacja*, no. 6 (2012): 133–138.
2. Paul Taylor, *Impresario: Malcolm McLaren and the British New Wave* (New York: New Museum of Contemporary Art; Cambridge, MA: MIT Press, 1988).
3. Marcus, *Lipstick Traces*. Savage's *England's Dreaming* also discusses the art background of London punk, especially with respect to Situationism.
4. Featherstone, *Global Culture*; Featherstone, *Undoing Culture*.
5. Muggleton, *Inside Subculture*. Astutely, Muggleton insists on distinguishing modernity from aesthetic modernism—the latter of which (like aesthetic postmodernism) often critiqued the former.
6. Monica Sklar, *Punk Style* (Oxford: Berg, 2013); Gololubov, "Immigrant Punk."
7. The Subcultures Network, *Fight Back*.
8. Ivan Gololubov, "Immigrant Punk."
9. Craig Bromberg, *The Wicked Ways of Malcolm McLaren* (New York: Perennial Library, 1989).
10. Savage, *England's Dreaming*.

11. Gilbert, *Passion Is a Fashion*.
12. McNeil and McCain, *Please Kill Me*.
13. Patti Smith, *Just Kids* (New York: Ecco, 2010).
14. Bromberg, *The Wicked Ways of Malcolm McLaren*.
15. Taylor, *Impresario*.
16. Bromberg, *The Wicked Ways of Malcolm McLaren*.
17. McNeil and McCain, *Please Kill Me*.
18. Taylor, *Impresario*.
19. McNeil and McCain, *Please Kill Me*.
20. Savage, *England's Dreaming*.
21. Urbańska, "Galeria Remont."
22. Patryk Wasiak, "Kontakty Kulturalne Pomiędzy Polską a Węgrami, Czechosłowacją i NRD W Latach 1970–1989 Na Przykładzie Artystów Plastyków" (PhD diss., Instytut Kultury i Komunikowania, Szkoła Wyższa Psychologii Społecznej, 2009).
23. Emmett Williams, Ay-o, and Ann Noël, *Mr. Fluxus: A Collective Portrait of George Maciunas, 1931–1978* (New York: Thames and Hudson, 1998); Astrit Schmidt-Burkhardt., *Maciunas' Learning Machines: From Art History to a Chronology of Fluxus* (Detroit: Gilbert and Lila Silverman Fluxus Collection in association with Vice Versa, 2003).
24. Eric Andersen, *Fluxus East: Fluxus-Netzwerke in Mittelosteuropa: Ausstellungskatalog = Fluxus Networks in Central Eastern Europe: Exhibition Catalogue* (Berlin: Künstlerhaus Bethanien, 2007).
25. Ivan Martin Jirous, "Report on the third Czech Musical Festival," in Martin Machovec, ed., *Views from the Inside: Czech Underground Literature and Culture 1948–1989* (Prague: Katedra české literatury a literární vědy, Univerzita Karlova v Praze, 2006).
26. Simon Ford, *Wreckers of Civilisation: The Story of COUM Transmissions and Throbbing Gristle* (London: Black Dog, 1999).
27. Ibid.
28. Penny Rimbaud, *Shibboleth: My Revolting Life* (Edinburgh: AK Press, 1998).
29. Crass, "General Bacardi," *The Feeding of the 5000*, Small Wonder 521984, 1978.
30. Andersen, *Fluxus East*.
31. Wasiak, "Kontakty Kulturalne."
32. Urbańska, "Galeria Remont."
33. Zora von Burden, *Women of the Underground: Music: Cultural Innovators Speak for Themselves* (San Francisco: Manic D Press, 2010).
34. Helen Reddington, *The Lost Women of Rock Music: Female Musicians of the Punk Era* (Aldershot: Ashgate, 2007); "Raincoats Profile; Legendary U.K. Band Interviewed," *Chicago Tribune*, September 14, 2014, http://articles.chicagotribune.com/2011-09-14/entertainment/chi-raincoats-profile-legendary-uk-band-interviewed-20110914_1_gina-birch-raincoats-riot-grrrl-movement.
35. Gajewski, "Punk," December 1979.
36. Barbara Dąbrowska, "Dzieci śmieci," *Na Przełaj*, January 4, 1981.
37. Dr. Avane, "Punky Reggae Party," *Non Stop*, February 1984.
38. Ibid.
39. Brylewski and Księżyk, *Kryzys w Babilonie*.
40. Ibid.
41. Ibid.
42. Liner notes to *Victim of Safety Pin: Polski Punk Underground 1977–82*.
43. Andersen, *Fluxus East*.
44. Jacek Lenartowicz, *Papier Białych Wulkanów*, no. 1 (1980), 11.
45. Jacek Lenartowicz, *Papier Białych Wulkanów*, no. 2 (1980), 8.
46. Matt Grimes and Tim Wall, "Punk 'zines: 'Symbols of Defiance' from the Print to the Digital Age," in *Fight Back, 287–303*.
47. Jonathyne Briggs, "Distortions in Distance: Debates over Cultural Conventions in French Punk, " in *Fight Back, 139–154*.
48. Ibid.

49. Diana Ozon, "Punkclub DDT666 door Diana Ozon," Nederpunk, October 27, 2007, http://nederpunk.punt.nl/content/2007/10/punkclub-ddt666-door-diana-ozon.
50. Gajewski, "Punk."
51. Ibid.
52. Ibid., 52–53.

Chapter 3

1. Wiesław Królikowski, "Antidotum: Rozmowa z Jackiem Sylwinem, impresariem i producentem płytowym," *Magazyn Muzyczny—Jazz*, October 1986.
2. Bałtycka Agencja Artystyczna, "Pop Session 1978 Program," 1978, http://www.jarocinfestiwal.com/historia/popsession/1978/folder/wstep.html.
3. Ibid.
4. Marek Wiernik, "W pieniądzu siła," *Non Stop*, September 1978.
5. Kasprzycki, *Dekada Buntu*.
6. Neil Nehring, *Popular Music, Gender, and Postmodernism: Anger Is an Energy* (Thousand Oaks, CA: Sage, 1997).
7. Pierre Bourdieu, "The Forms of Capital," in *Handbook of Theory and Research for the Sociology of Education*, ed. John Richardson (New York: Greenwood Press, 1986), 241–258.
8. Thornton, *Club Cultures*. Useful historiographical summaries of subcultural theory of are available in Nayak, *Race, Place and Globalization*; Hodkinson and Deicke, *Youth Cultures*; and The Subcultures Network, *Fight Back*.
9. Hodkinson and Deicke, *Youth Cultures*; Kasprzycki, *Dekada Buntu*.
10. Pilkington, *Russia's Skinheads*.
11. Simon Frith, *Sound Effects: Youth, Leisure, and the Politics of Rock 'n' roll* (New York: Pantheon Books, 1981).
12. Ibid.
13. For an account of the economics of punk in the West, see Stacy Thompson, *Punk Productions: Unfinished Business* (Albany: State University of New York Press, 2004).
14. McNeil and McCain, *Please Kill Me*.
15. See Alan O'Connor, *Punk Record Labels and the Struggle for Autonomy: The Emergence of DIY* (Lanham, MD: Lexington Books, 2008), for a thorough account of punk indie labels, especially in the United Kingdom, United States, and Canada.
16. Spitz, *We Got the Neutron Bomb*, 178.
17. O'Connor, *Punk Record Labels and the Struggle for Autonomy*.
18. Frith, *Sound Effects*.
19. Spitz, *We Got the Neutron Bomb*.
20. Mark Andersen, *Dance of Days: Two Decades of Punk in the Nation's Capital* (New York: Akashic Books, 2003).
21. Frith, *Sound Effects*, 153.
22. Ibid., 125.
23. Simon Reynolds, *Rip It Up and Start Again: Postpunk 1978–1984* (New York: Penguin Books, 2006).
24. Frith, *Sound Effects*.
25. John Peel, *Margrave of the Marshes* (London: Bantam, 2005).
26. Ken Garner, *The Peel Sessions* (London: BBC Books, 2007).
27. Ibid.
28. Ibid., 91.
29. Savage, *England's Dreaming*.
30. Ibid., 364.
31. Howe, *Typical Girls?*
32. For a more detailed approach to the Polish music industry and its conditions in the 1980s, see Raymond Patton, "The Communist Culture Industry: The Music Business in 1980s Poland," *Journal of Contemporary History* 47, no. 2 (April 2012): 427–449.

33. Jerzy Bojanowicz, "Rozmowa z Jerzym Bisiakiem, Wicedyrektórem Departmentu Teatru i Estrady MKiS," *Non Stop*, November 1981.
34. Peter Wicke, "The Times They Are A-changin': Rock Music and Political Change in East Germany," in *Rockin' the Boat: Mass Music and Mass Movements*, ed. Reebee Garofalo (Boston: South End Press, 1992), 86.
35. Marek Wiernik, "Co jest grane . . . w radiu?," *Non Stop*, April 1980.
36. "Kultura w Polskim Radiu i Telewizji," July 1985, 1354 Wydział Kultury PZPR, 1701, 982/47, Archiwum Akt Nowych, Warsaw, Poland.
37. Patton, "The Communist Culture Industry."
38. James Riordan, ed., *Soviet Youth Culture* (Bloomington: Indiana University Press, 1989).
39. "Czech Normalization," Balázs Trencsényi and Gábor Klaniczay, "Mapping the Merry Ghetto: Musical Countercultures in East Central Europe, 1960–1989," *East Central Europe* 38, no. 2 (2011): 169–179. See also Josef Skvorecky, "Hipness at Noon," *New Republic*, December 17, 1984, 27–35.
40. Paul Easton, "The Rock Music Community," in *Soviet Youth Culture*, ed. James Riordan (Bloomington: Indiana University Press, 1989).
41. *Opole 1980*, Telewizja Polska, July 1980; video available at http://www.tvp.pl/rozrywka/festiwale-i-koncerty/opole-2009/z-archiwum-opola/opole-1980-18-festiwal/maanam-boskie-buenos-1980.
42. Adam St. Trąbiński, "Bez rewelacji," *Non Stop*, August 1980.
43. Gajewski and Rypson, *Post*, September 10, 1980.
44. Gajewski and Rypson, *Post*, no. 6 (undated).
45. Rimbaud, *Shibboleth*, 74.
46. Crass, *The Feeding of the 5000*.
47. Gajewski and Rypson, *Post*, December 12, 1980.
48. Gajewski and Rypson, *Post*, December 20, 1980.
49. Crass, *Stations of the Crass*, Crass Records 521984, 1979.

Chapter 4

1. Jerzy Wertenstein-Żuławski, "Społeczne aspekty muzyki rockowej: znaczenie kultury młodzieżowej w społecznestwie," February 1981, 1354 Wydział Kultury PZPR, 315, 889/50, Archiwum Akt Nowych, Warsaw, Poland.
2. Ryback, *Rock around the Bloc*, 171.
3. Zhuk, *Rock and Roll in the Rocket City*.
4. Ibid.
5. Bruce J. Schulman, *The Seventies: The Great Shift in American Culture, Society, and Politics* (New York: Free Press, 2001).
6. "Consensus" has a long history in scholarship of the United Kingdom. See Brian Harrison, "The Rise Fall and Rise of Political Consensus in Britain since 1940," *History* 84, no. 274 (1999): 301–324. With respect to popular culture, see The Subcultures Network, ed., *Youth Culture, Popular Music and the End of "Consensus"* (London: Routledge, 2015).
7. James Millar, "The Little Deal: Brezhnev's Contribution to Acquisitive Socialism," *Slavic Review* 44, no. 4 (1985): 694–706.
8. Hobsbawm, *Age of Extremes*; Denning, *Culture in the Age of Three Worlds*.
9. On moral panics, see Stanley Cohen, *Folk Devils and Moral Panics: The Creation of the Mods and Rockers* (London: MacGibbon and Kee, 1972).
10. Hartman, *A War for the Soul of America*.
11. See Matthew Worley's "Shot by Both Sides," in *Youth Culture, Popular Music and the End of "Consensus,"* ed. The Subcultures Network (London: Routledge, 2015), 333–354, and "Oi! Oi! Oi!: Class, Locality and British Punk" in The Subcultures Network, *Fight Back*, 34–64.
12. The most prominent argument for punk's affiliation with the Right is Roger Sabin's in *Punk Rock, So What?* A constellation of cultural studies–influenced scholars have argued the opposing view, from Hebdige (*Subculture*) to Goodyer (*Crisis Music*).

13. See Martin Pugh, *State and Society Fourth Edition: A Social and Political History of Britain since 1870* (London: Bloomsbury Academic, 2012); Mark Hayes, *The New Right in Britain: An Introduction to Theory and Practice* (London: Pluto Press, 1994). For a comparative account, see Mazower, *Dark Continent*.
14. Cited in Andrew Adonis and Tim Hames, eds., *A Conservative Revolution? The Thatcher-Reagan Decade in Perspective* (Manchester: Manchester University Press 1994).
15. "Pop Concerts," Hansard, June 14, 1977, http://hansard.millbanksystems.com/commons/1977/jun/14/pop-concerts.
16. Matthew Arnold, *Culture and Anarchy* (1869; Oxford: Oxford University Press, 2006). For a useful introduction and excerpt, see John Storey, *Cultural Theory and Popular Culture: A Reader* (New York: Routledge, 2008). For more extensive analysis of Arnold, see Martin Ryle and Kate Soper, *To Relish the Sublime? Culture and Self-realisation in Postmodern Times* (New York: Verso, 2002).
17. *New Musical Express*, June 8, 1977; cited in Martin Cloonan, *Popular Music and the State in the UK: Culture, Trade, or Industry?* (Burlington, VT: Ashgate, 2007).
18. "Children and Young Persons Act 1969 (Amendment) Bill," Hansard, February 9, 1979, http://hansard.millbanksystems.com/commons/1979/feb/09/children-and-young-persons-act-1969#S5CV0962P0_19790209_HOC_33.
19. Savage, *England's Dreaming*.
20. *New Musical Express*, July 15, 1977.
21. Savage, *England's Dreaming*.
22. Lydon, Zimmerman, and Zimmerman, *Rotten*, 192.
23. Gilbert, *Passion Is a Fashion*, 177.
24. Edward Meadows, "Pistol-Whipped," *National Review*, November 11, 1977. Reprinted in Duncombe and Tremblay, *White Riot*, 54–56.
25. Goodyer, *Crisis Music*.
26. Ibid.
27. Gilbert, *Passion Is a Fashion*.
28. Ibid.
29. Quoted in Dorian Lynskey, *33 Revolutions per Minute: A History of Protest Songs, from Billie Holiday to Green Day* (New York: Ecco, 2011).
30. Goodyer, *Crisis Music*.
31. Sandy Robertson, "Sham 69: Son of Sham," *Sounds*, April 29, 1978. Cited in Duncombe and Tremblay, *White Riot*.
32. Worley, "Shot by Both Sides."
33. Jack M. Bloom, *Seeing through the Eyes of the Polish Revolution: Solidarity and the Struggle against Communism in Poland* (Chicago: Haymarket Books, 2014), 101.
34. R. J. Crampton, *Eastern Europe in the Twentieth Century* (London: Routledge, 1994), 367–376.
35. For the argument that Stalin inverted Marx's base-superstructure model, see Moshe Lewin, *The Making of the Soviet System: Essays in the Social History of Interwar Russia* (New York: Pantheon Books, 1985). For discussion of efforts to create a new Soviet man, see Jochen Hellbeck, *Revolution on My Mind: Writing a Diary under Stalin* (Cambridge, MA: Harvard University Press, 2006); for early Soviet debates on music, see Neil Edmunds, *The Soviet Proletarian Music Movement* (Oxford: Peter Lang, 2000); for culture in general, see David Hoffman, *Socialist Values: The Cultural Norms of Soviet Modernity, 1917–1941* (Ithaca, NY: Cornell University Press, 2003).
36. For a pioneering account of the debates over jazz, see S. Frederick Starr, *Red and Hot: The Fate of Jazz in the Soviet Union, 1917–1980* (New York: Oxford University Press, 1983).
37. Lisa Cooper Vest, "Shades of Cultural Backwardness: Negotiations between Composers and the State in Communist Poland, 1955–1958" (paper presented at the Annual Convention of the Association of Slavic, East European and Eurasian Studies, San Antonio, TX, November 2014).
38. Gregory Kveberg, "Shostakovich versus Boney M: Culture, Status, and History in the Debate over Soviet Diskoteki," in Risch, *Youth and Rock in the Soviet Bloc*.

39. "Festiwał nie wykorzystanych szans," *Walka Młodych*, August 27, 1978.
40. Andrzej "Ibis" Wróblewski, "Karaf Sound," *Literatura*, November 14, 1979; cited in Robert, "Co w prasie piszczy: Konflikt Pokoleń," *Non Stop*, January 1980.
41. Marian Butrym, "Zjawisko zwane MAANAM," *Razem*, April 19, 1981, 14–15.
42. Komitet Strajkowy, Pracownikow Kultury NSZZ "Solidarność," December 11, 1980, Number 52, Dissent in Poland, KARTA collection.
43. Jan Kubik, *The Power of Symbols against the Symbols of Power* (University Park: Pennsylvania State University Press, 1994), describes the culture wars between the party and Solidarity in detail.
44. PZPR, Komisja Zjazdowa, "Założenia programowe rozwoju socjalistycznej demokracji, umacniania przewodniej roli PZPR w budownictwie socjalistycznym i stabilizacji sytuacji społeczno-gospodarczej kraju," March 1981, 1354 PZPR KC w Warszawie Pion Środowiskowy, XL/1, Archiwum Akt Nowych, Warsaw, Poland.
45. Wydział Organizacji Społecznych, Sportu i Turystyki KC, "Informacja o wybranych problemach młodego pokolenia, sytuacji w ruchu młodzieżowym i zadaniach partii," January 1981, 1354 PZPR KC w Warszawie Pion Środowiskowy, XL/135, Archiwum Akt Nowych, Warsaw, Poland; Wydział Organizacji Społecznych, Sportu i Turystyki, "Tezy do wystąpienia nt: Młodzieży," 1981.
46. PZPR, Komisja Zjazdowa, "Założenia programowe rozwoju socjalistycznej demokracji, umacniania przewodniej roli PZPR w budownictwie socjalistycznym i stabilizacji sytuacji społeczno-gospodarczej kraju."
47. Roman Radoszewski, "Trzeci Etap Ekspansji," *Non Stop*, July 1980.
48. Jarocin 1981 Program, http://www.jarocin-festiwal.com/1981/folder81/folder81.html; Krzysztof Hipsz, "Na starcie—Jarocin 81," *Na Przełaj*, July 12, 1981.
49. Wydział Kultury KW PZPR Gdańsk, "Informacja dotycząca przebiegu I Przeglądu Piosenki Prawdziwej pt. "Zakazane Piosenki," August 1981, 1354 Wydział Kultury PZPR, 315, 889/50, Archiwum Akt Nowych, Warsaw, Poland. An electronic reproduction of the festival program can be found at http://www.dolinaradości.pl/pppp/03.htm.
50. Solidarity produced a cassette with recordings of the performance in 1981: *Zakazane piosenki—I Przegląd Piosenki Prawdziwej*, Radiową Agencję Solidarność Gdańsk, 1981. A version was also produced in the United States: *Piosenki Solidarności (Songs of Solidarity)* ECHO E 901-2, 1981.
51. Mikołaj Lizut, *Punk Rock Later* (Warsaw: Wydawnictwo Sic!, 2003).
52. Various Artists, *Niepokorni: I Przegląd Piosenki Prawdziwej*, Polskie Radio S.A., 2014.
53. Kenney, *A Carnival of Revolution*.
54. Lizut, *Punk Rock Later*, 54–55.
55. Gilbert, *Passion Is a Fashion*.
56. Lizut, *Punk Rock Later*.
57. MKiS: Department Teatru i Estrady, "Próba oceny sezonu 1980/81 w teatrach dramatycznych, lalkowych i na estradach," December 9, 1981, 1354 Wydział Kultury PZPR, 286, 889/21, Archiwum Akt Nowych, Warsaw, Poland.

Chapter 5

1. The Ruts, "Jah War / SUS," Virgin 2141 248, 1979.
2. Lynskey, *33 Revolutions per Minute*.
3. Andrzej Turczynowicz, "Number 3," *Kanal Review*, 1980.
4. Stuart Hall, "The Great Moving Right Show," *Marxism Today*, January 1979.
5. Barbara Dąbrowska, "Dzieci śmieci," *Na Przełaj*, January 4, 1981.
6. *Maximum Rocknroll*, no. 1 (July–August 1982): 3.
7. Lydon, Zimmerman, and Zimmerman, *Rotten*.
8. Berlant, *The Queen of America Goes to Washington City*.
9. Kazimierz Poznanski, *Poland's Protracted Transition: Institutional Change and Economic Growth 1970–1994* (Cambridge: Cambridge University Press, 1996).

10. Matthew Worley, "Oi! Oi! Oi!."
11. Alexis Patridis, "Ska for the Madding Crowd," *The Guardian*, March 8, 2002; cited in Thompson, *Wheels Out of Gear*.
12. Cited in Thompson, *Wheels Out of Gear*.
13. Burden, *Women of the Underground*.
14. Thompson, *Wheels Out of Gear*, 164.
15. Hayes, *The New Right in Britain*.
16. Ibid.
17. Thompson, *Wheels Out of Gear*.
18. Cited in Adonis and Hames, *A Conservative Revolution?*, 10.
19. Jimmy Carter, "Address to the Nation on Energy and National Goals," July 15, 1979, http://www.pbs.org/wgbh/americanexperience/features/primary-resources/carter-crisis/.
20. See Adonis and Hames, *A Conservative Revolution?*; and Sean Wilentz, *The Age of Reagan: A History, 1974–2008* (New York: Harper Perennial, 2009).
21. Gillian Peele, "Culture, Religion and Public Morality," in Adonis and Hames, *A Conservative Revolution?*; Wilentz, *The Age of Reagan*.
22. Anderson, *Dance of Days*.
23. Ibid.
24. Boulware and Tudor, *Gimme Something Better*.
25. Stevie Chick, *Spray Paint the Walls: The Story of Black Flag* (Oakland, CA: PM Press, 2011).
26. Gabriel Kuhn, *Sober Living for the Revolution: Hardcore Punk, Straight Edge, and Radical Politics* (Oakland, CA: PM Press, 2010).
27. David Ensminger, *Left of the Dial: Conversations with Punk Icons* (Oakland, CA: PM Press, 2012).
28. Ibid.
29. Ibid.
30. Lynskey, *33 Revolutions per Minute*.
31. *Maximum Rocknroll*, no. 1 (July–August 1982): 3.
32. Ibid.
33. Boulware and Tudor, *Gimme Something Better*.
34. Anderson, *Dance of Days*.
35. Wiesław Królikowski, "Ostry rock'n'roll," *Magazyn Muzyczny—Jazz*, January 1988.
36. Mikołaj Lizut, "Bezpieka w Jarocinie—rozmowa z Walterem Chełstowskim," *Gazeta Wyborcza*, November 25, 2003.
37. Footage can be seen in Mariusz Treliński, *Film o pankach* (Poland: Państwowa Wyższa Szkoła Filmowa Telewizyjna i Teatralna, 1983).
38. Kora Jackowska, "Rock 'n' Roll Rebellion in Poland: An Interview with Kora," interview by Piotr Westwalewicz, University of Michigan, Ann Arbor, MI, March 5, 2004.
39. Egzekutywa KMiG PZPR w Jarocinie, "Protokol nr 23/82: Posiedzenie Egzekutywy KMiG PZPR w Jarocinie z dnia 18.2.1982," February 18, 1982, 868 Komitet Miasto i Gmina PZPR w Jarocinie, 30, Archiwum Panstwowe w Kaliszu, Kalisz, Poland.
40. Egzekutywa KMiG PZPR w Jarocinie, "Protokol nr 24/82r.," February 25, 1982, 868 Komitet Miasto i Gmina PZPR w Jarocinie, 30, Archiwum Panstwowe w Kaliszu, Kalisz, Poland.
41. Wydział Kultury KK PZPR (Kraków), "Stan i rozmieszczenie sil Partii w środowisku kultury Krakówa," July 1982, 1354 Wydział Kultury PZPR, 936, 923/65, Archiwum Akt Nowych, Warsaw, Poland.
42. Jacek Korczakowski, "Notatka z narady w sprawie XX Festiwalu Polskiej Piosenki w dniu 13 lipca 1982," 1982, 1354 Wydział Kultury PZPR, 396, 891/14, Archiwum Akt Nowych, Warsaw, Poland.
43. Egzekutywa KMiG PZPR w Jarocinie, "Protokol nr 37/82r.," June 3, 1982, 868 Komitet Miasto i Gmina PZPR w Jarocinie, 30, Archiwum Panstwowe w Kaliszu, Kalisz, Poland.
44. Jacek Krzeminski, "Bunt kontrolowany," *Rzeczpospolita*, August 11, 2000.
45. "Perspektywy Polskiej Kultury," *Trybuna Ludu*, October 23, 1982.

46. Urszula Biełous, "Woodstock w Jarocinie," *Polityka*, no. 29, 1982; Rafał Szczęsny Wagnerowski, "Bania z festiwalami," *Non Stop*, October 1982.
47. L-P, "Punk-rock-Estrada w Lodzi," *Non Stop*, January 1983.
48. Sekretarz KW-G PZPR w Swiebodzinie, Miroslaw Algierski, "Opinia o pracy Swiebodzinskiego Domu Kutlury w Swiebodzinie," May 1983, 1354 Wydział Kultury PZPR, 489, 897/44, Archiwum Akt Nowych, Warsaw, Poland.
49. MKiS, "Informacja o sytuacji w przemyśle fonograficznym," June 1984, 1354 Wydział Kultury PZPR, 746, 908/125, Archiwum Akt Nowych, Warsaw, Poland.
50. Redakcja, "Zamiast Wstępu," *Forum Rozrywki*, 1983, 1.
51. Marek Wiernik, "Nadzieje: Kora i Maanam," *Forum Rozrywki*, 1983; Jerzy Wertenstein-Żuławski, "Semiotyka kultury młodzieżowej."
52. Wydział Organizacji Społecznych, Sportu i Turystyki, "Tezy do Wystąpienia nt: Młodzieży," 1981,1354 PZPR KC w Warszawie Pion Środowiskowy, XL/125, Archiwum Akt Nowych, Warsaw, Poland.
53. Zespół ds Młodzieży KC PZPR, "Program III Polskiego Radia," 1984, 1354 PZPR KC w Warszawie Pion Środowiskowy, XLIII/34, Archiwum Akt Nowych, Warsaw, Poland.
54. Marek Niedźwiecki, *Lista Przebojów Programu Trzeciego: 1982–1994* (Wrocław: W. Bagiński, 1996).
55. Ibid.
56. Ibid.
57. Ibid.
58. Wojciech Soporek, "Mister Pank: Rozmowa z Andrzejem Mogielnickim," *Non Stop*, November 1983.
59. Jolanta Dylewska, Aldona Krajewska, and Jacek Szmidt, "To Tylko Lady Pank," *Na Przełaj*, December 23, 1984, 3.
60. Witold Pawlowski, "I krzyk i płacz," *Magazyn Muzyczny—Jazz*, February 1984.
61. Dylewska, Krajewska, and Szmidt, "To Tylko Lady Pank."
62. Ensminger, *Left of the Dial*.
63. Andrzej Kołodziejski, "Różowy ciołg w Manhattanie," *Polityka*, no. 14, 1985.
64. Lizut, *Punk Rock Later*.
65. "Kochani nasi bracia cieszcie się z życia," *Brumu*, 1994.
66. Królikowski, "Ostry rock'n'roll."
67. Dezerter, *Ku przyszłości*, Tonpress N-65, 1983.
68. Ibid.

Chapter 6

1. Hebdige, *Subculture*.
2. Sławomir Gołaszewski, *Reggae-Rastafari* (Bydgoszcz: Wydawnictwo Pomorze, 1990).
3. Andrew Nash, "Third Worldism," *African Sociological Review* 7, no. 1 (2003): 94–116.
4. Quinones, "Mexico's Globophobe Punks."
5. George Lipsitz, *Dangerous Crossroads: Popular Music, Postmodernism, and the Poetics of Place* (New York: Verso, 1994); Homi K. Bhabha, *The Location of Culture* (London: Routledge, 1994); Bhabha, "The Third Space. Interview with Homi Bhabha," *Identity: Community, Culture, Difference*, ed. Jonathan Rutherford (London: Lawrence and Wishart, 1998), 207–221. See also Huq, *Beyond Subculture*.
6. See Carolyn Cooper, *Sound Clash* (New York: Palgrave Macmillan, 2004); Vijay Prashad, *The Darker Nations: A People's History of the Third World* (New York: New Press, 2007).
7. For a comparative account of the legitimacy crisis of states in the Second and Third Worlds, see Bogumil Jewsiewicki, V. Y. Mudimbe, Kathryn Barrett-Gaines, and Nadine LeMeur, "Meeting the Challenge of Legitimacy: Post-independence Black African and Post-Soviet European States," *Daedalus* 124, no. 3 (Summer 1995): 191–207.
8. Deborah A. Thomas, *Modern Blackness: Nationalism, Globalization, and the Politics of Culture in Jamaica* (Durham, NC: Duke University Press, 2004).

9. Ibid.
10. Stephen King and Renee Foster, "Revolutionary Words: Reggae's Evolution from Protest to Mainstream" (paper presented at the National Conference of the Popular Culture Association/American Culture Association, Washington, DC, March 2013).
11. Chang and Chen, *Reggae Routes*, 57.
12. For a fascinating account and analysis of the song and music video, see Lipsitz, *Dangerous Crossroads*.
13. Romek Rogowiecki, "Issiael: Pozytywna Wibracja," *Non Stop*, June 1983.
14. Lizut, *Punk Rock Later*.
15. Brygada Kryzys, *Brygada Kryzys*, Tonpress SX-T16, 1982.
16. Jacques de Koning, *I Could Live in Africa* (Poland: self-published, 1983); Lizut, *Punk Rock Later*.
17. Rogowiecki, "Issiael: Pozytywna Wibracja."
18. Andrzej Wójtowicz and Sławek Rogowski, eds., *Pamiętajcie o . . . Hybrydy* (Warsaw: BPiM Filmar, 2002).
19. Ibid.; Lizut, *Punk Rock Later*.
20. Jacek Słowiński. "Dziury w Głowie," *Razem*, January 29, 1984.
21. Naomi Marcus, "The Rooms Off Nevsky Prospect: A Decade in Aquarium," *Village Voice*, January 31, 1989, 27–33.
22. Timothy J. Cooley, *Making Music in the Polish Tatras: Tourists, Ethnographers, and Mountain Musicians* (Bloomington: Indiana University Press, 2005).
23. Rimbaud, *Shibboleth*.
24. Montgomery Wolf, "Dreaming of World War III" (paper presented at the Annual Meeting of the American Historical Association, Chicago, IL, January 2012).
25. Circle Jerks, *Wild in the Streets*, Faulty Products COPE 03, 1982.
26. Hayes, *The New Right in Britain*; Stanislao G. Pugliese, *The Political Legacy of Margaret Thatcher* (London: Politico's, 2003).
27. Rimbaud, *Shibboleth*.
28. Lynskey, *33 Revolutions per Minute*.
29. Thompson, *Wheels Out of Gear*.
30. Rimbaud, *Shibboleth*, 219.
31. Lynskey, *33 Revolutions per Minute*.
32. Westad, *The Global Cold War*.
33. Jeff Goldthorpe, "Intoxicated Culture: Punk Symbolism and Punk Protest," *Socialist Review* 22, no. 2 (1992) : 35–64.
34. Ibid.
35. Al Flipside, *Flipside*, Halloween 1984, 2; cited in Wolf, "Dreaming of World War III."
36. Lynskey, *33 Revolutions per Minute*.
37. Anderson, *Dance of Days*.
38. Ibid, 181.
39. Gilbert, *Passion Is a Fashion*.
40. Ibid.
41. Cited in Paul Gilroy, *There Ain't No Black in the Union Jack* (London: Hutchinson, 1987).
42. For a lucid discussion of the various uses and meanings of the term, see Paul James, *Globalism, Nationalism, Tribalism: Bringing Theory Back In* (London: Sage, 2006).
43. Greil Marcus, "Crimes against Nature," in Duncombe and Tremblay, *White Riot*, 80.
44. Chick, *Spray Paint the Walls*.
45. Ibid.
46. Ibid.
47. Tim Tonooka, "We Are Tired of Your Abuse Try to Stop Us It's No Use," *Ripper* 6 (October 31, 1981); posted at Kill from the Heart, https://files.nyu.edu/cch223/public/usa/info/blackflag_ripperinter.html.
48. Jonathyne Briggs, "Force de Frappe" (paper presented at the Annual Meeting of the American Historical Association, Chicago, IL, January 2012).

49. Jeffrey Kaplan, *Encyclopedia of White Power: A Sourcebook on the Radical Racist Right* (Walnut Creek, CA: AltaMira Press, 2000); Mattias Gardell, *Gods of the Blood: The Pagan Revival and White Separatism* (Durham, NC: Duke University Press, 2003).
50. See especially Timothy Scott Brown, "From England with Hate," in Brown and Anton, *Between the Avant-Garde and the Everyday*.
51. Kenney, *A Carnival of Revolution*, 185.
52. Sabrina Ramet, "Shake, Rattle, and Self-Management: Making the Scene in Yugoslavia," in Ramet, *Rocking the State*.
53. Biba Kopf, "Laibach—and Think of England!," *New Musical Express*, April 4, 1987, 24.
54. Siekiera, *Na wszystkich frontach świata* (Poland: Manufaktura Legenda, 2009).
55. Urszula Biełous, "Odchwaszczane Jarocina," *Polityka*, no. 33, 1984, 9.
56. Ibid.
57. Lizut, *Punk Rock Later*.
58. Jacek Korczak, *Non Stop*, July 1984.
59. Krzystof Masłoń, "Zakręcony Punk," *Razem*, April 14, 1985.
60. Kamil Sipowicz, "Mister Pank," *Razem*, January 13, 1985.
61. See Fenemore, *Sex, Thugs and Rock 'n' Roll*, for an account of East Germany.
62. Ryback, *Rock around the Bloc*; Laszlo Kurti, "How Can I Be a Human Being? Culture, Youth, and Musical Opposition in Hungary," in Ramet, *Rocking the State*.
63. Ryback, *Rock around the Bloc*.
64. Anna Pełka, *Z Politycznym Fasonem* (Gdańsk: Terytoria, 2013).
65. Interview with Iron Cross, *Touch and Go* 16 (December 1981); cited in Anderson, *Dance of Days*.
66. Anderson, *Dance of Days*.
67. Ibid.
68. Goldthorpe, "Intoxicated Culture."
69. Steve Waksman, *This Ain't the Summer of Love: Conflict and Crossover in Heavy Metal and Punk* (Berkeley: University of California Press, 2009).
70. Wojciech Soporek. "Plebiscyt Non Stopu: Najpopularniejsi w Roku 1984," *Non Stop*, January 1985.
71. Wojciech Soporek, "Wybralem Heavy Metal," *Non Stop*, October 1984, 6–7.

Chapter 7

1. Riordan, *Soviet Youth Culture*; Gregory Kveberg, "Moscow by Night: Musical Subcultures, Identity Formation, and Cultural Evolution in Russia, 1977–2008" (PhD diss., University of Illinois, 2012).
2. Eric Nuzum, *Parental Advisory: Music Censorship in America* (New York: Perennial, 2001).
3. Hartman, *A War for the Soul of America*.
4. Hunter, *Culture Wars*.
5. Joint Publications Research Service, *East Europe Report*, February 10, 1984.
6. Zhuk, *Rock and Roll in the Rocket City*.
7. Daniel Passent, "Elektrificacja plus epilepsja," *Polityka*, no. 28, 1983, 16.
8. Allan Bloom, *The Closing of the American Mind* (New York: Simon and Schuster, 1987).
9. Anna Romaszkan, "Grzywy i Czubki," *Polityka*, no. 13, 1984.
10. Urszula Biełous, "Nie tylko rock . . . ," *Trybuna Ludu*, June 28, 1984.
11. Adam Ciesielski, "Opole '84: Barometr Estrady," *Życie Warszawy*, June 30, 1984.
12. Stanislaw Kosicki, Główny Urzad Kontroli Publikacji i Widowisk, "Zgloszenie Z Gruszeckiego do młodzieżowych utworow wokalnych," May 1984, 1354 Wydział Kultury PZPR, 976, 923/105, Archiwum Akt Nowych, Warsaw, Poland.
13. Zespół Polskiego Radia, "Polskie Radio," May 1984, 1354 Wydział Kultury PZPR, 1271, 947/60, Archiwum Akt Nowych, Warsaw, Poland.
14. Kosicki, "Zgloszenie Z Gruszeckiego do młodzieżowych utworow wokalnych," May 1984, 1354 Wydział Kultury PZPR, 976, 923/105, Archiwum Akt Nowych, Warsaw, Poland.

15. Wydział Kultury KC PZPR, "Ocena Krajowego Festiwalu Polskiej Piosenki "Opole 1984," July 1984, 1354 Wydział Kultury PZPR, 685, 908/65, Archiwum Akt Nowych, Warsaw, Poland.
16. Ibid.; Wydział Kultury KC PZPR, Władz Opolskich, MKiS, ZSMP, "Ocena Przebiegu XXI Krajowego festiwalu Polskiej Piosenki—Opole '84," July 1984, 1354 Wydział Kultury PZPR, 685, 908/65, Archiwum Akt Nowych, Warsaw, Poland; Komisja Kultury KC PZPR, "Materialy z posiedzenia Komisji Kultury KC PZPR," June 11, 1984, 1354 Wydział Kultury PZPR, 746, 908/125, Archiwum Akt Nowych, Warsaw, Poland.
17. "Associated Press o festiwalu muzyki rockowej w Jarocinie," August 1984, 1354 Wydział Kultury PZPR, 684, 908/64, Archiwum Akt Nowych, Warsaw, Poland.
18. Zespół ds Młodzieży KC PZPR, "Informacja o zjawiskach patologii społecznej wśród młodzieży," August 1984, 1354 Wydział Kultury PZPR, 761, 908/141, Archiwum Akt Nowych, Warsaw, Poland.
19. A. Kaczmarek: Wydział Kultury PZPR KC, "Notatka Informacyjna," January 1985, 1354 Wydział Kultury PZPR, 1027, 924/49, Archiwum Akt Nowych, Warsaw, Poland.
20. Andrzej Kozlowski, Sekretarz ZG ZSMP, "Zarząd Główny Związku Socjalistycznej Młodzieży Polskiej prosi o wydanie zgody na wyjazd do NRD grup artystycznych "Budka Suflera" i "Combi" na światowy Festwial Pieśni Politycznej w Berlinie," February 1985, 1354 Wydział Kultury PZPR, 1066, 924/87, Archiwum Akt Nowych, Warsaw, Poland.
21. Zespół partyjny do sprawy Upowszechniania Kultury, "Kultura w radio i telewizji /Uwagi dotyczace centralnych programow PR i TV/," 1985, 1354 Wydział Kultury PZPR, 924/33, Archiwum Akt Nowych, Warsaw, Poland.
22. "Kultury w Polskim Radiu i Telewizji," July 1985, 1354 Wydział Kultury PZPR, 1701, 982/47, Archiwum Akt Nowych, Warsaw, Poland.
23. A. Kaczmarek: Wydział Kultury PZPR KC, "Estrada i rozrywka masów / Problemy do materialu na Biuro Polityczne/," March 1986, 1354 Wydział Kultury PZPR, 1325, 947/115, Archiwum Akt Nowych, Warsaw, Poland.
24. Hartman, *A War for the Soul of America*.
25. Linda Martin and Kerry Segrave, *Anti-rock: The Opposition to Rock 'n' Roll* (New York: Da Capo Press, 1993).
26. Ibid.
27. Nuzum, *Parental Advisory*.
28. Ibid.
29. Ibid.
30. Hartman, *A War for the Soul of America*.
31. Bernard Weinraub, "Rock Lyrics Irk Reagan," *New York Times*, October 9, 1985.
32. Nuzum, *Parental Advisory*.
33. Hunter, *Culture Wars*.
34. Nuzum, *Parental Advisory*.
35. Ibid. See also Steven Wishnia, "Of Punk and Pornography: Rockin' with the First Amendment," *Nation* 245, no. 13 (October 24, 1987): 444.
36. Nuzum, *Parental Advisory*.
37. Boulware and Tudor, *Gimme Something Better*.
38. Nuzum, *Parental Advisory*.
39. Michael Goodwin, "Parks Chief Says the Shows Will Go On, but with Changes," *New York Times*, July 26, 1983, http://www.nytimes.com/1983/07/26/nyregion/parks-chief-says-the-shows-will-go-on-but-with-changes.html.
40. *Ward v. Rock Against Racism*, 491 U.S. 781 (1989), https://supreme.justia.com/cases/federal/us/491/781/case.html.
41. Jeffrey Toobin, *The Oath: The Obama White House and the Supreme Court* (New York: Doubleday, 2012), supports the argument that this era was characterized by broader politicization and conservative ascendancy in the Supreme Court.
42. Michael McFaul, *Russia's Unfinished Revolution* (Ithaca, NY: Cornell University Press, 2001).
43. Hilary Pilkington, *Russia's Youth and Its Culture: A Nation's Constructors and Constructed* (New York: Routledge, 1994).

44. Cited in Paul Easton, "The Rock Music Community," in Riordan, *Soviet Youth Culture*.
45. Witold Nawrocki, Kierownik Wydziału Kultury KC PZPR, "Letter to Polish Radio," December 1985, 1354 Wydział Kultury PZPR, 1027, 924/49, Archiwum Akt Nowych, Warsaw, Poland.
46. Ibid.
47. "Punk podwojnie widziany," *Na Przełaj*, December 8, 1985, December 22, 1985, December 29, 1985.
48. "Punk podwojnie widziany," *Na Przełaj*, January 5, 1986.
49. "Punk podwojnie widziany," *Na Przełaj*, December 15, 1985; January 5, 1986.
50. "Punk podwojnie widziany," *Na Przełaj*, January 5, 1986.
51. "Punk podwojnie widziany," *Na Przełaj*, December 29, 1985.
52. "Punk podwojnie widziany," *Na Przełaj*, December 15, 1985.
53. "Punk podwojnie widziany," *Na Przełaj*, December 8, 1985, December 22, 1985, December 29, 1985.
54. "Punk podwojnie widziany," *Na Przełaj*, December 22, 1985.
55. Aldona Krajewska, "Koalang," *Na Przełaj*, March 16, 1986, 5.
56. Paweł Wyrzykowski, "Sztuka Podrywania," *Razem*, April 6, 1986, 6.
57. Ibid.
58. Piotr Lazarkiewicz, *Fala* (Poland: Studio Filmowe im. Karola Irzykowskiego, 1986).
59. Krzysztof Lesiakowski, *Jarocin w Obietywie Bezpieki* (Warsaw: Instytut Pamięci Narodowej, 2004).
60. Paweł Sito, "Centralne dożynki: Jarocin '86," *Magazyn Muzyczny—Jazz*, September 1986, 28–29.
61. Andrzej Kostenko, *My Blood, Your Blood* (UK: BBC, 1986).
62. Lesiakowski, *Jarocin w Obiektywie Bezpieki*.
63. Zbigniew Zaranek, "ODIUM SATANIZMU W WĄGROWCU," *Dwutygodnik Pałucki*, March 15, 1991, http://www.jarocin-festiwal.com/zespóły/tfk/j85-86/zaraneko.html.
64. Jacek Krzeminski, "Bunt kontrolowany," *Rzeczpospolita*, August 11, 2000.
65. Aleksander Kwaśniewski, May 1987, 1354 Wydział Kultury PZPR, 1536, 960/118, Archiwum Akt Nowych, Warsaw, Poland.
66. Forum Myśli Katolicko Społecznej, "List otwarty do Naczelnika Miasta i Gminy w Jarocinie," 1987, 1354 Wydział Kultury PZPR, 1555, 960/129-1, Archiwum Akt Nowych, Warsaw, Poland.
67. M. Slowinski, "Letter to Sekretarz KC PZPR," October 1987, 1354 Wydzial Kultury PZPR, 1556, 960/129-2, Archiwum Akt Nowych, Warsaw, Poland.
68. Ibid.
69. Ibid.
70. Wydział Kultury KC PZPR, "Notatka na temat Festiwalu Muzyki Rockowej 'Jarocin '88," April 1988, 1354 Wydział Kultury PZPR, 1799, 982/145, Archiwum Akt Nowych, Warsaw, Poland.
71. Mirosław Soliwoda, *Świata Młodych*, 1988; "Festiwal Rockowy Jarocin," *Non Stop*, September 1988, 3.

1989: Conclusion and Epilogue

1. Boulware and Tudor, *Gimme Something Better*.
2. See Timothy Garton Ash, *The Polish Revolution: Solidarity* (New York: Scribner, 1984); Ash, *The Magic Lantern: The Revolution of '89 Witnessed in Warsaw, Budapest, Berlin, and Prague* (New York: Random House, 1990).
3. Lizut, *Punk Rock Later*.
4. Stephen Kotkin, *Uncivil Society: 1989 and Implosion of the Communist Establishment* (New York: Modern Library, 2009).
5. McFaul, *Russia's Unfinished Revolution*.
6. Pilkington, *Russia's Youth and Its Culture*.

7. Artemy Troitsky, *Back in the USSR: The True Story of Rock in Russia* (Boston: Faber and Faber, 1987).
8. Lilia Shevtsova, "Russia's Post-communist Politics," in *The New Russia: Troubled Transformation*, ed. Gail W. Lapidus (Boulder, CO: Westview Press, 1995), 5–31.
9. Clover, *1989*.
10. Westad, *The Global Cold War*.
11. Boulware and Tudor, *Gimme Something Better*.
12. Lizut, *Punk Rock Later*, 147.
13. Ibid., 130.
14. Ibid.
15. Ibid., 13–21.
16. Ibid., 43.
17. Ibid., 46.
18. Anita Zuchora and Sebastian Łupak, "Zapomniani Buntownicy," *Wprost*, June 22, 2013, http://www.wprost.pl/ar/235392/Zapomniani-buntownicy/.
19. Anna Szemere, *Up from the Underground: The Culture of Rock Music in Postsocialist Hungary* (University Park: Pennsylvania State University Press, 2001).
20. See Jon F. Hale, "The Making of the New Democrats," *Political Science Quarterly* 110, no. 2 (1995): 207–232.
21. Rupa Huq, "Resistance or incorporation? Youth Policy Making and Hip Hop Culture," in Hodkinson and Deicke, *Youth Cultures*, 79–92.
22. Jen Angel, "David Solnit and the Arts of Change," *Journal of Aesthetics and Protest*, June 2009, http://joaap.org/webonly/solnit_angel.htm. See also Boulware and Tudor, *Gimme Something Better*.
23. See, for example, Emma Baulch, *Making Scenes: Reggae, Punk, and Death Metal in 1990s Bali* (Durham, NC: Duke University Press, 2007); Heather Hendman, "Anarchism Ke Ho" (paper presented at the National Conference of the Popular Culture Association/American Culture Association, Washington, DC, March 2013); and Keith Jones, *Punk in Africa* (US: MVD Visual, 2013).
24. Mike Lerner and Maxim Pozdorovkin, *Pussy Riot: A Punk Prayer* (UK: Roast Beef Productions, 2013).

Bibliography, Discography, and Videography

Archives and Government Documents

Archiwum Akt Nowych, Warsaw, Poland
Archiwum Panstwowe w Kaliszu, Kalisz, Poland
Dissent in Poland, KARTA Center Foundation Archives (microfilm)
East Europe Report, Joint Publications Research Service
Hansard, Parliament of the United Kingdom
Transcript, US Senate Committee on Commerce, Science, and Transportation

Newspapers and Magazines

Chicago Tribune (US)
Dwutygodnik Pałucki (Poland)
Forum Rozrywki (Poland)
Gazeta Wyborcza (Poland)
The Guardian (UK)
Los Angeles Times (US)
Magazyn Muzyczny (Jazz: Magazyn Muzyczny; Magazyn Muzyczny—Jazz) (Poland)
Na Przełaj (Poland)
New Musical Express (UK)
New Republic (US)
New York Times (US)
Non Stop (Poland)
Nowy Dziennik (US)
Polityka (Poland)
Prague Post (Czech Republic)
Razem (Poland)
Rzeczpospolita (Poland)
Sounds (UK)
Sztandar Młodych (Poland)
Świata Młodych (Poland)
Trybuna Ludu (Poland)
Village Voice (US)
Walka Młodych (Poland)
Wprost (Poland)
Życie Warszawy (Poland)

'Zines and Pamphlets

Brumu. Warsaw: 1994.
Flipside. Ed. Al Flipside. Los Angeles: 1984.
Kanal Review. Ed. Andrzej Turczynowicz. Warsaw: 1980.
Maximum Rocknroll. Ed. Tim Yohannan et al. San Francisco: 1982–1989.
Papier Białych Wulkanów. Ed. Jacek Lenartowicz. Warsaw: 1980–1981.
Post. Ed. Henryk Gajewski and Piotr Rypson. Warsaw: 1979–1981.
"Punk." Ed. Henryk Gajewski. Warsaw: 1979.
Ripper. Ed. Tim Tonooka. San Jose: 1981.

Books, Articles, and Dissertations

Adonis, Andrew and Tim Hames, eds. *A Conservative Revolution? The Thatcher-Reagan Decade in Perspective*. Manchester: Manchester University Press, 1994.

Adorno, Theodor. *The Culture Industry: Selected Essays on Mass Culture*. London: Routledge, 2001.

Andersen, Eric. *Fluxus East: Fluxus-Netzwerke in Mittelosteuropa: Ausstellungskatalog = Fluxus Networks in Central Eastern Europe: Exhibition Catalogue*. Berlin: Künstlerhaus Bethanien, 2007.

Andersen, Mark. *Dance of Days: Two Decades of Punk in the Nation's Capital*. New York: Akashic Books, 2003.

Anderson, Perry. *The Origins of Postmodernity*. New York: Verso, 1998.

Angel, Jen. "David Solnit and the Arts of Change." *Journal of Aesthetics and Protest*, June 2009. http://www.joaap.org/webonly/solnit_angel.htm.

Appadurai, Arjun. "The Ethnographic Imagination: Textual Constructions of Reality." *Theory, Culture and Society* 7 (1990), 295–310.

Appadurai, Arjun. *Modernity at Large: Cultural Dimensions of Globalization*. Minneapolis: University of Minnesota Press, 1996.

Arnold, Matthew. *Culture and Anarchy*. Oxford: Oxford University Press, 2006.

Ash, Timothy Garton. *The Magic Lantern: The Revolution of '89 Witnessed in Warsaw, Budapest, Berlin, and Prague*. New York: Random House, 1990.

Ash, Timothy Garton. *The Polish Revolution: Solidarity*. New York: Scribner, 1984.

Baulch, Emma. *Making Scenes: Reggae, Punk, and Death Metal in 1990s Bali*. Durham, NC: Duke University Press, 2007.

Belsito, Peter, and Bob Davis. *Hardcore California: A History of Punk and New Wave*. Berkeley: Last Gasp of San Francisco, 1983.

Berend, Ivan. *Central and Eastern Europe, 1944–1993: Detour from the Periphery to the Periphery*. Cambridge: Cambridge University Press, 1996.

Berlant, Lauren Gail. *The Queen of America Goes to Washington City: Essays on Sex and Citizenship*. Durham, NC: Duke University Press, 1997.

Bhabha, Homi K. *The Location of Culture*. London: Routledge, 1994.

Bloom, Allan. *The Closing of the American Mind*. New York: Simon and Schuster, 1987.

Bloom, Jack M. *Seeing through the Eyes of the Polish Revolution: Solidarity and the Struggle against Communism in Poland*. Chicago: Haymarket Books, 2014.

Bolton, Jonathan. *Worlds of Dissent: Charter 77, the Plastic People of the Universe, and Czech Culture under Communism*. Cambridge, MA: Harvard University Press, 2012.

Boulware, Jack, and Silke Tudor. *Gimme Something Better: The Profound, Progressive, and Occasionally Pointless History of Bay Area Punk from Dead Kennedys to Green Day*. New York: Penguin, 2009.

Bourdieu, Pierre. "The Forms of Capital." In *Handbook of Theory and Research for the Sociology of Education*, edited by John Richardson. New York: Greenwood Press, 1986, 241–258.

Bren, Paulina. *The Greengrocer and His TV: The Culture of Communism after the 1968 Prague Spring*. Ithaca, NY: Cornell University Press, 2010.

Bromberg, Craig. *The Wicked Ways of Malcolm McLaren*. New York: Perennial Library, 1989.

Brown, Timothy Scott, and Lorena Anton, eds. *Between the Avant-Garde and the Everyday: Subversive Politics in Europe from 1957 to the Present.* New York: Berghahn Books, 2011.

Brylewski, Robert and Rafał Księżyk. *Kryzys w Babilonie: Autobiografia.* Cracow: Wydawnictwo Literackie, 2012.

Burden, Zora von. *Women of the Underground: Music: Cultural Innovators Speak for Themselves.* San Francisco: Manic D Press, 2010.

Chang, Kevin O'Brien, and Wayne Chen. *Reggae Routes: The Story of Jamaican Music.* Philadelphia: Temple University Press, 1998.

Chick, Stevie. *Spray Paint the Walls: The Story of Black Flag.* Oakland, CA: PM Press, 2011.

Cloonan, Martin. *Popular Music and the State in the UK: Culture, Trade, or Industry?* Burlington, VT: Ashgate, 2007.

Clover, Jonathan. *1989: Bob Dylan Didn't Have This to Sing About.* Berkeley: University of California Press, 2009.

Cohen, Stanley. *Folk Devils and Moral Panics: The Creation of the Mods and Rockers.* London: MacGibbon and Kee, 1972.

Cook, James, ed. *The Cultural Turn in U.S. History: Past, Present, and Future.* Chicago: University of Chicago Press, 2008.

Cooley, Timothy J. *Making Music in the Polish Tatras: Tourists, Ethnographers, and Mountain Musicians.* Bloomington: Indiana University Press, 2005.

Cooper, Carolyn. *Sound Clash.* New York: Palgrave Macmillan, 2004.

Crampton, R. J. *Eastern Europe in the Twentieth Century.* New York: Routledge, 1994.

Dawson, Ashley. "Love Music, Hate Racism: The Cultural Politics of the Rock Against Racism Campaigns." *Postmodern Culture* 16, no. 1 (2005). https://muse.jhu.edu.

Denning, Michael. *Culture in the Age of Three Worlds.* London: Verso, 2004.

Denning, Michael. *Mechanic Accents: Dime Novels and Working-Class Culture in America.* London: Verso, 1987.

Donaghey, Jim. "Punk and Anarchism: UK, Poland, Indonesia." PhD diss., Loughborough University, 2016.

Duncombe, Stephen, and Maxwell Tremblay. *White Riot: Punk Rock and the Politics of Race.* New York: Verso, 2011.

Dunn, Kevin. *Global Punk: Resistance and Rebellion in Everyday Life.* London: Bloomsbury Publishing, 2016.

Edmunds, Neil. *The Soviet Proletarian Music Movement.* Oxford: Peter Lang, 2000.

Ensminger, David. *Left of the Dial: Conversations with Punk Icons.* Oakland, CA: PM Press, 2012.

Featherstone, Mike. *Global Culture.* London: Sage, 1990.

Featherstone, Mike. *Undoing Culture: Globalization, Postmodernism and Identity.* London: Sage, 1995.

Fehervary, Krisztina. "Goods and States: The Political Logic of State-Socialist Material Culture." *Comparative Studies in Society and History* 52, no. 2 (2009): 426–459.

Fenemore, Mark. *Sex, Thugs and Rock 'n' Roll: Teenage Rebels in Cold-War East Germany.* New York: Berghahn Books, 2007.

Ford, Simon. *Wreckers of Civilisation: The Story of COUM Transmissions and Throbbing Gristle.* London: Black Dog, 1999.

Frith, Simon. *Sound Effects: Youth, Leisure, and the Politics of Rock 'n' Roll.* New York: Pantheon Books, 1981.

Fulbrook, Mary. *Power and Society in the GDR, 1961–1979 the Normalisation of Rule?* New York: Berghahn Books, 2009.

Gardell, Mattias. *Gods of the Blood: The Pagan Revival and White Separatism.* Durham, NC: Duke University Press, 2003.

Garner, Ken. *The Peel Sessions.* London: BBC Books, 2007.

Garofalo, Reebee, ed. *Rockin' the Boat: Mass Music and Mass Movements.* Boston: South End Press, 1992.

Gilbert, Pat. *Passion Is a Fashion: The Real Story of the Clash.* Cambridge, MA: Da Capo Press, 2005.

Gilroy, Paul. *There Ain't No Black in the Union Jack*. London: Hutchinson, 1987.
Gołaszewski, Sławomir. *Reggae-Rastafari*. Bydgoszcz: Wydawnictwo Pomorze, 1990.
Goldthorpe, Jeff. "Intoxicated Culture: Punk Symbolism and Punk Protest." *Socialist Review* 22, no. 2 (1992): 35–64.
Goodyer, Ian. *Crisis Music: The Cultural Politics of Rock Against Racism*. Manchester: Manchester University Press, 2009.
Green, E. H. H. *Ideologies of Conservatism: Conservative Political Ideas in the Twentieth Century*. Oxford: Oxford University Press, 2002.
Hagen, Nina, Marcel Feige, and Jim Rakete. *Nina Hagen: That's Why the Lady Is a Punk*. Berlin: Schwarzkopf & Schwarzkopf, 2003.
Hale, Jon F. "The Making of the New Democrats." *Political Science Quarterly* 110, no. 2 (1995): 207–232.
Hall, Stuart. "The Great Moving Right Show," *Marxism Today*, January 1979.
Hall, Stuart. "Notes on Deconstructing the Popular." In *People's History and Socialist Theory*, edited by Raphael Samuel, 227–249. London: Routledge, 1981.
Hall, Stuart, and Tony Jefferson, eds. *Resistance through Rituals: Youth Subcultures in Post-war Britain*. London: Hutchinson, 1976.
Harrison, Brian. "The Rise Fall and Rise of Political Consensus in Britain since 1940." *History* 84, no. 274 (1999): 301–324.
Hartman, Andrew. *A War for the Soul of America: A History of the Culture Wars*. Chicago: University of Chicago Press, 2015.
Hayes, Mark. *The New Right in Britain: An Introduction to Theory and Practice*. Boulder, CO: Pluto Press, 1994.
Hebdige, Dick. *Subculture: The Meaning of Style*. London: Routledge, 1979.
Helbig, Adriana. *Hip Hop Ukraine: Music, Race, and African Migration*. Bloomington: Indiana University Press, 2014.
Hellbeck, Jochen. *Revolution on My Mind: Writing a Diary under Stalin*. Cambridge, MA: Harvard University Press, 2006.
Hobsbawm, Eric. *The Age of Extremes: A History of the World, 1914–1991*. New York: Pantheon Books, 1994.
Hodkinson, Paul, and Wolfgang Deicke, eds. *Youth Cultures: Scenes, Subcultures and Tribes*. New York: Routledge, 2007.
Hoffman, David. *Socialist Values: The Cultural Norms of Soviet Modernity, 1917–1941*. Ithaca, NY: Cornell University Press, 2003.
Howe, Zöe Street. *Typical Girls? The Story of the Slits*. London: Omnibus Press, 2009.
Hunter, James Davison. *Culture Wars: The Struggle to Define America*. New York: Basic Books, 1991.
Huq, Rupa. *Beyond Subculture: Pop, Youth, and Identity in a Postcolonial World*. London: Routledge, 2006.
James, Paul. *Globalism, Nationalism, Tribalism: Bringing Theory Back In*. London: Sage, 2006.
Jewsiewicki, Bogumil ,V. Y. Mudimbe, Kathryn Barrett-Gaines, and Nadine LeMeur, "Meeting the Challenge of Legitimacy: Post-independence Black African and Post-Soviet European States," *Daedalus* 124, no. 3 (Summer 1995): 191–207.
Kaplan, Jeffrey. *Encyclopedia of White Power: A Sourcebook on the Radical Racist Right*. Walnut Creek, CA: AltaMira Press, 2000.
Kasprzycki, Remigiusz. *Dekada Buntu: Punk w Polsce i Krajach Sasiednich w Latach 1977–1989*. Cracow: LIBRON, 2013.
Kenney, Padriac. *A Carnival of Revolution: Central Europe, 1989*. Princeton, NJ: Princeton University Press, 2003.
Kornai, Janos. *The Socialist System: The Political Economy of Communism*. Princeton, NJ: Princeton University Press, 1992.
Kotkin, Stephen. *Uncivil Society: 1989 and Implosion of the Communist Establishment*. New York: Modern Library, 2009.
Kubik, Jan. *The Power of Symbols against the Symbols of Power*. University Park: Pennsylvania State University Press, 1994.

Kuhn, Gabriel. *Sober Living for the Revolution: Hardcore Punk, Straight Edge, and Radical Politics*. Oakland, CA: PM Press, 2010.
Kveberg, Gregory. "Moscow by Night: Musical Subcultures, Identity Formation, and Cultural Evolution in Russia, 1977–2008." PhD diss., University of Illinois: 2012.
Lapidus, Gail, ed. *The New Russia: Troubled Transformation*. Boulder, CO: Westview Press, 1995.
Lesiakowski, Krzysztof. *Jarocin w Obietywie Bezpieki*. Warsaw: Instytut Pamięci Narodowej, 2004.
Letts, Don. *Culture Clash: Dread Meets Punk Rockers*. Edited by David Nobakht. London: SAF, 2007.
Lewin, Moshe. *The Making of the Soviet System: Essays in the Social History of Interwar Russia*. New York: Pantheon Books, 1985.
Lipsitz, George. *Dangerous Crossroads: Popular Music, Postmodernism, and the Poetics of Place*. New York: Verso, 1994.
Lizut, Mikołaj. *Punk Rock Later*. Warsaw: Wydawnictwo Sic!, 2003.
Lydon, John, Keith Zimmerman, and Kent Zimmerman. *Rotten: No Irish, No Blacks, No Dogs*. New York: Picador, 2008.
Lynskey, Dorian. *33 Revolutions per Minute: A History of Protest Songs, from Billie Holiday to Green Day*. New York: Ecco, 2011.
Machovec, Martin, ed. *Views from the Inside: Czech Underground Literature and Culture 1948–1989*. Prague: Katedra české literatury a literární vědy, Univerzita Karlova, 2006.
Marciniak, Marta. *Transnational Punk Communities in Poland: From Nihilism to Nothing Outside Punk*. Lanham, MD: Lexington Books, 2015.
Marcus, Greil. *Lipstick Traces: A Secret History of the Twentieth Century*. Cambridge, MA: Harvard University Press, 1989.
Martin, Linda, and Kerry Segrave. *Anti-rock: The Opposition to Rock 'n' Roll*. New York: Da Capo Press, 1993.
Mazower, Mark. *Dark Continent: Europe's Twentieth Century*. New York: Knopf, 1999.
McFaul, Michael. *Russia's Unfinished Revolution*. Ithaca, NY: Cornell University Press, 2001.
McNeil, Legs, and Gillian McCain. *Please Kill Me: The Uncensored Oral History of Punk*. New York: Grove Press, 1996.
Millar, James R. "The Little Deal: Brezhnev's Contribution to Acquisitive Socialism." *Slavic Review* 44, no. 4 (1985): 694–706.
Miller, G. Ann Stamp. *The Cultural Politics of the German Democratic Republic: The Voices of Wolf Biermann, Christa Wolf, and Heiner Müller*. Boca Raton, FL: Brown Walker Press, 2004.
Mitchell, Tony. "Mixing Pop and Politics: Rock Music in Czechoslovakia before and after the Velvet Revolution." *Popular Music* 11, no. 2 (1992): 187–203.
Muggleton, David. *Inside Subculture: The Postmodern Meaning of Style*. Oxford: Berg, 2000.
Nash, Andrew. "Third Worldism." *African Sociological Review* 7, no. 1 (2003): 94–116.
Nayak, Anoop. *Race, Place and Globalization: Youth Culture in a Changing World*. Oxford: Berg, 2003.
Nehring, Neil. *Popular Music, Gender, and Postmodernism: Anger Is an Energy*. Thousand Oaks, CA: Sage, 1997.
Niedźwiecki, Marek. *Lista Przebojów Programu Trzeciego: 1982–1994*. Wrocław: W. Bagiński, 1996.
Nuzum, Eric. *Parental Advisory: Music Censorship in America*. New York: Perennial, 2001.
O'Connor, Alan. "Local Scenes and Dangerous Crossroads: Punk and Theories of Cultural Hybridity." *Popular Music* 21, no. 2 (May 2002): 225–236.
O'Connor, Alan. *Punk Record Labels and the Struggle for Autonomy: The Emergence of DIY*. Lanham, MD: Lexington Books, 2008.
Ost, David. *The Defeat of Solidarity: Anger and Politics in Postcommunist Europe*. Ithaca, NY: Cornell University Press, 2005.
Ost, David. *Solidarity and the Politics of Anti-politics: Opposition and Reform in Poland since 1968*. Philadelphia: Temple University Press, 1990.
Patton, Raymond. "The Communist Culture Industry: The Music Business in 1980s Poland." *Journal of Contemporary History* 47 no. 2 (April 2012): 427–449.
Patton, Raymond. "Screamed Poetry: Rock in Poland's Last Decade of Communism." PhD diss., University of Michigan, 2011.

Payne, Anthony, and Paul K. Sutton. *Modern Caribbean Politics*. Baltimore: Johns Hopkins University Press, 1993.

Peel, John. *Margrave of the Marshes*. London: Bantam, 2005.

Pekacz, Jolanta. "Did Rock Smash the Wall? The Role of Rock in Political Transition." *Popular Music* 13, no. 1 (1994): 41–49.

Pełka, Anna. *Z Politycznym Fasonem*. Gdańsk: Terytoria, 2013.

Perkins, Lucian, and Henry Rollins. *Hard Art: DC 1979*. New York: Akashik Books, 2013.

Pilkington, Hilary. *Russia's Skinheads: Exploring and Rethinking Subcultural Lives*. London: Routledge, 2010.

Pilkington, Hilary *Russia's Youth and Its Culture: A Nation's Constructors and Constructed*. London: Routledge, 1994.

Piotrowski, Grzegorz. "Punk against Communism: The Jarocin Rock Festival and Revolting Youth in 1980s Poland." In *A European Youth Revolt*, edited by Knud Andresen and Bart van der Steen, 203–216. Houndmills, Basingstoke:: Palgrave Macmillan, 2016.

Poznański, Kazimierz. *Poland's Protracted Transition: Institutional Change and Economic Growth 1970–1994*. Cambridge: Cambridge University Press, 1996.

Prashad, Vijay. *The Darker Nations: A People's History of the Third World*. New York: New Press, 2007.

Pugh, Martin. *State and Society Fourth Edition: A Social and Political History of Britain since 1870*. London: Bloomsbury Academic, 2012.

Pugliese, Stanislao G. *The Political Legacy of Margaret Thatcher*. London: Politico's, 2003.

Purvis, Trevor, and Alan Hunt. "Discourse, Ideology, Discourse, Ideology . . ." *British Journal of Sociology* 44, no. 3 (September 1993): 473–499.

Quinones, Sam. "Mexico's Globophobe Punks." *Foreign Policy*, no. 138 (September–October 2003): 78–79.

Ramet, Sabrina Petra, ed. *Rocking the State: Rock Music and Politics in Eastern Europe and Russia*. Boulder, CO: Westview Press, 1994.

Reddington, Helen. *The Lost Women of Rock Music: Female Musicians of the Punk Era*. Aldershot: Ashgate, 2007.

Reynolds, Simon. *Rip It Up and Start Again: Postpunk 1978–1984*. New York: Penguin Books, 2006.

Rimbaud, Penny. *Shibboleth: My Revolting Life*. Edinburgh: AK Press, 1998.

Riordan, James, ed. *Soviet Youth Culture*. Bloomington: Indiana University Press, 1989.

Risch, William Jay. *The Ukrainian West: Culture and the Fate of Empire in Soviet Lviv*. Cambridge, MA: Harvard University Press, 2011.

Risch, William Jay, ed. *Youth and Rock in the Soviet Bloc: Youth Cultures, Music, and the State in Russia and Eastern Europe*. Lanham, MD: Lexington Books, 2015.

Rose, Tricia. *Black Noise: Rap Music and Black Culture in Contemporary America*. Hanover, NH: Wesleyan University Press of New England, 1994.

Rutherford, Jonathan, ed. *Identity: Community, Culture, Difference*. London: Lawrence and Wishart, 1998.

Ryback, Timothy W. *Rock around the Bloc: A History of Rock Music in Eastern Europe and the Soviet Union*. New York: Oxford University Press, 1990.

Ryle, Martin, and Kate Soper. *To Relish the Sublime? Culture and Self-realisation in Postmodern Times*. New York: Verso, 2002.

Sabin, Roger, ed. *Punk Rock, So What? The Cultural Legacy of Punk*. New York: Routledge, 1999.

Salewicz, Chris. *Redemption Song: The Ballad of Joe Strummer*. New York: Faber and Faber, 2007.

Savage, Jon. *England's Dreaming: Anarchy, Sex Pistols, Punk Rock, and Beyond*. London: Faber, 1991.

Schmidt-Burkhardt, Astrit. *Maciunas' Learning Machines: From Art History to a Chronology of Fluxus*. Detroit: Gilbert and Lila Silverman Fluxus Collection in association with Vice Versa, Berlin, 2003.

Schulman, Bruce J. *The Seventies: The Great Shift in American Culture, Society, and Politics*. New York: Free Press, 2001.

Sklar, Monica. *Punk Style*. Oxford: Berg, 2013.

Smith, Patti. *Just Kids*. New York: Ecco, 2010.

Spitz, Marc. *We Got the Neutron Bomb: The Untold Story of L.A. Punk.* New York: Three Rivers Press, 2001.
Starr, S. Frederick. *Red and Hot: The Fate of Jazz in the Soviet Union, 1917–1980.* New York: Oxford University Press, 1983.
Storey, John. *Cultural Theory and Popular Culture: A Reader.* New York: Routledge, 2008.
Subcultures Network, The, ed. *Fight Back: Punk, Politics, and Resistance.* Manchester: Manchester University Press, 2015.
Subcultures Network, The, ed. *Youth Culture, Popular Music and the End of "Consensus."* London: Routledge, 2015.
Suri, Jeremi. *Power and Protest: Global Revolution and the Rise of Détente.* Cambridge, MA: Harvard University Press, 2003.
Szemere, Ann. *Up from the Underground: The Culture of Rock Music in Postsocialist Hungary.* University Park: Pennsylvania State University Press, 2001.
Taylor, Paul. *Impresario: Malcolm McLaren and the British New Wave.* New York: New Museum of Contemporary Art; Cambridge, MA: MIT Press, 1988.
Thomas, Deborah A. *Modern Blackness: Nationalism, Globalization, and the Politics of Culture in Jamaica.* Durham, NC: Duke University Press, 2004.
Thompson, Dave. *Wheels Out of Gear: 2 Tone, the Specials and a World in Flame.* London: Helter Skelter, 2004.
Thompson, Stacy. *Punk Productions: Unfinished Business.* Albany: State University of New York Press, 2004.
Thornton, Sarah. *Club Cultures.* Hanover, NH: University Press of New England, 1996.
Toobin, Jeffrey. *The Oath: The Obama White House and the Supreme Court.* New York: Doubleday, 2012.
Trencsényi, Balázs, and Gábor Klaniczay. "Mapping the Merry Ghetto: Musical Countercultures in East Central Europe." *East Central Europe* 38, no. 2 (2011): 169–179.
Troitsky, Artemy. *Back in the USSR: The True Story of Rock in Russia.* Boston: Faber and Faber, 1987.
True, Everett. *Hey Ho Let's Go: The Story of the Ramones.* London: Omnibus, 2005.
Urbańska, Katarzyna. "Galeria Remont. Nieznana Awangarda Lat Siedemdziesiątych." *Sztuka i Dokumentacja*, no. 6 (2012): 133–138.
Waksman, Steve. *This Ain't the Summer of Love: Conflict and Crossover in Heavy Metal and Punk.* Berkeley: University of California Press, 2009.
Wasiak, Patryk. "Kontakty Kulturalne Pomiędzy Polską a Węgrami, Czechosłowacją I NRD W Latach 1970-1989 Na Przykładzie Artystów Plastyków." PhD diss., Instytut Kultury i Komunikowania Szkoła Wyższa Psychologii Społecznej, 2009.
Westad, Odd Arne. *The Global Cold War: Third World Interventions and the Making of Our Times.* Cambridge: Cambridge University Press, 2005.
Wilentz, Sean. *The Age of Reagan: A History, 1974–2008.* New York: Harper Perennial, 2009.
Williams, Emmett, Ay-o, and Ann Noël. *Mr. Fluxus: A Collective Portrait of George Maciunas, 1931–1978.* New York: Thames and Hudson, 1998.
Wishnia, Steven. "Of Punk and Pornography: Rockin' with the First Amendment." *Nation* 245, no. 13 (October 24, 1987): 444–446.
Wójtowicz, Andrzej, and Sławomir Rogowski, eds. *Pamiętajcie o . . . Hybrydy.* Warsaw: BPiM Filmar, 2002.
Zhuk, S. I. *Rock and Roll in the Rocket City: The West, Identity, and Ideology in Soviet Dniepropetrovsk, 1960–1985.* Baltimore: Johns Hopkins University Press, 2010.
Zieliński, Przemysław. *Scena Rockowa w PRL: Historia, Organizacja, Znaczenie.* Warsaw: Wydawnictwo Trio, 2005.

Conference Papers and Interviews

Briggs, Jonathyne. "Force de Frappe." Paper presented at the annual meeting of the American Historical Association, Chicago, IL, January 2012.

Hendman, Heather. "Anarchism Ke Ho." Paper presented at the National Conference of the Popular Culture Association/American Culture Association, Washington, DC, March 2013.
Jackowska, Kora. "Rock 'n' Roll Rebellion in Poland: An Interview with Kora." Interview by Piotr Westwalewicz, University of Michigan, Ann Arbor, MI, March 5, 2004.
King, Stephen, and Renee Foster. "Revolutionary Words: Reggae's Evolution from Protest to Mainstream." Paper presented at the National Conference of the Popular Culture Association/American Culture Association, Washington, DC, March 2013.
Vest, Lisa Cooper. "Shades of Cultural Backwardness: Negotiations between Composers and the State in Communist Poland, 1955–1958." Paper presented at the Annual Convention of the Association of Slavic, East European and Eurasian Studies, San Antonio, TX, November 2014.
Wolf, Montgomery. "Dreaming of World War III." Paper presented at the annual meeting of the American Historical Association, Chicago, IL, January 2012.

Websites and Blogs

Brightest Young Things. http://brightestyoungthings.com.
CNN Online. http://www.cnn.com.
Jarocin Festival Unofficial Website. http://www.jarocin-festiwal.com.
Justia US Supreme Court Center. https://supreme.justia.com/.
Kill From the Heart. Chris Hubbard. www.killfromtheheart.com.
Nederpunk. Kees Smit and Bert Broodje. http://nederpunk.punt.nl/.
PBS Online. http://www.pbs.org.
Punk w Polsce. Michał Szymański. http://www.mitologie.pl/michasz/main.php.

Audio

Akvarium. *Radio Afrika*. Melodia 26701, 1983.
Black Flag. *Damaged*. Unicorn/SST 9502, 1981.
Brygada Kryzys. *Brygada Kryzys*. Tonpress SX-T16, 1982.
Circle Jerks. *Wild in the Streets*. Faulty Products COPE 03, 1982.
Clash, The. *The Clash*. CBS 82000, 1977.
Clash, The. *Sandinista!* CBS FSLN 1, 1980.
Crass. *The Feeding of the 5000*. Small Wonder 521984, 1978
Crass. *Stations of the Crass*. Crass Records 521984, 1979.
Dead Kennedys. "Nazi Punks Fuck Off / Moral Majority." Alternative Tentacles VIRUS 6, 1981.
Deadlock. *Victim of Safety Pin: Polski Punk Underground 1977–82*. Supreme Echo SE 01, 2003.
Dezerter. *Ku przyszłości*. Tonpress N-65, 1983.
KSU. "Nocą." Bootleg from I Festiwał Nowa Fala, 1980.
Lady Pank. *Lady Pank*. Tonpress SX-T26, 1983.
Maanam. *Maanam*. Wifon LP-028, 1981.
Minor Threat. *Minor Threat*. Dischord 12. 1983.
Misty in Roots. *Poor and Needy*. Tonpress S-536. 1985.
New York Dolls. *New York Dolls*. Mercury SRM-1-675, 1973.
Ramones. *Ramones*. Sire SASD-7520, 1976.
Republika. *Nowe Sytuacja*. Polton LPP003, 1983.
Ruts, The. *Babylon's Burning*. Virgin VS 271, 1979.
Ruts, The. "Jah War / SUS." Virgin 2141 248, 1979.
Sex Pistols. "Anarchy in the UK." UK: EMI 2566, 1976.
Sex Pistols. "God Save the Queen." A&M AMS 7284, 1977.
Sex Pistols. *Never Mind the Bullocks Here's the Sex Pistols*. Virgin V 2086. 1977.
Siekiera. *Na wszystkich frontach świata*. W Moich Oczach ML 8, 2008.
Slits, The. *Cut*. Virgin ILPS9573, 1979

Specials. *Specials*. 2 Tone Records CDL TT 5001, 1979.
Various Artists. *Fala*. Polton LPP-014, 1985.
Various Artists. *Niepokorni: I Przegląd Piosenki Prawdziwej*. Polskie Radio S.A., 2014.

Video

Jones, Keith, *Punk in Africa*. US: MVD Visual, 2013.
Koning, Jacques de. *I Could Live in Africa*. Poland (self-published), 1983
Kostenko, Andrzej. *My Blood, Your Blood*. UK: BBC, 1986.
Lady Pank. "Fabryka Małp." Poland: Telewizja Polska, 1983.
Lazarkiewicz, Piotr. *Fala*. Poland: Studio Filmowe im. Karola Irzykowskiego, 1986.
Lerner, Mike, and Maxim Pozdorovkin. *Pussy Riot: A Punk Prayer*. UK: Roast Beef Productions, 2013.
Mirkovic, Ivan. *Sretno Dijete*. Croatia: Gerila DV Film, 2003.
Opole 1980. Poland: Telewizja Polska, 1980.
Treliński, Mariusz. *Film o pankach*. Poland: Państwowa Wyższa Szkoła Filmowa Telewizyjna i Teatralna, 1983.

Index

Akvarium, 9, 68, 133–134, 164–165
Andropov, Iurii, 151, 162, 164
Ari Up. *See* Forster, Ariane "Ari Up"
Arnold, Matthew, 78–79, 82, 88–89, 91, 93, 96, 101, 116, 176, 179
art school, 14, 16–17, 36–38, 43–44, 46, 48–50, 61, 86

Baker, Clarence, 99, 128
BBC, 3, 61–63, 65, 83, 107
Beatles, 14, 22–24, 41, 65, 89, 162
Berlin, 1, 3, 13–14, 22–25, 27–29, 51, 62, 144, 157, 175
Biafra, Jello, 111–112, 143, 162–163
Biermann, Wolf, 22–25, 28
big beat, 23, 53
Black Flag, 110, 123, 142, 146, 148
Brezhnev, Leonid, 77, 87, 151, 164
Brygada Kryzys. *See* Kryzys / Brygada Kryzys
Brylewski, Robert
   conversion to punk, 1–3, 46–48
   and first wave punk band Kryzys, 3, 50, 70
   political views of, 173, 182
   and reggae band Izrael, 131–132, 146
   and second wave punk band Brygada Kryzys, 93–95
Budzyński, Tomasz, 114, 145–146, 182

CBGB, 15–16, 29, 39, 58–61
Centre for Contemporary Cultural Studies (CCCS), 4–6, 8, 14, 55–56, 75, 101, 104, 188n19
Charter 77, 87
Chełstowski, Walter, 92, 114, 169
the Clash
   and black culture, 20–21, 99, 106, 128, 140
   global views and connections of, 17, 18, 19, 22, 30, 76, 105, 135, 153
   and Joe Strummer, 13, 16, 18
   and the music industry, 55, 60, 63–64, 71, 125

politics of, 81, 83–85, 95, 163
and Rock Against Racism, 2, 84–85, 87 (*see also* Rock Against Racism)
the Cold War
   culture of, 35–36, 41, 123
   and globalization, 13–14, 30–31, 103, 110, 129, 134–135, 140, 175
   ideology and politics of, 8–10, 57, 102, 133, 148, 160, 170–171, 177–178, 181
   punk transgressing boundaries of, 49–50, 147, 176, 181
   scholarship on, 5–7, 11, 153, 179, 187n3
   and the Second World, 64, 115
   and the three worlds framework, 2–3, 8, 16–17, 24, 26, 29–31, 34, 128, 137
   transition from, 175, 183, 185
Colvin, Douglas "Dee Dee Ramone", 13–16, 38
communism
   cultural politics of, 84, 88
   fall of, 5, 62, 153, 173–175, 180–183, 185
   as a global ideological framework, 2–3, 17, 153–154, 156, 167, 178–179, 185
   in the Second World, 5, 22–24, 77, 103, 164, 180
Communist Party
   of East Germany, 23
   of Poland, 24, 49, 51, 67, 70, 75, 101, 115, 156, 169–170, 175, 182
   as a transnational institution, 2, 77, 88, 95, 152–153, 178
   of the USSR, 151, 174
Conservative Party (UK), 8, 80–84, 86, 100, 136, 143
conservatives
   cultural, 23, 60, 72, 88, 94–95, 101–102, 107–108, 115, 151, 154–160, 163–164, 177–178
   in Eastern Europe, 91, 94, 101, 103, 115, 154–158, 165–174, 176, 183, 185
   global, 136, 177

213

conservatives (*cont.*)
    as neoconservatives, 80, 100–101, 103, 107, 115, 128–130, 140
    and punks, 103, 126, 143, 148
    and realignment, 79, 102, 126, 154–157, 160, 165–168, 170–176, 179–181
COUM (art group), 44–46, 49
counterculture. *See* the 1960s
Crass (band)
    and avant-garde art, 44
    and the music industry, 61, 71–72
    politics of, 44, 72–73, 129, 135–138, 142, 152, 162–163
    transnational connections of, 44–46, 71–73, 139–140
culture wars, 10, 151, 153, 170–171, 178
Czechoslovakia, 16, 23, 29, 41, 42, 68–69, 77, 87, 143, 151, 165
Czezowski, Andy, 21, 45–46, 49, 61

Dadaism, 34, 36–39, 41–42, 44, 49, 176
Dammers, Jerry, 105, 107, 139
Danicki, Lesław "Walek Dzedzej," "Cyril," 13, 27–29, 47, 176
Dead Kennedys, 110–112, 137, 143–144, 159, 162–163, 173
Democratic Party (US), 75, 108, 138, 148, 158, 160, 181, 183
Dezerter (SS-20), 113–114, 121, 124–125, 144–145, 182
Dictor, Dave, 111, 173, 181
Dudanski, Richard. *See* Nother, Richard "Dudanski"
Dylan, Bob, 24–25, 28, 136
Dzedzej, Walek. *See* Danicki, Lesław "Walek Dzedzej," "Cyril"

East Germany, 13, 23–26, 29, 65, 68–69, 87, 107, 146, 165. *See also* Hagen, Nina
Elliott-Said, Marianne Joan "Poly Styrene", 2, 21, 84
Erdélyi, Tamás "Tommy Ramone", 15–16
ethnoscapes, 5, 9, 13–15, 29–31, 34, 43, 175

fanzines
    as discursive practice, 50
    global circulation of, 4, 34, 101, 137
    in the Netherlands, 50
    in Poland, 49–50, 100
    in the UK, 55, 61, 84
    in the US, 60–61, 101, 107, 111–112, 137–138
Fluxus, 34, 36, 41–47, 49–50, 72, 176
folk (culture and music)
    cultural politics of, 75, 89, 93–95
    in Eastern Europe, 23, 28, 47, 89, 93–95, 119, 134
    globally, 18–19, 47
    punk connections to, 28–29, 48, 75
    in the US, 15

Forbidden Songs festival, 93–94
Forster, Ariane "Ari Up", 13, 22, 25–27

Gajewski, Henryk. *See also* Remont gallery;
    avant-garde art, 33–34, 36–38, 40–42, 45–46, 50, 176
    international connections of, 33, 40, 42, 50–51, 72–73, 101
    and the music industry, 36, 55, 71–72, 110, 112, 121, 176
    and Remont gallery, 40, 45, 47–49, 53, 70, 92, 100–101, 144
Gdańsk (Poland), 19, 22, 28, 48, 88, 114
gender, 6
    dynamics of in punk scenes, 26, 86, 104, 109, 112, 124, 141–148, 154, 167
    politics of, 26, 84, 102, 106, 152, 158, 162
    in punk performances and songs, 70, 162, 167
    and scholarship on punk, 6–7, 56, 79, 180
    and the Slits, 25–26, 84 (*see also* the Slits)
Gierek, Edward, 87–88, 91
Ginsberg, Allen, 41, 44
globalization. *See also* ethnoscapes; third cultures
    and the Cold War, 9, 11, 77, 103, 126, 128–129, 134, 140–141, 152, 175
    contestation of, 7, 34, 110, 129, 182, 184
    and the music industry, 9, 119, 148, 176–177
    politics of, 129, 136, 138
    scholarship on, 7, 9, 13, 34, 77, 129, 180
Gorbachev, Mikhail, 164–165, 174
Groenveld, Diana "Ozon", 50–51

Hagen, Nina, 13–14, 22–29, 40, 48, 50–51
Hall, Stuart, 5, 8, 100
hardcore (punk subgenre)
    in Eastern Europe, 103, 113–115, 119, 121–127, 144–146, 154, 165, 167
    politics of, 109–112, 126, 141–148, 152, 154, 159, 165
    sound and style of, 48, 114, 122, 145
    in the US, 107–110, 112, 141–143, 147–148, 159
heavy metal, 148, 152, 154, 158–159, 168, 170–171, 174
Hell, Richard, 16, 39
hippies, 16, 84, 111–112, 138
Hungary
    and avant garde art, 41–42
    cultural politics of, 76–77, 87
    early punk scene, 29
    and market reforms, 64–65, 177
    music industry of, 67–69, 183
    rock and roll scene, 25, 28, 65, 68
    skinheads in, 146–147
    and Tommy Ramone, 15

immigrants and immigration
    in Eastern Europe, 13, 27–28, 69, 70–71, 131, 134
    and politics, 20, 80, 85, 106, 146

in punk bands, 14, 21, 35, 46
  in the UK, 2, 18–21, 25–26, 30, 101
  in the US, 15–16, 41, 47
independent record labels, 59–61, 162–163
International Monetary Fund (IMF), 77, 79, 103, 130
Iron Curtain
  cultural connections across the, 45, 62, 148
  emigration across, 22, 27
  origin of the, 22
  punk connections across the, 1, 50–51, 72–73, 100, 131, 181
  similarities across the, 1, 29, 57, 72–73, 77, 100, 151–152, 160, 175–177
Iron Maiden, 148

Jackowska, Olga "Kora", 70, 90. *See also* Maanam
Jamaica
  culture of, 2, 18–20, 30, 62, 99, 105, 127, 131–132, 134, 139 (*see also* reggae)
  immigrants in the UK from, 2, 18, 20–21, 26, 30, 86, 99, 105, 127, 131 (*see also* Donovan Letts)
  politics of, 130
  punk inspiration from, 27, 30, 99–101, 105, 127, 147 (*see also* Rock Against Racism)
  and Rastafarianism, 2, 20, 131
  and the Third World, 10, 20, 130–131
Jarocin Festival, 92–93, 113–119, 124, 144, 156, 167–170, 173, 181
Jaruzelski, Wojciech, 99–103, 113, 116, 126, 130, 143, 170, 177
jazz
  clubs, 41, 127–128
  cultural politics of, 22, 89, 123, 162
  musical influence of, 28, 54, 134
  unions, 28, 66, 68–69, 153
Johnson, Linton "Kwesi", 86, 99–100

Khrushchev, Nikita, 41, 77
Knížák, Milan, 42
Kozlowski, Jarosław, 45–46
Král, Ivan, 16
Kryzys / Brygada Kryzys. *See also* Robert Brylewski
  cultural politics of, 96, 132, 182
  global connections of, 50, 132
  origins of, 3, 29, 44, 47–48
  performances and recordings of, 50–52, 70, 125, 132
  and Remont gallery, 47–48
  and Solidarity, 93–94
Kwaśniewski, Aleksander 169

Labour Party (UK), 79–84, 86, 95, 148
Lady Pank
  breakup of, 158
  cultural politics of, 122, 154–155, 165
  fans of, 122–123, 146
  and gender, 124, 145–146
  and the Hits List, 121, 124

and the music industry, 119, 121–124, 132, 154–155, 182
  punk animosity toward, 124–125, 145–146, 167, 182
  in the US, 123–124
Laibach, 143–144, 146, 199
Lenartowicz, Jacek "Luter", 48–50
Letts, Donovan
  as Acme Apparel manager, 18, 61
  global background of, 19–21, 26–27, 30, 106, 133, 140, 176
  influence on punk, 18–21, 51, 140
  as Roxy DJ, 13, 21, 38, 47
Lipiński, Tomasz "Franz," "Lipa", 46, 49, 52, 182
London
  and avant garde art, 33, 38–39, 43–46, 50, 52
  as a destination for punks, 10, 22, 25
  global connections of, 1–2, 10, 13, 16, 18–22, 25–30, 38–39, 43, 45–46, 52, 62, 101, 134–135, 138–140, 176
  politics of, 62–63
  popular unrest in, 99–101, 106, 136–138
  punk scene of, 16, 18–22, 25–27, 29–30, 44, 46, 61, 63–64
Lydon, John "Johnny Rotten". *See also* Sex Pistols
  global connections of, 1, 25, 27, 29–30, 140
  politics of, 84, 102
  and the Sex Pistols, 40, 82–84, 104

Maanam. *See also* Jackowska, Olga "Kora"
  and cultural politics, 96, 114, 120–121
  global connections of, 28, 123
  performances and recordings of, 70–71, 117, 123
  popular success of, 28, 54–55, 70–71, 119–123, 146, 158, 182
  and Solidarity, 93–94
  views on punk, 90
Maciunas, George, 41–42, 45
Manley, Michael, 130
Marley, Bob, 20, 30, 62, 85, 127, 130
martial law (*stan wojenny*), 99–103, 113–128, 132
Maximum Rocknroll, 101, 107, 111–113, 129, 137–138, 147–148, 162
McLaren, Malcolm. *See also* Sex Pistols
  and avante garde art, 16, 33–47, 176
  and hip-hop, 140
  and the London shop Sex, 18–19, 46, 61
  and the music industry, 36, 62, 64, 71, 125
  as punk impresario, 2, 21, 34, 121
MDC (band), 111–112, 147, 173, 181
Mellor, John "Woody," "Joe Strummer". *See also* the Clash
  global connections of, 13, 16–19, 20–21, 25, 27, 30, 46, 105, 135, 176
  politics of, 20–21, 27, 81, 83, 85, 95, 176
  punk origins of, 16–21, 27, 38, 43, 62, 81
Misty in Roots, 2, 99, 127–128, 131–134
Moral Majority, 108–110, 143, 158

moral panics, 78, 175
Music of the Young Generation (MMG), 53–54, 69, 71, 75, 89, 92, 114

National Front, 80, 84–86, 99, 106, 176
neoliberalism, 9–10, 101, 148, 175, 181, 183, 185
neo-nazism, 6, 87, 104, 106, 142–147, 159, 178
new wave
  cultural politics of, 81, 93–96, 151–152, 154–159, 164–165, 167–168
  in the East, 30, 47, 69–71, 76, 90, 93–96, 103, 115, 119–132, 134, 144–147, 151, 154–158, 164–165, 167–168, 182
  and the music industry, 54, 60, 103, 115, 119–132, 141, 144–147, 152, 167
  in the West, 29, 81, 84, 159
New York City
  and avant garde art 33, 38–39, 41–43, 45, 50–52
  cultural politics in, 112, 163
  early punk scene, 3, 15–16, 18–19, 33, 38–40, 47, 58, 58–61, 76
  global connections, 13, 15–17, 19, 28–30, 38–43, 45, 50–52, 123, 135, 176
  hip-hop in, 139–140
  and the music industry, 58–61, 64
the New York Dolls, 3, 15–19, 38–39, 143
the 1960s
  and avant-garde art, 40–41, 43
  counterculture of, 16, 24, 27, 33, 36, 39–40, 42, 62, 82, 109, 112
  culture and politics of, 77–79, 141, 152, 158–159
  and global upheaval, 24, 76
  music of, 19, 23–24, 28, 48, 53–54, 89, 134, 136
1968, global rebellions of, 9, 17, 24, 37. *See also* Prague Spring
the 1970s
  and avant-garde art, 33, 42–45
  and crisis, 3, 15, 48
  culture and politics of, 8–9, 66, 77–80, 86, 91, 96, 102, 104, 108, 141, 152, 160
  and global transformation, 129–130, 170, 177–179
  music of, 33, 58–59, 71, 75, 89 (*see also* progressive rock)
  and recession, 65, 87
  subcultures of, 87
Nother, Richard "Dudanski", 21, 46

Oi!, 103–109, 142, 146–147

Palmolive. *See* Romero, Paloma
Parents' Music Resource Center (PMRC), 159–163, 169, 183
Parliament (UK), 4, 45, 80–83, 136, 169, 174
Peach, Blair, 99–101
Peel, John, 3, 62–63, 120, 124

Plastic People of the Universe 23, 29, 41–42, 68
Poland
  avant garde art in, 33, 40–42, 45–46
  cultural politics of, 4–5, 47, 64–69, 75–76, 79, 82, 89–92, 95–96, 116–120, 123–125, 153–158, 165–170, 179
  and the end of communism, 174–177, 180–183
  global connections of, 1–2, 10, 28–30, 45–46, 51, 72–73, 77, 99–102, 115, 130–134, 173
  music industry in, 53–55, 64–71, 103, 110, 119–123 (*see also* Music of the Young Generation)
  politics of, 87–88, 100–102, 119, 165, 173–174, 177, 180–182
  punk bands and performances in, 28–30, 70, 92–93, 112, 121–122, 143–145, 158, 165, 175
  punk scenes of, 1, 28, 48, 101, 103, 112–114, 118, 124–126, 143–146, 158 (*see also* Gdańsk; Warsaw)
  and reggae, 127–128, 131–134
  rock and roll in, 23–24, 48, 53
  scholarship on, 5–6, 115, 174
Poly Styrene. *See* Elliott-Said, Marianne Joan "Poly Styrene"
Pop Art, 33–34, 36–39, 41–42, 176
Porter, John, 13, 27–28, 70–71
postmodernism and postmodernity
  and avant garde art, 36, 38–40, 42
  definitions and theories of, 9, 35–36
  punk as an instance of, 35–36, 49, 55–56, 78, 144, 176
Prague, 2, 16, 22–24, 41–43, 69, 143
Prague Spring, 16, 24, 77, 143
progressive rock
  cultural politics of, 67, 89, 148
  in the East, 28, 48, 54, 65, 67–68, 89, 124, 157
  and the music industry, 58
  in the West, 3, 16, 63

race
  and culture, 17, 19, 22, 24–25, 62
  political relevance of, 20, 102, 104, 139, 177
  punk's relationship to, 21, 30, 84–87, 100, 105–106, 112, 128, 139–141, 143, 147, 184 (*see also* Rock Against Racism; 2 Tone; Oi!)
  in scholarship of punk, 5, 7, 56, 79, 180
radio
  Hits List (Poland), 120–122, 155
  in the UK, 3, 62–63, 107
  in the US, 60–61, 159
  and the music industry, 53–55, 60–62, 65
  in Poland, 23, 47, 53–54, 65, 117, 155, 157, 165, 170
  punk played on the, 3–4, 60, 62, 119 (*see also* Peel, John)
  transnational reach of, 4, 22, 29, 62, 134, 151
the Raincoats, 1–2, 46–48
Ramone, Dee Dee. *See* Colvin, Douglas

Ramone, Tommy. *See* Erdélyi, Tamás
Ramones, 15–16, 19, 30, 38–39, 58–60, 62, 64, 189
Rastafarianism, 2, 20, 84, 127, 130–133, 147, 149, 168
Ratter, Jeremy John "Penny Rimbaud", 44–45, 71–72, 137
Reagan, Ronald
  cultural politics of, 154, 158, 160–161
  in global context, 102, 113, 126, 130, 154, 177
  and militarism, 135, 137
  political rise of, 108
  punk opposition to, 103, 111–113, 129, 137–138, 148
  social politics of, 10, 101–103, 107, 126, 130, 155, 180, 183
reggae. *See also* Rastafarianism; Rock Against Racism
  in Eastern Europe, 30, 47, 51, 127–128, 131–134, 146, 165, 168–170
  and the global music industry, 130–131
  influence on punk, 2, 19–21, 26–27, 30, 51, 85–86, 105, 135, 140, 147
  in Jamaica, 19, 21, 130–131
  in the UK, 18–21, 27, 62, 84–86, 99
Remont gallery, 40, 45, 47–49, 53, 70, 92, 100–101, 144. *See also* Gajewski, Henryk
Republican Party (US), 108, 158, 160, 181
Republika, 119, 121–123, 132, 146, 154, 157–158
rhythm and blues (R&B), 13, 17, 19, 38, 133
Rimbaud, Penny. *See* Ratter, Jeremy John
Robinson, Thomas Giles "Tom", 84, 107, 183
Rock Against Racism
  concerts, 2, 84, 99
  connections to Eastern Europe, 76, 127, 131
  and cross-racial alliances, 21, 30, 86, 105, 107
  and Oi!, 104
  origins of, 84–85
  politics of, 84–87, 127
  in the US, 111–112, 163
rock and roll, 13, 17, 22–25, 27, 28, 48, 54, 57–58, 109, 120
Rolling Stones, 13–14, 24, 40, 51
Romero, Paloma "Palmolive", 21, 25, 29, 46
Rotten, Johnny. *See* Lydon, John "Johnny Rotten"
the Roxy (punk club), 13, 19, 21, 38, 45–47, 61, 64, 85
the Ruts, 99, 104, 125, 128
Rypson, Piotr, 49

San Francisco. *See also* Dead Kennedys; *Maximum Rocknroll*
  early punk scene in, 16, 52, 60
  global connections of, 103
  politicized punk scene of, 107, 111–113, 137–138, 142–143, 148, 152, 173, 184
Seaga, Edward, 130
Sex Pistols. *See also* Lydon, John "Johnny Rotten"; McLaren, Malcolm
  controversy over, 3, 62–64, 70, 80–81, 83, 136, 163
  cultural politics of, 80–81, 83, 96, 102, 143–144, 160
  global connections of, 1–2, 19
  influence of on punks in the East, 28, 40, 47–48, 125
  influence of on punks in the West, 18, 25, 43–44, 46, 50, 61, 145
  and McLaren, Malcolm, 16, 34, 37, 40
  and the mass media, 3, 62–64, 71, 121, 132
  music of, 3, 28, 40, 63
  popularity of, 3, 57, 63
Siekiera, 114, 144–146, 152, 156, 167, 182
Simonon, Paul, 18–22, 30, 85, 106, 140
Situationism, 34, 36, 39, 41–42, 84, 176
Skrewdriver, 142
The Slits. *See also* Forster, Ariane "Ari Up"
  Ari Up of, 13
  gender politics of, 26, 84
  global connections of, 21–22, 25–27, 29–30, 46, 85, 99
  and the mass media, 62–63
  and Nina Hagen, 25–26
Smith, Patti, 16, 18, 21, 30, 37–39, 58, 60
Socialist Workers Party, 85–86, 176
Solidarity (labor union)
  after the fall of communism, 175, 181–183
  challenge to communist authority by, 87–88, 100, 103, 107, 113, 116–117, 173–174
  cultural politics of, 4, 90–96, 116–117, 174
Southall (UK), 73, 99–100, 106
Special Patrol Group (SPG), 99, 101, 128
the Specials, 100, 105, 107, 136, 139
SS-20. *See* Dezerter
Stalin, Josef, 16, 22, 24, 67, 77, 89, 114, 137, 155, 165, 179, 181, 185
straightedge, 103, 107–109
Strummer, Joe. *See* Mellor, John "Woody," "Joe Strummer"
Styrene, Poly. *See* Elliott-Said, Marianne Joan
subculture
  in Eastern Europe, 75, 155–157, 166, 170, 174
  predecessors to punk, 17–19, 83
  punk as a form of, 9, 34, 55–56, 102–104, 125, 152–153, 162, 171, 178
  and race, 18–19, 141
  theories of, 4–6, 14, 55–56 (*see also* Centre for Contemporary Cultural Studies)
sung poetry, 89, 93
Surrealism, 34, 36–37
Suspicious Persons act (SUS), 20, 99
Sylwin, Jacek, 53

Television (band), 16, 39–40, 58, 60
Thatcher, Margaret. *See also* neoliberalism
  in global context, 102, 108, 126, 130, 154, 177, 183

Thatcher, Margaret (*cont.*)
  and immigrants, 106 (*see also* immigrants and immigration)
  interaction with punk, 102, 113, 128, 136–137, 140
  and militarism, 108, 135–136
  and neoconservatism, 80, 100, 102–103, 107
  and neoliberalism, 80, 100, 107
  politicization of culture under, 102, 108, 113, 162
  sociopolitics of, 8, 100, 106–107, 180
third culture, 34, 37, 56, 176
tiermondisme
  and opposition to apartheid, 139
  and opposition to racism, 143
  origins of, 126, 128–129
  as a subset of punk, 10, 130–140, 149, 177
Tilt (band), 44, 47–49, 51–52, 93, 175, 182
tribalism, 10, 129, 140–149, 177
Turczynowicz, Andrzej "Amok", 47, 100–101
2 Tone Records, 8, 21, 30, 103–107, 136, 139

Ukraine, 30, 76, 151, 153
Union of Soviet Socialist Republics (USSR)
  and avant garde art, 41
  cultural politics of, 22–23, 76, 88–89, 151
  end of, 181, 185
  influence on punk, 30
  music industry in, 68–69
  politics of, 77, 87, 134, 151, 164, 174, 179, 181
  punk in, 30, 69, 76, 133–134, 183
  reggae in, 2, 133–134
  and regimes of the Second World, 16, 23–24, 89–90, 93, 95, 113, 165
  rock and roll in, 22, 65, 68
  subcultures in, 22
United Kingdom
  and avant garde art, 37, 44–45
  cultural politics in, 72, 78–84, 87, 102–107, 109, 152, 162–164, 175, 179
  empire of, 2, 19, 80
  global connections of, 10, 18, 27, 40, 47, 50–51, 76–77, 100, 105, 123, 126, 131, 134, 139, 147, 183
  music industry in, 54, 60–65, 69–71, 122, 124, 132
  politics of, 77, 87–88, 100, 126, 136–137, 177, 181, 183
  punk bands and performances in, 2, 17, 27, 43, 48, 71–72, 123, 135–137, 143
  punk scenes in, 103–107, 114–115, 136
  and race, 20, 30, 84–85, 99, 104–107, 128, 131, 139–140, 142, 184 (*see also* Rock Against Racism)
  reggae and ska in, 19, 125, 128
  rock and roll in, 17, 22–24
  scholarship on, 4, 55, 77, 124
United States
  and avant garde art, 41–42

  cultural politics in, 114, 151–155, 158–164, 175, 179, 181
  global connections of, 10, 14, 20, 24, 29, 42, 62, 65, 68, 103, 123–124, 139
  immigrants in (*see* immigrants and immigration)
  music industry in, 29, 54, 57–61, 69–70, 123
  politics of, 77, 107–108, 126, 135, 137–138, 141, 177, 183
  punk scenes in, 103, 107–113, 115, 136, 138, 147–148
  and race, 20, 30, 142, 184
  rock and roll in, 17, 22, 114
  scholarship on, 7, 77, 152, 175

Vičs, Ivar "Dr. Rat", 50–51

Warhol, Andy, 33, 37–39, 41–44
Warsaw (Poland)
  avant garde art in, 33, 37, 40, 42–46, 51 (*see also* Remont gallery)
  global connections of, 13, 22–24, 27–29, 40, 42–43, 51–52, 101, 176
  origins of punk in, 1–2, 27–28, 46–48
  punk scene of, 2, 28, 44, 46–48, 51, 53–54, 70, 89, 92, 101, 103, 121, 132, 155, 167
  reggae in, 127–128, 131, 133–134
  rock and roll in, 23–24, 48
Washington, D.C., 103, 107–108, 112, 139, 148, 159
West Germany, 21–22, 24, 27, 42, 142
Westwood, Vivienne, 38–39
white nationalism, 106, 146–147

X-Ray Spex, 2, 21, 84

Yohannan, Tim, 111–113
Yoko Ono, 41, 46
youth
  and culture, 7, 22, 53, 66, 69, 71, 88–89, 92, 96–97, 101, 118–119, 152, 160, 164, 168, 179
  organizations, 23, 28, 45, 47, 66, 69, 75–76, 92–93, 115–117, 122, 125, 157, 167–168, 176 (*see also* youth unions)
  as punks, 113, 115, 155–161, 166–167
  and race, 20, 26, 128, 159
  social concern about, 1, 4–5, 23, 56, 75, 80–81, 90, 92, 97, 101, 115–120, 151–153, 156–161, 166–167, 169, 174, 179
  and subcultures, 4–5, 17, 19, 55, 155, 170 (*see also* subculture)
youth unions (SZSP, ZSMP, ZHP), 28, 45, 47, 66, 76, 92–93, 115–118, 153, 157, 167, 176
Yugoslavia, 2, 29, 48, 69, 132, 144

Zappa, Frank, 161–162
Zermati, Marc, 50
'zines. *See* fanzines